Disability Inclusion in Africa is an eye-opening and transformative work that redefines how disability is perceived within theological and cultural contexts in Africa. The authors blend academic rigor with practical insights, offering an inclusive, compassionate approach that challenges traditional views. The book emphasizes the urgent need for the African church to redefine its relationship with disability by addressing harmful narratives and providing practical solutions. Hence, it lays the groundwork for transformative change, offering a strategy toward a more just and compassionate society across Africa. Through its powerful exploration of deeply rooted stigmas, it makes significant contributions to the fields of disability studies and theology, providing readers with essential tools to engage in compassionate and inclusive practices, particularly for those working in theology, development, and disability advocacy. This book is essential reading for scholars, practitioners, and advocates committed to creating more inclusive communities in the faith realm.

Nicodeme Hakizimana, PhD
Executive Director,
Organization for Integration and Promotion of Persons with Albinism (OIPPA), Rwanda

Disability Inclusion in Africa: From Harmful to Life-Giving Theologies is a groundbreaking work that enriches the growing scholarship of theology and disability studies in the African context. By deftly intertwining theological perspectives with the social and cultural realities unique to the continent, the authors present thorough and weighty analysis from varied perspectives. This book is a must-read for scholars, practitioners, and anyone interested in understanding the intricate and multifaceted nature of disability in Africa. It stands out not only for its rich scholarship but also for its inclusive approach, making it a significant contribution to the field.

Esther Mombo, PhD
Professor, School of Theology,
St Paul's University, Kenya

It is encouraging to see a title of this sorts being published. An attempt to move from harmful (and yes, Christian) theologies to life-giving theologies. For persons living with disabilities, this is not merely a matter of being accepted but a matter of being recognised and included. This book is both theological and practical. This work is an important read for all who are working and living in this space of disabilities.

Nico Mostert, PhD
Executive Director,
Network for African Congregational Theology (NetACT)

A dialogue between disability and theology in the African context is long overdue. I cannot wait to read this book thoroughly, because at first glance it begins to answer many of my questions. It is thorough, balanced and scholarly without being off-puttingly academic. I know many others will be desperate to read it and I hope we can all put the inclusivity it advocates for into practice. I have no hesitation in recommending this work.

Tom Shakespeare, PhD
Professor of Disability Research,
London School of Hygiene and Tropical Medicine, UK

Disability Inclusion in Africa

Disability Inclusion in Africa

From Harmful to Life-Giving Theologies

Editors
**Madleina Daehnhardt,
Nina G. Kurlberg, Sas Conradie and
Emmanuel Murangira**

Foreword by Samuel Kabue

© 2024 Madleina Daehnhardt, Nina G. Kurlberg, Sas Conradie and Emmanuel Murangira

Published 2024 by HippoBooks, an imprint of ACTS and Langham Publishing.
Africa Christian Textbooks (ACTS), TCNN, PMB 2020, Bukuru 930008, Plateau State, Nigeria
www.actsnigeria.org

Langham Publishing, PO Box 296, Carlisle, Cumbria CA3 9WZ, UK
www.langham.org

ISBNs:
9781786411617 Large Print

Madleina Daehnhardt, Nina G. Kurlberg, Sas Conradie and Emmanuel Murangira hereby assert their moral right to be identified as the Author of the General Editor's part in the Work in accordance with sections 77 and 78 of the Copyright, Designs and Patents Act 1988.

All rights reserved. No part of this publication may be reproduced, stored in a retrieval system or transmitted, in any form or by any means, electronic, mechanical, photocopying, recording or otherwise, without the prior written permission of the publisher or the Copyright Licensing Agency.

Requests to reuse content from Langham Publishing are processed through PLSclear. Please visit
www.plsclear.com to complete your request.

All Scripture quotations, unless otherwise indicated, are taken from the Holy Bible, New International Version®, NIV®. Copyright ©1973, 1978, 1984, 2011 by Biblica, Inc.™ Used by permission of Zondervan.

Scripture quotations in Chapter 1 are taken from **The Message**, copyright © 1993, 2002, 2018 by Eugene H. Peterson. Used by permission of NavPress. All rights reserved. Represented by Tyndale House Publishers.

Scripture quotations in Chapter 2, unless otherwise stated, are from the New Revised Standard Version Bible, copyright © 1989 National Council of the Churches of Christ in the United States of America. Used by permission. All rights reserved. All other translations in Chapter 2 are authors own.

Scripture quotations marked (ESV) are from The

Holy Bible, English Standard Version® (ESV®), copyright © 2001 by Crossway, a publishing ministry of Good News Publishers. Used by permission. All rights reserved.

British Library Cataloguing-in-Publication Data
A catalogue record for this book is available from the British Library
ISBN: 978-1-78641-161-7

Cover & Book Design: projectluz.com
Cover Artwork: Tafadzwa Gwetai

Langham Partnership actively supports theological dialogue and an author's right to publish but does not necessarily endorse the views and opinions set forth here or in works referenced within this publication, nor can we guarantee technical and grammatical correctness. Langham Partnership does not accept any responsibility or liability to persons or property as a consequence of the reading, use or interpretation of its published content.

Contents

List of Contributors xiii
Acknowledgements xxi
Foreword xxiii
    Samuel Kabue

Introduction: Disability Inclusion in Africa. 1
Introducing the Contexts and Contents of
the Volume
    Madleina Daehnhardt

Part 1: Rethinking Theologies of Disability

1. Disability, Beliefs and Theologies in
African Contexts 55
    Madleina Daehnhardt and
    Nina G. Kurlberg

2. Disability and the Bible 115
The Challenge of Reading Responsibly
    Grant Macaskill

3. Am I Being Punished? 165
Reimagining Sin Alongside People with
Disabilities in Southern Africa
    Selina Palm

4. Holistic Healing in Acts 3:1–10 211
A Transformative Church for All People
    Micheline Kamba

Part 2: Different Perspectives on Disability: Transforming Church and Institutional Practice

5 An African Community Perspective in Positive Dialogue with Disability and Christianity..................................241
    Edwin Zulu

6 Being Different........................ 285
   Imago Dei in Light of Disability in Africa
    David Tarus

7 From Exclusion to Divine Accommodation of People with Profound Intellectual Disabilities 321
    Jill Harshaw

8 Attitudes and Accessibility................ 379
   The Church's Response to People with Disabilities in Ghana
    Dan Nyampong Asihene

9 Worshippers with Disabilities in the Nigerian Church Community 411
   The Role of Inclusive Theological Education
    Tongriang Daspan and Noah Daspan

   Epilogue: Towards an Inclusive Theology of Disability for Africa.................... 469
    Emmanuel Murangira and Sas Conradie

   Appendix 1: The Use of Terms Describing People and Places 491

List of Contributors

Editors
Madleina Daehnhardt

Madleina Daehnhardt is a social researcher with an interest in disability, health and well-being. She has been a post-doctoral researcher, tutor, senior teaching associate and affiliated lecturer at the University of Cambridge, from where she also holds an MPhil in Social Anthropology and a PhD in Development Studies. Madleina currently supports a social enterprise in rural Cambridgeshire, providing meaningful work and skills opportunities for people with learning disabilities and autism on an organic care farm. Previously, Madleina was Impact and Research Advisor for Tearfund. She is (co-)editor and (co-)author of a number of published works, including **Ageing in Rwanda: Challenges and Opportunities for Church, Nation and State** (Tearfund in Rwanda and the University of Birmingham, 2019).

Nina Kurlberg

Nina Kurlberg is a postdoctoral research associate at Durham University in the UK, where she is working on diversifying the Common Awards curriculum. From 2019 to 2023, she worked for Tearfund UK, developing theology in the area of equality, diversity and inclusion. She is co-editor of **Theologies and Practices of Inclusion** (SCM, 2021) and author of **Institutional Logics within Faith-Based Aid** (Routledge, 2024).

Sas Conradie

Dr. Sas Conradie is currently the Tearfund International Partnerships Manager having served for six years as the Tearfund Theology and Networking Engagement Manager for Africa. Sas has had a varied career including being Assistant International Director of World In Need (a UK mission organization), Global Mission Fund Manager of CMS and Coordinator of the Global Generosity Network. Sas is an ordained minister of the Dutch Reformed Church Pretoria-Oosterlig congregation in South Africa. He has held various leadership positions in the World Evangelical Alliance and Lausanne Movement. Sas holds a doctor of divinity from the University of Pretoria and has contributed a number of articles and chapters to publications. He edited a generosity edition of the **Evangelical Review of Theology**.

Emmanuel Murangira

Emmanuel is Tearfund's Country Director for Rwanda. He is co-editor of **Jubilee: God's Answer to Poverty** (Regnum, 2020) and co-author of **Ageing in Rwanda: Challenges and Opportunities for Church, State and Nation** (Tearfund and University of Birmingham, 2019). Emmanuel is a PhD candidate in Transformational Theology through the Oxford Centre for Religion and Public Life. His thesis is titled "Revival, Regression and Renewal: The Church in Spiritual, Social and Economic Transformation in Post-Genocide Rwanda." Emmanuel is an ordained minister and an itinerant preacher.

Authors
Dan Nyampong Asihene

Dan Nyampong Asihene is an ordained minister of the Church of Pentecost in Ghana. He holds a bachelor of theology degree from Canada Christian College and a master of arts degree from the University of Ghana. He is currently a PhD student. His research interests are in the area of Theology in Disability Studies. Dan has authored one book. He is married to Abigail.

Noah Daspan

Noah Daspan is a teacher, an independent researcher and a freelance editor. Currently, he is a lecturer at the Plateau State College of Education Gindiri. Previously, he taught English language and literature at the Gindiri Theological Seminary and the Theological College of Northern Nigeria, Bukuru. He has also served as a Master Trainer for many non-governmental organizations and has discipled/mentored youths, including persons with disabilities. Noah holds an MA (Literature in English) at the University of Jos, where he is currently a doctoral student. Together with his wife, Tongriang, he advocates for the inclusion of persons with disabilities in church and society.

Tongriang Daspan

Tongriang Daspan is a sign language interpreter and staff member of the Theological College of Northern Nigeria, Bukuru. She holds an MEd (Science Education) from the National Open University of Nigeria. Currently, she is a PhD (Science Education) student at Western Michigan University, USA. Her interests include curriculum development, STEM identity, and inclusion of persons with disabilities in science and worship. Previously, she served as a science teacher at Demonstration School for the Deaf Children, Kaduna; part-time lecturer (Integrated Science) at Plateau State College of Education Gindiri; coordinator, TCNN Centre for Continuing Education; and director, Academic Planning, TCNN College of Education.

Jill Harshaw

Jill Harshaw is Adjunct Professor of Disability Theology at Western Theological Seminary MI, where she is consultant to the Centre for Disability Ministry, and is Executive Director of Tio Associates, a not-for-profit organization that equips the church to honour and welcome the contributions of people with intellectual disabilities. She was previously lecturer in Practical and Disability Theology at Queens University Belfast. Jill has spoken widely on academic and practically focused disability theology. She holds an MTh and a PhD from Queens University and has published a number of academic articles. Her book, **God Beyond Words**, was shortlisted for the 2019 Archbishop Ramsey Prize for Theological Writing.

Micheline Kamba

Dr. Micheline Kamba Kasongo was the Francophone Africa coordinator of the WCC's Ecumenical Disability Advocates Network (EDAN). She was a member of the WCC's central committee from 2006 and a professor at the Faculty of Theology at the Université Protestante au Congo. She also led IMAN'ENDA Ministries (a pastoral ministry for people with disabilities) in the Democratic Republic of Congo. (note 1)

Grant Macaskill

Grant Macaskill is the Kirby Laing Chair of New Testament Exegesis at the University of Aberdeen, where he is also co-director of the Centre for Autism and Theology. He is the author of several books, including **Union with Christ in the New Testament** (Oxford University Press, 2013) and **Autism and the Church: Bible, Theology, Community** (Baylor University Press, 2019).

Selina Palm

Selina Palm is a Senior Researcher based at the Unit for Religion and Development at Stellenbosch University, South Africa. She has twenty years of project and empirical research experience working with marginalized groups and faith actors, especially across the African continent. She holds an MA in Human Rights from the University of Essex and a PhD in Theology and Development

---

1. World Council of Churches, "WCC Grieves Passing of Rev. Dr Micheline Kamba Kasongo," 6 August 2020, https://www.oikoumene.org/news/wcc-grieves-passing-of-rev-dr-micheline-kamba-kasongo.

from the University of Kwa-Zulu Natal. She has published widely in academic journals on faith and violence against women, children, people with disabilities, and gender and sexual minorities. She is also a lay faith leader in her church.

David Tarus

David Kirwa Tarus currently serves as Executive Director of the Association for Christian Theological Education in Africa (ACTEA), a project of the Association of Evangelicals in Africa. Previously, he served as a lecturer and Deputy Principal at AIC Missionary College, an affiliate institution of Scott Christian University. David is a graduate of McMaster Divinity College (PhD in Christian Theology), Wheaton College Graduate School (MA, Historical and Systematic Theology) and Scott Christian University (bachelor of theology). He is the author of **A Different Way of Being: Toward a Reformed Theology of Ethnopolitical Cohesion for the Kenyan Context** (Langham Academic, 2019), co-editor of **Christian Responses to Terrorism: The Kenyan Experience** (Wipf & Stock) and has written many articles. His research interests are theological anthropology, ecclesiology and social issues. He is an ordained minister of the Africa Inland Church, Kenya.

Edwin Zulu

Edwin Zulu holds a doctorate in Old Testament from the University of Stellenbosch, South Africa. Previously a Research Fellow at the University of Stellenbosch and Senior Lecturer at Africa University, Mutare, Zimbabwe, he also served as Vice Chancellor and professor at Justo Mwale University, Lusaka. He is currently the Deputy Vice Chancellor of the Zambian Open University, Lusaka, Zambia. His research interests are in the areas of Bible and contemporary issues and disability.

Acknowledgements

This volume has been the result of vision, determination and patience. The editors would like to thank all the authors for their commitment and patience with multiple revisions and with the long editorial process. Due to unexpected editor illness and absence, the process leading to finalizing the manuscript was prolonged.

We would like to acknowledge Ellie Hall who has skilfully, patiently and professionally project managed this book project from start to finish. Ellie has been a tremendous support and managed stakeholder communications with authors, editors and publishers. She has carried herself with poise, patience and kindness.

Thanks also to Shannon Thomson for copy-editing the manuscript, and for her flexibility throughout the process, and to Mark Arnold at Langham for his continued support.

Finally, our thanks go to all reviewers and key supporters who have – in one way or another – been generous with their time and financial resources in supporting the vision of this book.

Tearfund's Theology and Network Engagement team in particular has been instrumental in pursuing the idea of this book and has backed it with financial and moral support.

Foreword

Samuel Kabue

To be human is to live a life that is marked both by the God-given goodness of creation and the brokenness that is a part of human life. We experience both sides of human life with disabilities. To interpret disability from one of these perspectives is to deny the ambiguity of life and to create an artificial ontological split in the heart of our understanding of disability.

Until very recently, and possibly still the case in some parts of the world, as pointed out in the WCC document **A Church of All and for All**, disability has been interpreted as a punishment for sins, committed either by the persons with disabilities themselves or by their relatives in earlier generations. It has also been understood as a sign of lack of faith that prevents God from performing a healing miracle, or as a sign of demonic activity, in which case exorcism is needed to overcome the disability. Such interpretations have led to the oppression of people with disabilities in the church. In that respect, churches' attitudes have reflected attitudes in societies as a whole. Structures of oppression within societies and within churches have mutually reinforced each other.

When new understandings of disabilities emerge in society, traditional theological interpretations are challenged. In some churches, this has raised awareness that people with disabilities were not seen as equal. In many churches, traditional ways of treating people with disabilities have then been perceived as oppressive and discriminatory, and actions towards people with disabilities have moved from "charity" to recognition of their human rights. Changing attitudes have led to new questions and interpretations. Awareness has slowly grown that people with disabilities have experienced that which can enrich churches themselves. In the search for unity and inclusion, some have acknowledged that people with disabilities must be included in the life and the witness of the church. Often, this has been connected to the language about weakness found in the New Testament, especially in the two Epistles to the Corinthians.

But even this insight has been challenged. Is disability really something that shows the weaknesses in human life? Is that in itself a limiting and oppressive interpretation? Do we not have to take another, more radical step? Is disability really something that is limiting? Is the language of disability as a "loss" an adequate one at all, despite it often being a stage of the journey undertaken by persons with disabilities themselves? Is a language of plurality not more adequate?

One of the most harmful practices in the church is that of emphasis on physical healing and the lack of distinction between disability and sickness. If your disability is as a result of sickness or accident, the term "healing" comes with the yearning and hope for recovery for as long as you have not accepted that as a new condition in your life. To those who have been disabled since birth or for a long time and have gone through the necessary processes of adjustment, the term "healing" often has little to do with their disabilities until others remind them of this understanding. To them, disability and sickness might be two very different things, with "healing" applying to sickness but not to disability.

Let me make it clear at this point that there is no doubt in my mind, and in the minds of many persons with disabilities whom I know, that divine healing is biblical and applicable in the Christian faith. However, its understanding in relation to persons with disabilities is made complex by differing teaching, doctrines and theology. Some of these have made the word "healing" an anathema in the ears of persons with disabilities. This is especially the case where persons with disabilities become vulnerable to easy commercial fixes and religious groups, which offer miraculous healing in the setting of superficial acceptance and friendship. Two scenarios can illustrate this.

Take the case of a well-known evangelist from abroad who flies with his whole team of assistants to a city in Africa. Prior to his arrival, the city is alight with posters and media announcements about his powers to heal and inviting all those vexed with all manner of infirmities for healing. An entire school for children with physical disabilities turns up at the stadium where the evangelical crusade is taking place, with many hopes of being cured. An altar call for those with needs is made after the sermon and the enthusiastic ushers push forward all the children in their wheelchairs and on crutches to the front. A moving prayer is made and everyone is called upon to receive healing by jumping out of their wheelchairs and throwing off their crutches. The ushers assist the children by pulling them out of their wheelchairs and taking away their crutches. In the confusion some get badly hurt, no cure takes place and the crowd scatters away, some carrying with them the crutches as evidence of some imagined cure, in the process inflicting more suffering on those children left in the stadium unable to move.

The other case is that of a mature Christian with a disability who turns up to such an evangelical gathering with the simple objective of listening to the word of God from the reputed evangelist and thereby receiving spiritual blessings. An altar call is made for those who would like to accept the Lord and those who have needs requiring prayers. Believing, rightly or wrongly, that the Christian with the disability must have come to seek healing, the enthusiastic ushers push him to the front without any consultation or even consent. No healing takes place, and as the crowd scatters away the "poor" man is left alone, still with his disability, the given reason being that he had no faith.

Hypothetical as these may seem, they are lived experiences in the part of the world where I come from and I have personally been a victim of such circumstances. As can therefore be seen, while healing can bring joy and relief, it can also bring pain, frustration and serious theological questions.

The healing stories in the New Testament, and especially those in the gospels, have a hidden dimension that modern society should consider as it deals with disability in light of the contemporary concepts of healing and reconciliation. Jesus set a precedent in including the sick and those with disabilities as a focus of concern in his ministry. He chose to use healing to unite them with the rest of the society. Prior to his time, they were excluded, ignored and considered unclean. His reconciling mission meant good news for the poor, release for captives, recovery of sight to the blind and freedom for the oppressed (Luke 4:18).

Healing as a means of reconciliation in respect to Jesus's ministry to persons with disabilities had two complementary, but distinct, dimensions: cure and restoration. His mission had to take into consideration the aspect that the society of the day best understood. That was the cure, though it was only a means to the end and not necessarily the end. What was, and still is, most important in our reconciliation message is acceptance, inclusion and restoration into the mainstream of society. For example, when Bartimaeus (Mark 10:46–52) received his sight, we are told that he joined with the rest of the crowd who followed Jesus. He became one of them and was no longer isolated, excluded and ignored. He was no longer the blind man begging on the roadside. Not only was he cured of his blindness, but he was also restored to and reconciled with the rest of the society which had previously rebuked him, screamed at him, spoken **at** him instead of **to** him, and considered him different, inferior and imperfect.

There are approximately twenty-six different scriptures in the gospels referencing people with such infirmities as paralysis, blindness, deafness or physical disabilities. There are, in accordance with the Jewish and Christian culture and practice of the day, some important and shared characteristics among all these people. They have no names, they are poor, unemployed, beggars or servants. They are patronized, treated with contempt, publicly rebuked and humiliated. It was from this state of affairs that Jesus declared that he had come to set the captives free and to give release to the oppressed. His healing mission, though at times using the language of forgiveness of sin as this is what the Jews could understand, was precisely to set free those who had lived in the bondage of oppression, ridicule and humiliation. He invited them to his banquet table contrary to the expectations of the prevailing norm and practice.

Disability work in our churches will need to be inclusive and seen from the perspectives of the wider meaning of mission. "Mission" carries a holistic understanding: the proclamation and sharing of the good news of the gospel by word (**kerygma**), deed (**diakonia**), prayer and worship (**leiturgia**) and the everyday witness of the Christian life (**martyria**); teaching as building up and strengthening people in their relationship with God and each other; and healing as wholeness and reconciliation into **koinonia** – communion with God, communion with people, and communion with creation as a whole. This encompasses well what the church is expected to be and to do.

We are challenged to make our theological understanding so broad, so spacious, that it can take into account every aspect of human life in relation to Christ's saving grace. We are challenged to view life in its full richness and complexity. In relation to disability, theology is challenged to talk about God, faith and life in a way that is open to God's future that can unite and transcend every human existence.

The church is by definition a place and a process of communion, open to and inviting all people without discrimination. It is a place of hospitality and a place of welcome, in the manner in which Abraham and Sarah received God's messengers in the Old Testament (Gen 18). It is an earthly reflection of a divine unity that is at the same time worshipped as Trinity. It is a community of people with different yet complementary gifts. It is a vision of wholeness as well as of healing, of caring and of sharing. We all accept and proclaim that this is what the church is and stands for. It is the basis of our unity as Christians.

Inclusion and meaningful participation are what many persons with disabilities strive for. They need to be in the process of give and take and not remain those who receive what other people give. Interdependence is the key here. Even though the secular world stresses independence, we are called to live as a community dependent on God and one another. Nobody among us should be considered a burden for the rest; and nobody among us is simply a burden-bearer. We all bear one another's burdens in order to fulfil the law of Christ (Gal 6:2). Paul writes: "For as in one body we have many members, and the members do not all have the same function, so we, though many, are one body in Christ, and individually members one of another" (Rom 12:4–5, ESV). This calls for recognition of the fact that we are incomplete, we are less than whole, without the gifts and talents of all people. We are not a full community without one another.

This edited volume, which comprises contributions from authors situated in several African countries and the UK, centres on disability inclusion and harmful practices that should be considered as we move towards life-giving theologies. It is another step towards reconciliation and building the church as a communion by upholding persons with disabilities as members on an equal basis with others. It is a step towards a theology of inclusion and meaningful participation of all despite their bodily or psychological conditions. It reflects a stage in our togetherness in a pilgrimage of justice and reconciliation.

Introduction

Disability Inclusion in Africa

Introducing the Contexts and Contents of the Volume

Madleina Daehnhardt (note 1)

Disability, Church Practice and Theologies in African Contexts: Why It Matters

The former Malawian Minister for Disability and Elderly Affairs, the late Rachel Kachaje – who was a wheelchair user – spoke of once visiting

---

1. Many thanks to Nina Kurlberg for her detailed input into the introduction, and to Sas Conradie, Tom Shakespeare, Ruth Reinecke and David Ford for reviewing it. Thanks to Seren Boyd for final copy-edits.

her sister who had been admitted to a referral hospital. She was met by pastors from her sister's church with great amazement. They asked if she was OK and what was wrong with her as she was in a wheelchair, demonstrating an underlying assumption that she needed medical attention. Kachaje recorded this encounter:

> When I entered the hospital [to visit my sick sister], the nurse enquired which ward was I admitted in. I responded that I was not a patient, but that I was visiting my sister who was [unwell and] admitted. Then she said: "But you are in the wheelchair." I said, "Yes, this wheelchair is for my mobility." (note 2)

The above glimpse from Kachaje's life story shows the challenges of dealing with prevailing narratives of disability being perceived as sickness in church and public life. This is in the context of the contemporary church having become a powerful social movement shaping public perceptions in the African continent. Like few other institutions, it influences the thinking and actions of millions of people at grassroots levels. At the same time, the church's engagement with disability seems to have been inconsistent: empowering and transformative

---

2. Kachaje, "'I Know the Plans,'" 330.

at best, but patchy and problematic at worst. As will become clear through the chapters in this volume, we argue that attitudinal changes must involve a critical assessment of cultural and religious messages and practices on all levels, which is why this book focuses on holistic and liberative theologies. Since the teaching of the church is so crucial in shaping attitudes and perceptions on disability in the African context, it is not an option for theological education and pastoral practice to treat disability as a side topic. This insight is especially important in the context of Christian relief and development organizations that work with churches to bring transformation to those living in poverty. According to the Kenyan practitioner–scholar Phitalis Were Masakhwe,

> The church's stand on anything is taken very seriously. . . . It is therefore important that the church's stand on the place, role, rights and dignity of [people living with disabilities] be made unequivocally clear. Any ambiguities . . . can greatly damage public perception on disability and hence the image and dignity of those born with various forms of impairments. (note 3)

---

3. Masakhwe, "Disability Concerns," 113.

4   Disability Inclusion in Africa

This volume seeks to foster dialogue, stimulating fresh thinking and deep introspection in regards to beliefs held and theologies preached. The idea for this book emerged in 2019 during a conference hosted by Tearfund in the Democratic Republic of Congo on disability and the church. At this conference there was a request for theological resources that could facilitate a better understanding of how churches and Christian relief and development organizations could respond to disability in their communities.

Consequently, a call for papers was extended beyond the participants of the conference. This volume brings together a range of voices – including disability theologians and practitioners from across Africa and the UK. Our aim is to contribute to promoting a movement away from potentially harmful attitudes towards liberative and holistic approaches, which are important to disability inclusion. Although the book contributions are largely rooted in the discipline of theology – broadly speaking – they also have multidisciplinary elements, exploring disability inclusion and disability theologies with reference to disability studies, development studies and cultural anthropology. This partly reflects my own editorial positionality as a non-theologian, and as a multidisciplinary researcher with a background in languages, anthropology and development studies. The relationship between theology and the social sciences – anthropology in particular – has traditionally been awkward and filled with tensions. (note 4) Drawing on the work of anthropologists, this volume is trying to work with the uneasy disciplinary divide. Of particular note in this engagement are the ways in which book contributions "ground theology within lived experience" and draw from insights offered in ethnographic studies on the topic. (note 5)

By "inclusion," in this volume we refer to practices that go beyond access and participation to address power imbalances – hidden as well as visible. (note 6) Disability inclusion is also seen as an evolving journey towards belonging, requiring continued change. (note 7) There are several dimensions to this move towards disability inclusion – and this book does not stand in isolation, but is rather part of a wider recent and encouraging development in African church networks to engage with the topic. This is in dialogue with the work of global disability theologians who challenge the church to engage positively with disability and to become more

_____

4. Robbins, "Anthropology and Theology."
5. Lemons, **Theologically Engaged Anthropology**, 8.
6. See Kurlberg and Daehnhardt, "Introduction."
7. Kurlberg and Daehnhardt.

inclusive communities of faith. (note 8) The 2019 work of South African disability theologian Louise Kretzschmar on inclusion and participation has been invaluable in efforts to create disability-friendly churches. (note 9) This very practical publication focuses on theological interpretations, sociocultural issues and practical circumstances of people living with disabilities in Southern Africa and their full inclusion in churches. In 2011, Samuel Kabue et al., pioneers in disability theology in African contexts, published **Disability, Society, and Theology: Voices from Africa** – the first edited volume of its kind. Kabue identified three main aspects hindering the full inclusion in church life of people living with disabilities: paternalistic and patronizing attitudes; exclusion from participation and leadership; and unjustified theological emphasis on physical healing. (note 10)

A number of further resources on disability theology have been promoted through the World Council of Churches (WCC) Ecumenical Disability Advocates Network (EDAN) since then. In 2016, two resource books for theology and religious studies

---

8. Eiesland, **Disabled God**; Creamer, **Disability and Christian Theology**; Swinton, "God We Worship"; Yong, **New Vision**.
9. Kretzschmar, **Church and Disability**.
10. Kabue, "Persons with Disabilities," 8.

were developed by Kabue et al. and supported by EDAN in Nairobi. The textbook **Disability in Africa** covers African Traditional Religions, biblical views, and psychological, sociological, theological, pastoral and legal perspectives on disability, alongside practical dimensions, gender and emerging issues. (note 11) In a similar vein, the textbook **Perspectives on Disability** discusses concepts and definitions of disability; theoretical perspectives; matters of inclusion and exclusion; disability in relation to gender, children, worship, African Traditional Religions and cultural perspectives; the problem of evil; and many more topics. (note 12) These are key advances regarding disability and the church, and the book is a much-needed resource for learning and teaching in theological education institutions. Written from within the context, it engages with important aspects of African cultures, traditions, customs and rituals, which are all significant for understanding the disability discourse on the continent. The development of disability theology by African scholars shows that "practical theologians and the wider church community have taken serious notice of the realities and

---

11. Kabue, Amanze and Landman, **Disability in Africa.**
12. Kabue, Ishalo-Esan and Ayegboyin, **Perspectives on Disability.**

experiences of persons with disabilities in our time." (note 13) As Anjeline Okola, a representative of EDAN, mentions in Kabue et al.'s latest volume in this series, **The Changing Scenes of Disability in Church and Society** (2021), "the idea is to promote a theology of inclusion despite our abilities as all people who have been created in the image and likeness of God." (note 14)

Structure of the Introduction

This introduction can only briefly touch on the wider scene of disability theology in African contexts; we devote chapter 1 to discussing African beliefs, religion, theologies and disability. Initially this introduction and chapter 1 were written as one piece, but in order to do justice to both perspectives – disability theology and wider contexts – they were split in two and then developed in greater depth. The remainder of this introduction now discusses a range of contexts – contexts which are not necessarily discussed directly in the chapters that follow, nor central to disability theology, but which are nevertheless crucial to understanding disability. We start with a

---

13. Okola, introduction to Kabue et al., **Changing Scenes**, xvi.

14. Okola, foreword to Kabue et al., **Changing Scenes**, vii.

brief discussion of the challenges of understanding disability in context, followed by a discussion of the policy context, and the intersectional context of poverty, which highlights disability as a social justice issue. This is followed by a discussion on how the volume engages with and contributes to disability models. The next major section introduces the book structure and each chapter, highlighting contributions to the field. Lastly, a reflection on the overall contributions and limitations of the volume highlights gaps and future research agendas.

The Challenge of Understanding Disability in Context

Such a volume as this has the task of defining what is meant by disability. This is important, as disability is a widely used and yet vague term with complex realities and heterogeneous meanings. Even the World Health Organization (WHO) and World Bank's **World Report on Disability** describe disability as "complex, dynamic, multidimensional and contested." (note 15) It has been highlighted that "the lack of homogeneity among 'people with disabilities' makes creating a valid taxonomy

---

15. WHO and the World Bank, **World Report on Disability**, 3.

under this term difficult." (note 16) Aggregating persons with disabilities in one homogeneous group can be problematic as respect for difference diminishes, since "people with impairments differ from one another as much as people in any other segment of society differ." (note 17) Yet despite the contention and complexity surrounding disability as a concept or construct, its value lies in enabling connection and constructive dialogue on a common aspect of human experience, especially in relation to shared experiences of discrimination and marginalization on account of disabilities.

The challenge of establishing standardized classifications and measurements of disabilities was revealed by a major cross-cultural, multi-country study – including African countries – commissioned by the WHO. (note 18) The study acknowledges that "it is difficult to arrive at a common language on a topic as culture-bound as disability." (note 19) This is because concepts of functioning and what constitutes disability may differ markedly across contexts. Cultural diversity poses a "fundamental dilemma" when researching disability: although impairments are

---

16. Wehymeyer, "Beyond Pathology," 4.
17. Kabue et al., **Disability in Africa**, 8.
18. Üstün et al., "Cultural Variation," 3–19.
19. Üstün et al., ix.

"a universal trait of human beings," they are also experienced by individuals uniquely and influenced by a range of complex combinations of factors, from personal, psychological and intellectual, to differences in the physical, social and cultural environments. (note 20) As earlier work of anthropologists on disability and culture shows, disability as a category does not exist in many contexts and languages; in the words of Susan Reynolds Whyte and Benedicte Ingstad, "there are blind people, and lame [**sic**] people and 'slow' people, but 'the disabled' as a general term does not translate easily into many languages." (note 21) In that sense, disability is an external construct in many cultures and one that also has a very recent history. To some degree, this also relates to the ancient cultures and languages of Israel: biblical Hebrew does not have a word equivalent to the English term "disability"; the Hebrew word **mum** comes closest to referring to conditions that we may consider disabilities today, and is usually translated as "blemish." (note 22) In this context, rather than dismissing disability as a modern concept foreign to ancient societies in Israel, Hebrew Bible scholars Nyasha Junior and Jeremy

---

20. Üstün et al., 9.
21. Whyte and Ingstad, "Disability and Culture," 7.
22. Junior and Schipper, "Disability Studies," 32.

Schipper point out that "these differences invite us to consider the cultural associations present in biblical representations of disability." (note 23)

In this volume, we do not attempt to work towards a pan-African definition of disability. Instead, we engage with the plurality of perceptions of disability, and highlight the importance of contextual understandings. Nevertheless, for clarity and pragmatic reasons, we need to work with some sort of broad working definition of disability. In short, we define disability as any long-term impairment which leads to social and economic disadvantage and to the denial of rights and equal participation in society. (note 24) Generally, the authors in this volume understand disability as a social condition affecting the person living with that disability, as well as his or her household and wider social relations. (note 25) We do not focus on or limit the discussion to specific types of disability; instead we include both general and specific chapters. In other words, some chapters discuss disability in conceptual terms, while others draw from specific examples across physical, intellectual or psychosocial disabilities. The use

---

23. Junior and Schipper, 32.
24. United Nations, CRPD.
25. Harris-White and Sridhar, "Disability and Development," 126–30.

of the terms "disability" and "impairment" and their differences need clarification. Impairment is defined as any loss of physiological, psychological or anatomical structure or function. (note 26) An impairment on its own does not need to be a disability; instead it is "the interaction between persons with impairments and attitudinal and environmental barriers" that result in disability. (note 27) As this volume highlights, socio-religious beliefs and sociocultural attitudes to impairments can lead to disability.

The Public Policy and Intersectional Contexts

This volume is set in a wider, ever-emerging public policy context. For policy discussions about disability inclusion, access and participation are key, and infrastructure and education are vital. A comprehensive analysis of these important aspects of disability inclusion is not the focus of this book: zooming in on the under-researched aspects of beliefs and theologies is. However, this wider policy context is very important to note, as progress on policy in African contexts has been comparatively slow, and this impacts everything else. In 2018, a conference held in Botswana – which resulted in a

---

26. Harris-White and Sridhar, 127.
27. UN Human Rights Office of the High Commissioner, CRPD.

publication comprising twenty-seven essays – was held to "address the injustices, discrimination and exclusion that people with disabilities face in their daily life" in Southern and Central Africa. (note 28) The organizers of the conference, Botswana-based theologian–academics James Amanze and Fidelis Nkomazana, acknowledged that although understandings and acceptance of disability in Africa had come a long way, "we still cannot say with certainty how much has been achieved in regard to [the] spiritual, economic, political, legal and social emancipation [of people with disabilities]." (note 29)

The contextual discrepancy between good policy intentions and the experience of grassroots-level realities globally is also worth noting. Since 2008, many countries have ratified the Convention on the Rights of Persons with Disabilities (CRPD) and may even have initiated reform legislation – and this is a step in the right direction. However, at the same time, in 2021, when we started to write this book, far less seemed to have changed in practice on the ground to address discrimination against people living with disabilities. (note 30) Colin Barnes, one of the key advocates of disability studies in the

---

28. Amanze and Nkomazana, "Introduction," 26.
29. Amanze and Nkomazana, 26.
30. Nyangweso, "Disability in Africa," 134.

UK, acknowledges that "policies have had only a marginal impact on the everyday experience of disablement." (note 31) This wide gap between intended policy ratifications and implementation realities also affects the African church and societal context, despite fifty-four of fifty-five African countries having signed the African Charter on Human and Peoples' Rights. (note 32)

We now turn to discuss a specific policy concern: the disability–poverty linkage. This connection is of particular importance to relief and development organizations and the faith-based organizations they partner with in designing disability-inclusive programmes. More broadly, the significance of disability theology in Africa is to be understood as a social justice issue – relevant for the mission of the church – in its intersectional context. Intersectionality is to be understood as a set of mutually reinforcing and amplifying factors in the experience of inequality. Poverty – like gender – is a key intersectional factor in relation to disability both in public policy and practice. We also focus on the intersection between disability and poverty here, as the holistic well-being and flourishing of humans is a core concern of the integral mission of the church. In other words, if the church is to

---

31. Barnes, "Social Model," 26.
32. ACHPR, "African Charter."

address human need holistically, it must first show awareness of the stark realities of disadvantage pertaining to disability.

Overall, prevalence of different forms of disabilities across the African continent is difficult to assess, due to incomplete data and lack of statistical information. According to research by the African Child Policy Forum (ACPF), Africa as a continent has one of the largest populations of children with disabilities in the world, as a result of widespread armed conflicts, household poverty and lack of adequate health care services. (note 33) What is clear is that worldwide, as many as 50 percent of disabilities are preventable and linked to poverty. (note 34) Thinking about disability and its lived experience in faith communities is therefore connected to wider socio-economic issues and part of a web of interconnections. (note 35) These

---

33. African Child Policy Forum, **Children with Disabilities**.
34. Harris-White and Sridhar, "Disability and Development," 126.
35. **The Routledge Handbook of Disability in Southern Africa**, an edited volume by Chataika (2019), is a good starting point to understand intersectionality as it covers a range of important areas in relation to disability in the Southern African region: inclusion and development, access

include a range of factors from macro-level social policies to micro-level household dynamics, which are beyond the scope of this introduction.

Both disability and poverty are dynamic phenomena, with several interrelated, evolving and contextually rooted mechanisms at play. An edited volume by anthropologists Arne Eide and Benedicte Ingstad confirms further the persistent interconnections between poverty and disability which result from social, cultural, political and structural processes. (note 36) The vicious cycle manifests itself in severe disadvantages in opportunities in education, employment, health care and income security. A two-way influence has been noted: disability can create or worsen poverty, but poverty can also create disability. Poverty is often linked to malnutrition, poor housing and hygiene conditions, ill health, and inadequate access to preventive and curative medical care, which can all result in physical disabilities. For example, in the absence of financial resources, some curable conditions may be left untreated and result in permanent visual

---

to primary, secondary and higher education, employment, religion, gender and parenthood, access to travel and sports.

36. Ingstad and Eide, "Introduction: Disability and Poverty."

or hearing impairments. (note 37) Inequalities are amplified when children born into low-income households do not have access to medical and educational opportunities, while their peers born into high-income families may have access to private specialist health care and special needs education, or educational support in mainstream education, providing optimal environments for them to flourish. (note 38)

This, of course, is not to assume that all persons living with disabilities also live in poverty. (note 39) However, research clearly shows that most people living with disabilities in the Majority World – including Africa – are confronted with

---

37. Ingstad and Eide, 5.
38. Ingstad and Eide, 6.
39. It is important here to highlight the significance of family (broadly conceived) "as a critical source of survival for disabled people particularly in low-income countries." As Addlakha rightly emphasizes, "disability is often lived as a family experience" (Addlakha, "Kinship Destabilized!," S46). Those fortunate enough to be born into wealthy families may enjoy high levels of education and high living standards, alongside high levels of accommodation.

poverty and lower living standards. (note 40) The authors of a study of households across fifteen countries found that disability was linked with lower educational attainment, lower employment rates, asset deprivation and higher medical expenditure. (note 41) The study concluded that "persons with disabilities, on average, experience multiple deprivations at higher rates and in higher breadth, depth, and severity than persons without disabilities." (note 42) This finding supports the hypothesis that, "in developing countries, disability is associated with multidimensional poverty." (note 43) The earlier article of UK-based social researchers Rebecca Yeo and Karen Moore provides an important piece of evidence supporting the vicious cycle of poverty and disability in the Majority World: "poverty within poverty" and the

---

40. For example, Eide et al.'s study "Living Conditions" on four countries in the Southern African region (Namibia, Zimbabwe, Malawi and Zambia) indicates that living conditions among people living with disabilities – in comparison with the general population – are lower in all areas being studied: school attendance, literacy, employment, access to information and access to service delivery.
41. Mitra et al., "Disability and Poverty," 1–18.
42. Mitra et al., 11.
43. Mitra et al., 11.

widespread exclusion of people with disabilities in the work of development institutions. (note 44) As part of overall development efforts, disability researchers Shakespeare et al. have also argued for the importance of investing in the training of people with disabilities in Africa, "for economic reasons, not solely to achieve social justice goals." (note 45)

The Use of Disability Models in This Volume

The authors in this volume broadly refer to three common models in understanding disability: the medical model, the charity model and the social model. (note 46) The medical model emphasizes the medical condition of the impairment involved, and seeks medical or technical solutions to

---

44. Yeo and Moore, "Including Disabled People."

45. Shakespeare et al., "Success in Africa," 1.

46. There are other models worth mentioning, which have not been main lenses employed in this volume but have indirectly informed the thinking of some authors. For example, the human rights model, which although connected to the social model is distinct: "Whereas the social model merely explains disability, the human rights model encompasses values for disability policy that acknowledge the human dignity of disabled persons" (Degener, "New Human Rights Model," 43).

improve or alleviate the impairment. This model underpins much of medical and occupational rehabilitation interventions. The charity model focuses on helping people with disabilities through offering elementary welfare. The global church, including the church and its missions across the African continent, has historically drawn from these models in the establishment of hospitals, schools and charitable organizations. In this volume we are making a case for the church to engage more intentionally with the social model in its theology and practice, and to develop awareness of cultural–religious models. The church in Africa has been criticized for being a "reluctant reformer" in failing to embrace ideas from the disability movement and for not going beyond the charity model; it has been argued that "the church must do more than just building institutions for the disabled. It should be more rights-based, holistic and adopt a developmental understanding and appreciation of disability." (note 47)

The social model was developed in the wake of the disability movement by those living with disabilities, to address the shortcomings in the medical and charity models which tended to see people as passive recipients. It has been described as "a tool with which to provide insights into the

---

47. Masakhwe, "Disability Concerns," 115.

disabling tendencies of modern society in order to generate policies and practices to facilitate their eradication." (note 48) The idea that persons with impairment become disabled only when social and environmental barriers limit their opportunities and rights is central to the social model. (note 49) It emphasizes three major types of social discrimination: institutional, environmental and attitudinal. (note 50) Institutional discrimination runs through laws, strategies, policy and practice, and the absence thereof. (note 51) Environmental discrimination refers to the physical environment and its inaccessibility. Attitudinal discrimination includes values and beliefs that are harmful. Although the different chapters in this volume engage with the three different aspects of social discrimination, the attitudinal aspect underpins most chapters. Overall, most authors engage with (variations and extensions of) the social model, "a powerful and life-affirming model" which aligns

---

48. Barnes, "Social Model," 20.
49. Harris-White and Sridhar, "Disability and Development," 126–30.
50. Yeo and Moore, "Including Disabled People," 571–90.
51. Yeo and Moore, 572.

with the purpose of the volume. (note 52) Some authors in this volume attempt to contextualize existing models in African contexts.

An additional model that is worth highlighting in the context of this volume is the moral/religious model of disability, which sees disability as a consequence of moral/religious infractions. (note 53) Much of the theological reflection on disability within the church in Africa, and within the global church too, arguably engages with this model. (note 54) Engagement with the moral/religious model of disability is therefore present to varying degrees in a number of the contributions in this volume, even if not explicitly stated as such.

What is more, European-based disability researchers have been working on formulating a cultural model of disability – using culture as an analytical category for the study of disability. Belgium-based anthropologist Patrick Devlieger frames a perspective on disability through the lens of culture. (note 55) According to Devlieger, a cultural perspective emphasizes that disability

---

52. Vehmas and Watson, "Disability Studies," 4.
53. Retief and Letsosa, "Models of Disability," n.p.
54. Reynolds, "Protestant Christianity."
55. Devlieger, "Cultural Model."

is a cultural reality that is both time- and place-bound; "the assertion that disability is culturally created and stands as a reflection of a society's meaning of the phenomenon it created" is its starting point. (note 56) Devlieger has argued that the social model must be expanded with "components of disability that are reflected in identity, culture, and worldview." (note 57) German-based sociologist Anne Waldschmidt sums up the cultural model as starting with "the premise that impairments and dis/abilities are structuring culture(s) and are concurrently structured and lived through culture." (note 58) At the same time Devlieger and colleagues in their work on world perspectives acknowledge that the cultural model needs continued rethinking and "remains an unfinished project." (note 59) Waldschmidt similarly points out that the cultural model is emerging and without a uniform definition to date, one reason being that the definition of culture itself is contested terrain. (note 60) She also highlights that the model remains unacknowledged: "the cultural model of disability is rather implicit

---

56. Devlieger, "Rejoinder," 526.
57. Devlieger, "Cultural Model," 2.
58. Waldschmidt, "Disability-Culture-Society," 76.
59. Devlieger et al., **Rethinking Disability**, 19.
60. Waldschmidt, 71.

amidst an ongoing discussion on the implications of culture for disability constructions." (note 61) Although the authors in this volume do not directly engage with this body of work on developing a cultural model, several chapters in part 2 engage with cultural context. We also explore the theme of attitudes, beliefs, religion and culture in greater depth in the first half of chapter 1. In summary, the volume adds to discussions about some aspects of culture in seeking to understand disability contextually, such as through "symbols and values, meanings and interpretations, narratives and histories, traditions, rituals and customs, social behaviour, attitudes and identities." (note 62)

It is important to reflect on the fact that all models have limitations, and to reiterate that they were developed within individualistic societies in Europe and the USA. As editors, we realize the dangers of dichotomies, such as the potential polarization of the medical model

---

61. Waldschmidt, 74.

62. Waldschmidt here is summarizing the broad approach to culture by German-based cultural anthropologist Vester (**Kompendium der Soziologie I**), according to which "culture refers to the totality of 'things' created and employed by a particular people or a society, be they material or immaterial." Waldschmidt, 71.

versus the social model. Such dichotomies are not helpful, especially given the context. (note 63) Shakespeare, who is critical of the social model, has made a case for disability studies to "achieve a complex, multi-factorial account of disability." (note 64) The 2020 revised edition of the **Routledge Handbook of Disability Studies** – which has served as a major reference text in the development of the discipline globally – makes a case for "the multidisciplinary future" of disability studies. (note 65) The handbook describes the decade since its first edition as a "cooperative period," one when "different approaches have co-existed, ideas have been shared, and new ways of looking at disability have emerged." (note 66) Since we intend to make a contribution by encouraging interdisciplinary engagement between theology and disability studies, this allows for the coexistence and intertwining of models, going beyond the use of any one conceptual model.

Book Structure and Chapter Overview

This volume consists of nine chapters structured in two parts. Part 1 sets out holistic frameworks

---

63. Shakespeare, **Rights and Wrongs**.
64. Shakespeare, 1.
65. Vehmas and Watson, "Disability Studies," 3–13.
66. Vehmas and Watson, 5.

for rethinking disability and disability theology in African contexts. This first part draws from work written (or reframed for this volume) by both UK-based and African-based theologians, practitioners and thinkers. This framing is pursued by setting the wider scene for a discussion of disability, beliefs and theologies, in reference to principles for reading the Bible responsibly, by untangling harmful theologies that associate disability with sin, and by aiming at more liberative and holistic understandings of and preaching about "healing" in church contexts. Part 2 offers a range of perspectives for understanding disability more helpfully in context, through the different lenses of **ubuntu** and **imago Dei**, and through a theology of accommodation. While all chapters draw from practical and/or pastoral examples – and advocate in different ways for the transformation of church and institutional practice – the last two chapters are most focused on this endeavour. They reflect the need for church communities to adjust attitudes and accessibility, and for educators to better incorporate disability theology in the curriculum in theological education across Africa.

What now follows in this section is a summary of each chapter, focusing on the main contributions to the volume.

Part 1

In the opening chapter on disability, beliefs and theologies in the context of the African continent, Madleina Daehnhardt and Nina Kurlberg, the UK-based editors of this volume, engage with the existing literature on religion and disability relevant to African contexts. The chapter discusses the important values–beliefs–behaviours linkage. The significance of etiology is highlighted here: African beliefs regarding the causal origin of disability as documented in earlier and more recent anthropological studies are discussed. An exploration of these contexts is instrumental for a meaningful engagement with disability in African Traditional Religion and African Protestant Christianity, which follows. Based on a literature review of African theological publications, supplemented with literature from outside Africa, the authors identify key relevant themes of research in disability theology: purity and sin, healing, liberation and dignity, as well as church practice and theological education. The different chapters in this volume engage with many of these topics to varying degrees, and the opening chapter sets the scene for the volume as a whole.

Grant Macaskill then provides the reader with a constructive framework for reading the Bible responsibly on disability. The chapter highlights that a serious effort to "think biblically" about disability brings with it a body of further blessings for the church. Macaskill, who is based in Scotland and is a specialist in autism, starts with disentangling misreading the Bible in relation to autism. He then introduces the reader to six helpful principles putting interpretations of disability (and illness) in the Bible into context. The principles that the author outlines can be traced back to the earliest centuries of the church, when its centres of spiritual and intellectual leadership were particularly associated with northern Africa, Asia Minor and the Middle East. This is important to note because in today's context, these rich principles of biblical reading have widely been replaced by interpretative practices that are popular in contemporary evangelicalism, the advocates of which consider themselves uniquely faithful to the Bible. As the author highlights, their interpretative approach is, however, much more affected by the values of the West than they typically recognize. Macaskill's six principles can be summarized as reading the Bible in a way that is governed by the person and story of Jesus Christ; reading the Bible as a complex whole; respecting the historical particularities of the time when the Bible was written; reading the Bible within the communion of the church; reading the Bible humbly as a fallible community; and reading the Bible with the Spirit who illumines. While Macaskill's examples draw from the condition of autism, the principles outlined are widely applicable, and relevant to the chapters that follow.

Selina Palm's chapter disentangles harmful theological scripts around sin and healing in the Southern African context where the author is based and writes from an academic theological viewpoint. Her chapter shows how these scripts sadly often underpin the lived experiences of harm of people living with disabilities and their families within religious settings and faith communities. Here, she argues that the prevalent disability/sin/curse nexus must be tackled at its theological roots within local congregations where it has led to distorted approaches to healing and prayer, wrongly transferring blame and guilt to people with disabilities and their families. Palm makes a case for developing liberating theologies of disabilities including addressing Bible interpretations, drawing from theological voices within Southern Africa and beyond. She makes a case for the need for churches to move towards redemptive biblical interpretations of disability and to be Spirit-filled communities of embrace for people living with disabilities.

The late Micheline Kamba, from her position of professor at the Université Protestante au Congo (UPC), and a person living with a visible disability, examines holistic theologies on the basis of Acts 3:1–10, which records the healing of a man with lifelong mobility impairments. First, she offers to the reader an autobiographical reading of the text. Kamba views this text as a source of holistic healing – beyond just the physical – because it also reveals emotional, social and spiritual healing. Kamba's chapter concludes that the text challenges the church to deal with the issue of disability holistically. Second, the text of Acts 3:1–10 is at the centre of an exploratory contextual Bible study with church leader participants. This was conducted for her PhD research on "Developing a Holistic Educational Programme through Contextual Bible Study with People with Disabilities in Kinshasa, DRC." The Bible study participants came to understand their attitudes towards people with disabilities and opted for change. Kamba's chapter argues that the church needs to adopt the aspect of holistic healing to become a church of all and for all, which is what she refers to as a "transformative church." The rereading of the text focuses on a reconstructed view of people with disabilities to be realized with the support of church leaders. The support is understood as involving the use of education, which serves as a source of empowerment and as the means of liberation for people with disabilities.

Part 2

Edwin Zulu's chapter reflects on the positive contribution that an African perspective on community can bring to understanding disability, in an attempt to shape a more positive perspective on disability in the African church. He writes from the perspective of a Zambian theologian–academic and church leader. The chapter introduces four perspectives on disability that can be found in Africa and shows how, when a community perspective – underpinned by the concept of **ubuntu** – is brought into dialogue with the Bible, negative perspectives on disability can be deconstructed, while positive perspectives can be brought to the fore. The chapter is grounded in an understanding that as the creator of all, God is the source of human dignity and diversity.

David Tarus, from the perspective of a leading thinker in Christian theological education in Africa, offers reflections from Kenya on the concept of **imago Dei** in light of disability. Tarus argues that people living with disabilities are created fully in the image of God and should be honoured as full persons capable of contributing to the flourishing of the church and society in Africa. The chapter presents three views of the image of God: the substantial view, the functional view and the relational view. Each of these views simply highlights different aspects of the image of God, and no one view is sufficient on its own. The relational view seems to resonate with an African approach to prefer communion over individuality. However, African communality alone is not sufficient for a correct theological anthropology that esteems people living with disabilities. A christocentric anthropology is necessary here. Thus, the chapter shows the central place of Christ in the formation of image bearers who can take on an alternative way of being. Tarus presents three ecclesial implications of the doctrine of the image of God in the African context in regard to treatment of disability: the sacredness of human life; cultivation of an enabling environment for the flourishing of people living with disabilities; and empowerment of people living with disabilities as equal partners in the flourishing of the world.

Jill Harshaw's chapter helps us to rethink the possible spirituality and inclusion of people living with profound intellectual disabilities, through the doctrine of divine accommodation. "Intellectual disability" refers to those who are nonverbal and/or with restricted cognitive functions due to an IQ below 30 from birth or early infancy. She sets herself a difficult task, as the spirituality of intellectual disability cannot be explored through first-hand accounts from people who have severe linguistic and cognitive limitations. Harshaw's point of reference is her own daughter Rebecca, and her writer positionality is that of a Northern Ireland-based academic. Nevertheless, her insights into the theology of accommodation have wider global applicability to people living with profound intellectual disabilities, their families and faith communities, also in the African context. Harshaw claims that genuine inclusion means recognizing and valuing people's relationships, not only with other members of the community, but also with God. She delves into ways of divine revelation and the theology of accommodation, which has been described as the act of God, in his self-revelation to humanity, accommodating himself to the mental and spiritual capacity of human beings, so that they can come to know and love him. Harshaw challenges the widespread assumption that his self-disclosure must be confined within the biblical text, and asks why it should not be possible for God, out of the reservoirs of the same love that motivated God's accommodated communication found within the biblical text, to be capable of self-revelation in ways appropriate to potential recipients of his revelation. In the context of profound intellectual disability, this means that because human beings cannot know God as he is revealed though the Scriptures, he sees fit to reveal to them as and what he wants them to know of himself.

Dan Nyampong Asihene explores attitudes and accessibility in the Ghanaian church context. His chapter shows that prevailing attitudes towards people with disabilities are a major concern in Ghanaian society, with a number of reasons accounting for these varied attitudes. These include social, cultural and religious factors, as well as the real or perceived causes of disability. The chapter discusses inherent cultural and religious beliefs which Asihene describes as "unhealthy"; these manifest themselves in the use of Akan language terms, and tend to express and influence people's attitudes towards people with disabilities. The chapter explores disability models in the African/Ghanaian context and argues that the sociocultural attitudes of the church in Africa, and society at large, have influenced people's views of disabled people. The author points out that previous research in the field of disability studies relied predominantly on the medical and social models of disabilities. Whereas these models consider psychosocial attitudes to disability, this chapter emphasizes that cultural and religious beliefs significantly affect attitudes and in turn influence actions towards people with disabilities.

Tongriang Daspan and Noah Daspan's chapter, from the perspective of an academic planning practitioner in theological education in Nigeria, makes a case for the important role of inclusive theological disability education. The chapter uses an original small-scale survey, presenting experiences of worshippers with disability in churches which are part of the Fellowship of Churches of Christ in Nigeria (TEKAN) network, as well as of educators and key informants in theological college education. Daspan and Daspan argue for the need for a theological education that is inclusive and considerate of people living with disabilities. The authors argue that theological education holds the greatest potential and yet owes both church and society the greatest responsibility for building an inclusive worship community, through which all worshippers reach maturity and unity of faith and maximize their calling and potential. In contrast, their interviews with worshippers with visual, hearing and mobility impairments highlight the reality that many of them do not enjoy the same opportunities as others for growth, service or participation because of discrimination in different aspects of society, including places of worship. Daspan and Daspan's analysis concludes that, despite the commendable efforts of some churches in providing educational and rehabilitation services to people living with disabilities, the church in Nigeria is generally not very inclusive. This is linked to the fact that theological education in Nigeria is not adequately preparing clerics for ministerial assignments that consider worshippers with disabilities in the church. As their study shows, the curricula of the sampled theological institutions have minimal or no disability studies included in them. This can unintentionally lead to graduates being ignorant, insensitive or unable to create the right environment for the spiritual growth and participation of worshippers in the church.

Contributions, Limitations and Future Research

Lastly, it is important to reflect on the contributions, special features and limitations of this volume.

The synthesis of published work in dialogue across different disciplines is an important contribution to the field. We have pulled together current strands and perspectives in relation to disability and disability theology in Africa, in deep engagement with the existing literature. The extensive bibliography consulted in chapter 1 provides the reader with further references to engage with. In this volume we have attempted to give space to a range of theological and practitioner voices. We have allowed for different approaches in writing, including those that are academic, reflective and pastoral. Bringing the diversity of approaches together into one coherent whole is a significant achievement of the volume.

US-based African studies scholars Toyin Falola and Nic Hamel claim that the discipline of disability studies in the context of Africa is an "identifiably important field." (note 67) In their recently edited volume **Disability in Africa**, they suggest three ways to enable the flourishing of Africans living with disabilities, one being "a critical evaluation of African cultures and belief systems with regard to disability." (note 68) The contributions in this volume, interrogating theologies and beliefs based on interpretations of biblical texts pertaining to disability, have largely emerged from within Africa, and offer a unique contribution to

---

67. Falola and Hamel, "Africanizing Disability," 3. Falola and Hamel's work, situated within African studies, recognizes the prevalence of indigenous spiritual and religious approaches to disability in Africa, as well as the influence of Islamic and Christian conceptions of disability which are also substantial, although there is recognition that these vary widely depending on context.

68. While this point on critical evaluation is conceptual, the other two measures the editors suggest are practice-oriented: "an investment in local communities of families, caregivers and disabled peoples' organisations; and productive cooperation among national governments, NGOs, and the international humanitarian community." Falola and Hamel, 3.

the field. This contribution is twofold: it offers insights for the church in Africa and for African theological education institutions, and contributes to the wider global field of disability studies. Contributions from the African continent have a lot to offer; as Shakespeare concludes in his synthesis of disability in the Majority World, "disability studies cannot focus solely on Western experiences. It would be deeply regrettable if researchers spent their time exploring theoretical issues while neglecting practical and applied research to support social change." (note 69)

Therefore, the emphasis on context in our volume is a major contribution to the existing global literature. The works of medical anthropologists have repeatedly emphasized the importance of context when studying disability. Whyte and Ingstad highlight that circumstance and comparison are fundamental principles of anthropology, which help to tease out understanding of complex phenomena, such as disability in context. (note 70) This is important, as it is also often a disconnection from contextual understanding that renders policies and

---

69. Shakespeare, "Disability in Developing Countries," 330.
70. Whyte and Ingstad, "Introduction: Disability Connections," 1.

interventions inefficient. (note 71) In our volume we argue that disability in "the context of local worlds" needs to be understood through the context of local religions, which have been influenced by contextual interpretations of Christianity and contextual theological understandings. (note 72) As we have pointed out, secular anthropologists often fail to make this connection at the required level of depth, and this is where our volume can make a contribution.

One important goal of this volume is to enable the readership to identify, rethink and critique harmful theological approaches and to work towards more holistic understandings of disability for themselves. We hope this will contribute to enabling churches in Africa to respond better theologically to those living with disabilities, and especially to people with disabilities living in poverty in their

---

71. In the words of Whyte and Ingstad, "it is our argument that the energizing potential of human-rights declarations, progressive policies, and national statements of intent towards disabled citizens has to be measured in the context of local worlds. For that is where people are acting to make things work, and where the potentials may (or may not) be effected and effective as they were intended to be" (25).

72. Whyte and Ingstad, 25.

communities. Here it is so important for readers to be aware of their own positionality, which they will without doubt bring to reading and understanding the text.

Similarly, it is important to reflect on writer positionality in the context of a volume of this complexity. Editor positionality is not necessarily a weakness – or limitation – but rather a feature of this project. Different characteristics in terms of the places and spaces where the authors and editors are situated come with a range of experiences and perspectives.

Here it is important to reiterate that some of the authors and editors of this volume are or have been located in Africa, while others are located outside Africa, and the latter positionality comes with limitations in contextual understanding. Moreover, some are living with a disability or have first-hand experience of limiting conditions, while others have close experience of disability through living with a disabled family member. Yet others without first-hand or close experience of disability see themselves as allies of the disability rights movement. It is important to bear in mind the influence of these different positionalities on the writing process, including the personal and educational background of each writer, while recognizing that every contributor has something valuable to offer.

There is always the critique that individual experiences and expressions of people living with disabilities can get "buried in the representations of others," which is why collaborative research and genuine co-production of knowledge is so important. (note 73) Further, in-depth grassroots work can "provide the material to sketch out concepts of personhood, causality, and value that constitute local and moral worlds." (note 74) This present volume has limitations in all these areas. We would like to see more pioneering approaches using innovative research methods at grassroots levels in the future.

Lastly, the volume offers limited engagement with a number of topics and disability studies subdisciplines. For example, while other edited volumes have focused on studying disability through the life-course approach, our volume does not employ life-cycle perspectives. (note 75) Chapter contributions do not differentiate between the stages of the life course: infancy, childhood,

---

73. Whyte, "Discourse and Experience," 276.
74. Whyte, 281.
75. Heller, Harris and Albrecht, **Life Course**.

youth, adulthood, old age, death and dying. In future research, it would be valuable to apply a theological lens to understanding the spirituality of disability across the life-cycle stages in African contexts. More work also is needed to develop understanding in the suggested move from healing to flourishing, using narrative approaches and working with positive life stories on matters of importance raised in this volume: such as the experiences of disabled people of dignity, intrinsic worth and positive contribution within community and church. Other future research agendas include deeper hermeneutical work on biblical interpretations of disability in the African context, possibly in dialogue with African-Jewish theologians; under-researched types of disabilities and the African church; the role of the church in advocacy; and how the church can partner with the disability rights movement in the African context going forward.

Bibliography

Addlakha, Renu. "Kinship Destabilized! Disability and the Micropolitics of Care in Urban India." **Current Anthropology** 61, no. 21 (February 2020): S46–S54.

African Child Policy Forum. **The African Report on Children with Disabilities.** Addis Ababa: ACPF, 2014.

African Commission on Human and Peoples' Rights (ACHPR). "African Charter on Human and Peoples' Rights." Accessed 7 June 2022. https://achpr.au.int/en.

Amanze, James N., and Fidelis Nkomazana. "Introduction." In **Disability Is Not Inability: A Quest for Inclusion and Participation of People with Disability in Society**, edited by James N. Amanze and Jonathan S. Nkhoma, 26–29. Mzuzu: Muzuni Press, 2020.

Barnes, Colin. "Understanding the Social Model of Disability: Past, Present and Future." In **Routledge Handbook of Disability Studies**, edited by Nick Watson and Simo Vehmas, 14–31. London: Routledge, 2020.

Chataika, Tsitsi. "Introduction: Critical Connections and Gaps in Disability and Development." In **The Routledge Handbook of Disability in Southern Africa**, edited by Tsitsi Chataika, 3–13. London: Routledge, 2019.

Creamer, Deborah Beth. **Disability and Christian Theology: Embodied Limits and Constructive Possibilities.** Oxford: Oxford University Press, 2009.

Degener, Theresia. "A New Human Rights Model of Disability." In **The United Nations Convention on the Rights of Persons with Disabilities: A Commentary**, edited by Valentina Della Fina et al., 41–59. Cham: Springer, 2017.

Devlieger, Patrick J. "Generating a Cultural Model of Disability." Paper presented at the 19th Congress of the European Federation of Associations of Teachers of the Deaf (FEAPDA), 14–16 October 2005.

———. "Rejoinder: The Culture and Disability Perspective on Disability." **Disability and Rehabilitation** 22, no. 11 (2000): 526–27.

Devlieger, Patrick, Beatriz Mairanda-Galarza, Steven E. Brown and Megan Strickfaden. **Rethinking Disability: World Perspectives in Culture and Society**. 2nd ed. Antwerp: Garant, 2016.

Eide, Arne H., and Benedicte Ingstad. "Epilogue: Some Concluding Thoughts – The Way Ahead." In **Disability and Poverty: A Global Challenge**, edited by Arne H. Eide and Benedicte Ingstad, 225–31. Bristol: Policy Press, 2011.

Eide, Arne H., Mitch E. Loeb, Sekai Nhiwatiwa, Alister Munthali, Thabale J. Ngulube and Gert van Rooy. "Living Conditions among People with Disabilities in Developing Countries." In **Disability and Poverty: A Global Challenge**, edited by Arne H. Eide and Benedicte Ingstad, 55–70. Bristol: Policy Press, 2011.

Eiesland, Nancy. **The Disabled God: Towards a Liberatory Theology of Disability**. Nashville: Abingdon, 1994.

Falola, Toyin, and Nic Hamel. "Africanizing Disability: Toward an Articulation of African Disability Studies." In **Disability in Africa:**

Inclusion, Care, and the Ethics of Humanity, edited by Toyin Falola and Nic Hamel, 1–46. Rochester: University of Rochester Press, 2021.

Harris-White, Barbara, and Devi Sridhar. "Disability and Development." In **The Elgar Companion to Development Studies**, edited by David A. Clark, 126–30. Cheltenham: Elgar, 2006.

Heller Tamar, Sarah Parker Harris and Gary L. Albrecht. **Disability through the Life Course.** London: Sage, 2012.

Ingstad, Benedicte, and Arne H. Eide. "Introduction: Disability and Poverty: A Global Challenge." In **Disability and Poverty: A Global Challenge**, edited by Arne H. Eide and Benedicte Ingstad, 1–14. Bristol: Policy Press, 2011.

Junior, Nyasha, and Jeremy Schipper. "Disability Studies in the Bible." In **New Meanings for Ancient Texts: Recent Approaches to Biblical Criticisms and Their Applications**, edited by Steven L. McKenzie and John Kaltner, 21–37. Louisville: Westminster John Knox, 2013.

Kabue, Samuel. "Introduction." In **Disability in Africa: A Resource Book for Theology and Religious Studies,** edited by Samuel Kabue, James Amanze and Christina Landman, viii–ix. Nairobi: Acton, 2016.

———. "Persons with Disabilities in Church and Society: A Historical and Sociological Perspective." In **Disability, Society, and Theology: Voices from Africa**, edited by Samuel Kabue,

Esther Mombo, Joseph Galgalo and C. B. Peter, 3–25. Limuru: Zapf Chancery Publishers Africa, 2011.

Kabue, Samuel, James Amanze and Christiana Landman. **Disability in Africa: A Resource Book for Theology and Religious Studies**. Nairobi: Acton, 2016.

Kabue, Samuel, Helen Ishalo-Esan and Deji Ayegboyin. **Perspectives on Disability: A Resource Book for Theological and Religious Studies in Africa.** Nairobi: EDAN, 2016.

Kabue, Samuel, Edison Kalengyo, John Ndavula and Anjeline Okala. **The Changing Scenes of Disability in Church and Society: A Resource Book for Theological and Religious Studies**. Nairobi: EDAN, 2021.

Kabue, Samuel, Esther Mombo, Joseph Galgalo and C. B. Peter. **Disability, Society, and Theology: Voices from Africa**. Limuru: Zapf Chancery Publishers Africa, 2011.

Kachaje, Rachel K. "'For I Know the Plans That I Have for You': The Story of My Life." In **The Routledge Handbook of Disability in Southern Africa**, edited by Tsitsi Chataika, 330–35. London: Routledge, 2019.

Kretzschmar, Louise. **The Church and Disability: Inclusion and Participation.** KwaZulu-Natal: Cluster, 2019.

Kurlberg, Nina, and Madleina Daehnhardt. "Theologies and Practices of Inclusion: Introduction." In **Theologies and Practices of Inclusion: Insights from a Faith-Based Relief, Development and Advocacy Organization**, edited by Nina Kurlberg and Madleina Daehnhardt, 3–20. London: SCM, 2021.

Lemons, J. Derrick, ed. **Theologically Engaged Anthropology**. Oxford: Oxford University Press, 2018.

Masakhwe, Phitalis Were. "The Church, Public Policy and Disability Concerns in Kenya." In **Disability, Society, and Theology: Voices from Africa**, edited by Samuel Kabue, Esther Mombo, Joseph Galgalo and C. B. Peter, 111–20. Limuru: Zapf Chancery Publishers Africa, 2011.

Mitra, Sophie, Alexandra Posarac and Brandon Vick. "Disability and Poverty in Developing Countries: A Multidimensional Study." **World Development** 41 (2013): 1–18.

Nyangweso, Mary. "Disability in Africa: A Cultural/Religious Perspective." In **Disability in Africa: Inclusion, Care and the Ethics of Humanity**, edited by Toyin Falola and Nic Hamel, 115–36. Rochester: University of Rochester Press, 2021.

Retief, Marno, and Rantoa Letsosa. "Models of Disability: A Brief Overview." **HTS Teologiese Studies/Theological Studies** 74, no. 1 (2018): a4738.

Reynolds, Thomas E. "Protestant Christianity and Disability." In **Disability and World Religions: An Introduction**, edited by Darla Y. Schumm and Michael Scholtzfus, 137–66. Waco: Baylor University, 2016.

Robbins, Joel. "Anthropology and Theology: An Awkward Relationship?" In **Anthropological Quarterly** 79, no. 2 (2006): 286, 292–3.

Shakespeare, Tom. "Disability in Developing Countries." In **Routledge Handbook of Disability Studies**, edited by Nick Watson and Simo Vehmas, 321–33. London: Routledge, 2020.

———. **Disability Rights and Wrongs Revisited**. London: Routledge, 2014.

Shakespeare, Tom, Anthony Mugeere, Emily Nyariki and Joseph Simbaya. "Success in Africa: People with Disabilities Share Their Stories." **African Journal of Disability** 8, no. 6 (2019): 1–7.

Swinton, John. "Who Is the God We Worship? Theologies of Disability; Challenges and New Possibilities." In **International Journal of Practical Theology** 14, no. 2 (2011): 273–307.

UN Human Rights Office of the High Commissioner. Convention on the Rights of Persons with Disabilities (CRPD). Resolution A/RES/61/106. 12 Dec. 2006. https://www.ohchr.org/en/instruments-mechanisms/instruments/convention-rights-persons-disabilities.

Üstün, T. Bedirhan, Somnath Chatterji, Jerome E. Bickenback, Robert T. Trotter II and Shekhar Saxena. "Disability and Cultural Variation: The Icidh-2 Cross-Cultural Applicability Research Study." In **Disability and Culture: Universalism and Diversity**, edited by T. Bedirhan Üstün et al., 3–19. Seattle: Hogrefe & Huber, 2001.

Vehmas, Simo, and Nick Watson. "Disability Studies: Into the Multidisciplinary Future." In **Routledge Handbook of Disability Studies**, edited by Nick Watson and Simo Vehmas, 3–13. London: Routledge, 2020.

Vester, Heinz-Günter. **Kompendium der Soziologie I: Grundbegriffe**. Wiesbaden: VS Verlag für Sozialwissenschaften, 2009.

Waldschmidt, Anne. "Disability-Culture-Society: Strengths and Weaknesses of a Cultural Model of Dis/ability." In **European Journal of Disability Research** 12 (2018): 67–80.

Wehmeyer, Michael. "Beyond Pathology: Positive Psychology and Disability." In **The Oxford Handbook of Positive Psychology and Disability**, edited by M. Wehmeyer, 3–6. Oxford: Oxford University Press, 2013.

Whyte, Susan Reynolds. "Disability between Discourse and Experience." In **Disability and Culture**, edited by Benedicte Ingstad and Susan Reynolds Whyte, 267–91. Berkeley: University of California Press, 1995.

Whyte, Susan Reynolds, and Benedicte Ingstad. "Disability and Culture: An Overview." In **Disability and Culture**, edited by Benedicte Ingstad and Susan Reynolds Whyte, 3–35. Berkeley: University of California Press, 1995.

———. "Introduction: Disability Connections." In **Disability in Local and Global Worlds**, edited by Benedicte Ingstad and Susan Reynolds Whyte, 1–32. Berkeley: University of California Press, 2007.

World Health Organization (WHO) and the World Bank. **World Report on Disability.** Geneva: WHO, 2011. https://www.who.int/teams/noncommunicable-diseases/sensory-functions-disability-and-rehabilitation/world-report-on-disability.

Yeo, Rebecca, and Karen Moore. "Including Disabled People in Poverty Reduction Work: 'Nothing about Us, without Us.'" **World Development** 31, no. 3 (2003): 571–90.

Yong, Amos. **The Bible, Disability and the Church: A New Vision of the People of God**. Grand Rapids: Eerdmans, 2011.

Part 1

Rethinking Theologies of Disability

1

Disability, Beliefs and Theologies in African Contexts

Madleina Daehnhardt and Nina G. Kurlberg (note 1)

Introduction

This introductory chapter – which draws from a multidisciplinary literature review – sets the wider scene for disability and disability theology in African contexts. The chapter draws from relevant work across disability theology, disability studies, African studies, development studies and anthropology. While this body of literature is vast, we have narrowed our focus to work

---

1. The authors would like to thank Sas Conradie, Jonas Kurlberg, Fohle Lygunda li-M, Grant Macaskill and Selina Palm for their insights which have helped improve the chapter.

that is relevant in African contexts. One main insight from our engagement with the literature is an unfortunate disciplinary separation: the mainstream disability literature does not often engage with religion and theologies, just as the broader discipline of theology does not often engage with disability. This is not an entirely new insight. Disability theologians have long noted that disability studies thus far has shown little interest in religion, which makes a mutually critical and constructive conversation difficult. (note 2) As John Swinton laments, "theology's public voice is inevitably silenced if its dialogue partner [disability studies] is not participating in the conversation." (note 3)

The chapter lays the ground for the volume as a whole by highlighting important themes and areas of research. The thread that runs through this book is that while religious and theological beliefs about disability can be a source of great harm to disabled people, they also hold the potential to be a source of healing and transformation. The life and testimony of the late Micheline Kamba illustrates this well. Contracting polio at the age of two left Micheline with paralysed legs. While her family

---

2. Swinton, drawing from Deborah Creamer, in "Who Is the God We Worship?," 288.
3. Swinton, 288.

was incredibly supportive of her, she experienced significant stigma throughout her childhood on account of her disability, which led her to attempt suicide. As she explained, "it was so difficult to be accepted as God's creation." (note 4) Micheline was able to come through this period with the support of her sister: "My sister helped to show me that I am God's creation and am loved by him. In Isaiah 49:15 God asks Israel, 'Can a mother forget her baby?' I realised this is impossible. In the same way, God cannot forget me. Understanding this was my liberation." (note 5)

Micheline then spent the rest of her life working to encourage those with impairments to "rise up and walk" spiritually, while also challenging harmful attitudes towards them within the church. In an interview the year before her death, she explained:

> I know that nothing is impossible for God: if he told me today to leave my crutches and walk, I would not be surprised. But it is difficult when church leaders just see a disability, not a person. . . . Churches need

---

4. World Council of Churches, "WCC Grieves."
5. Tearfund Learn, "I Am Not Sick."

to involve people with disabilities. They should look beyond the disability to who they are in Christ. (note 6)

Micheline's words underscore the importance of engaging with beliefs and theologies around disability.

Chapter Overview

The aim of this chapter is twofold.

First, in order to understand the wider implications of disability in African contexts, it is crucial to gain an understanding of African Traditional Religion and its associated beliefs, both of which can influence theology and practice. The chapter shows that one cannot engage holistically with Christian disability theologies and practices without also engaging with the wider contextual socio-cultural-religious belief systems of etiology: beliefs around the causal origin of disability. Moreover, the literature review highlights important linkages between values, beliefs and behaviours.

Second, in the context of the African continent, we analyse existing harmful theologies and aim to move the reader towards theologies that enable the flourishing of disabled people in

---

6. Tearfund Learn.

faith communities. Our survey – which focuses specifically on the literature emerging from Africa – identifies a number of key themes in relation to disability and theology which call for deeper engagement: purity and sin; normalcy and healing; liberation and dignity.

In summary, the chapter's key message is that while architectural and attitudinal barriers are (for the most part) acknowledged to be the key factor preventing disability inclusion, (note 7) these are underpinned by harmful beliefs and theologies. The main purpose of this chapter is thus to survey contextual theological beliefs, and to understand their intersection with attitudes and practices (the focus being churches and theological education institutions). This underscores the argument that in order to challenge and remove the barriers to genuine inclusion, it is critical to engage in a constructive way with deeply ingrained beliefs and theologies around disability.

---

7. As noted in the introduction to this volume, "inclusion" refers to practices that go beyond access and participation to address power imbalances – hidden as well as visible (Kurlberg and Daehnhardt, **Theologies and Practices**).

Disability and Religion in the African Context
Important Links: Values, Beliefs and Behaviours

As established in the introduction, disability on a global level is linked to poverty and exclusion. The religion–disability intersection is important, because of inclusion–exclusion dynamics that take place in religious contexts, based on religious teaching and beliefs. (note 8) In line with a cultural model of disability, these dynamics are underpinned by underlying beliefs and value systems which can create stigma, and attitudes and practices of exclusion. For religious organizations and institutions to create positive environments for people living with disabilities, there is thus a need to interrogate and address harmful cultural and religious beliefs about disability, and to reinforce positive narratives in faith communities.

Negative attitudes towards disability can be found in all world religions. James Amanze, who analysed attitudes towards people with disabilities within six world religions – including African Traditional Religion, Christianity and Judaism – found negative attitudes present across all religions "on the basis of their belief systems, teachings, ethics,

---

8. Chataika, "Introduction."

spirituality and practice." (note 9) In their edited work **Disability and Poverty**, anthropologists Arne Eide and Benedicte Ingstad also identified "established and culturally rooted discriminatory practices that affect individuals with disabilities and their families." (note 10) Engaging with what we identify as the "beliefs and behaviours linkage" is also key for breaking the poverty–disability cycle. Eide and Ingstad consider as one of the major lessons from **Disability and Poverty** the insight that levels of explanation for poverty and disability should not be viewed in isolation: "policy changes with the best of intentions may fail or even be counterproductive if people's cultural beliefs or structural barriers are not considered." (note 11) The editors rightly make a case for what they call "a culture-sensitive approach," which considers contextual attitudes towards disability. (note 12)

___

9. Amanze, "Attitudes," 62.
10. Eide and Ingstad, "Epilogue," 226.
11. Eide and Ingstad, 230.
12. "[A] culture-sensitive approach to disability and poverty . . . quite simply requires an understanding of individuals, values, interpretations and understanding, as these are fundamental aspects to influence, utilise and/or incorporate for any sustainable change to take place. Attitudes . . . represent established patterns for understanding to a phenomenon" (Eide and Ingstad, 226).

Anthropologists, however, often do not explore in sufficient depth how **religious beliefs** and local theologies are very much part of **cultural beliefs** in the African context, where religion and culture are so intertwined. As the chapters in this volume demonstrate, in Africa, one cannot engage with culture without deeply engaging with religion, and one cannot engage deeply with religion without understanding the underlying theologies that inform socio-religious thought and practice. This includes all levels: from macro policy levels to micro community and household levels. The belief–behaviour linkage within the church also operates on all levels, although our focus in this chapter is mostly on individual, household and community levels. It is worth noting that "relatively less is known about how disability is constructed within the context of collectivist societies in the Global South where an individual's identity is closely tied to the family or community," and this includes faith communities. (note 13)

---

13. Rao also notes that "while perceptions of disability that are tied to collectivist orientations are acknowledged to some extent, they are often deemed to be negative" (Rao, "Disability," 315).

The Significance of Etiology: Beliefs around the Origins of Disability

We know that impairments are complex and can be caused by many different factors, such as genetics, illness, accidents, violence, malnutrition, harmful lifestyles and hazardous environments. In this section we examine a number of key anthropological and ethnographic studies from the African region which have shed light on people's cultural beliefs on etiology: beliefs regarding the causal origin of impairments. This is highly important because of the significant impact of beliefs on behaviour – as well as the connection to the interpretations of scriptural texts shaping (misguided) beliefs on causation. Etiology has been an important narrative in ethnographic accounts of disability; "the discourse on cause is relevant and current." (note 14) According to Susan Reynolds Whyte, in ethnographic accounts "there is far greater concern with etiology [i.e. beliefs of causation] than there is with coping, stigma, adjustment, or social integration [or inclusion]." (note 15) This has been observed in African ethnographies (and beyond), "where a strong tradition in ethnographic writing emphasizes explanations of misfortune." (note 16)

---

14. Whyte, "Disability," 273.
15. Whyte, 273.
16. Whyte, 273.

In Mary Nyangweso's study – on perceptions, attitudes and behaviours towards people living with disabilities in African sociocultural contexts – it is evident that underlying beliefs regarding the origin of disability shape behaviours towards people living with disabilities. Simply put, in communities where beliefs prevail that those with disabilities are "sacred," a "reincarnation of a deity," "pacifiers of evil spirits," or a "gift from God," this results in acceptance and kindness towards them. (note 17) For example, Ingstad's study among one specific community in Botswana showed complete acceptance of persons living with a disability as full persons, where seeing a child born with a disability as a "divine gift" was a means to overcome stigma. (note 18) In contrast, where disability is viewed as a curse from God or

---

17. Nyangweso, "Disability in Africa," 119.

18. Ingstad, "'Mpho ya Modimo,'" 254. Ingstad observes that "to avoid the stigmatizing label is to claim that the child is 'mpho ya modimo,' a gift from God. In line with Tswana tradition of giving children a name that is meaningful for the life situation of a child born into, or for the parents' wishes or expectations, several of the children [in the sample] born with visible impairments had been given this name. The Tswana traditional God Modimo, and even the Christian counterpart that has taken over the same name, is mainly seen as

the gods, this results in cruel and discriminating behaviours against those living with disabilities and their family members. (note 19)

A cross-cultural study commissioned by the World Health Organization (WHO) in sixteen locations shows that there are significant differences in attitudes and beliefs about the origin of disability according to cultural context. This then manifests itself in the different language terms used to describe people, the different ways in which individual societies attach relative stigma to different types of disability, how they evaluate the need for assistance and how they evaluate the severity of different kinds of health conditions. (note 20) This comprehensive study provides strong evidence that levels of sympathy and stigma differ according to beliefs concerning the origination and causation of disability. The results from the study show that people in cultures which maintain a strong belief that bad outcomes reflect misbehaviour in the past – whether by the individual concerned or by his or

---

an omnipotent power that demonstrates trust in people by giving them such special challenges" (Ingstad, 254).

19. Nyangweso, "Disability in Africa," 119.
20. Üstün et al., "Cultural Variation."

her parents – are far less sympathetic towards people whose disabilities have been present from birth. (note 21)

The WHO's Nigeria country study provides the clearest example of this causation between etiology beliefs and behaviour. The majority of informants associated a "mobility problem" or "mental disorder" with a divine sign that the parents of the child did something wrong in the past: they assumed "he is a sinner," "the parents did something wrong," and "it is a curse from God," or even "[it was] sent from the devil." (note 22) Disabilities resulting from road accidents were viewed with more sympathy and less stigma, as these were viewed not as "a result of someone's own faults," but as something that "could happen to anybody." (note 23) Because Nigerian society

---

21. Room et al., "Cross-Cultural Views."
22. Room et al., 259.
23. Room et al., 259. These causations made by people based on their beliefs are relevant beyond the African context. Key informants gave similar explanations in India, where disability was seen as a "sign of fate or supernatural punishment" or a "problem due to a person's past sins" (252). Stigma for the family from a presumed genetic defect was further implied in the data from Greece, Japan and Turkey.

largely believes that congenital disabilities – conditions that are present before or at birth – occur as a result of sin committed by the parents, the family and person affected are viewed with great suspicion and lack of pity. According to key informants, this can even lead to such persons being abandoned by the family. (note 24) Interviews with the general population reconfirm such trends, as the informants believe that "gaining employment, getting married and having a family" would be severely affected by disability status. (note 25) In summary, the WHO research provides strong evidence for how cultural–religious beliefs surrounding causation can lead to negative attitudes and discriminatory behaviours, and this is most pronounced for persons with congenital and mental disabilities. (note 26)

The Place of Religion in Relation to Disability in Africa

Globally, religion has always played a crucial role in how disability is conceptualized. This is partly because historically religions "establish cultural representations for what is deemed normal human

---

24. Omigbodun, Odejide and Morakinyo, "Nigeria," 193.
25. Omigbodun, Odejide and Morakinyo, 192.
26. Omigbodun, Odejide and Morakinyo, 185.

physical and mental behaviour." (note 27) Darla Schumm and Michael Stoltzfus's work exploring cross-cultural and interreligious perspectives on disability collates evidence showing that "religion, in its multiple manifestations, plays a critical role in determining how disability is understood and how persons with disabilities are treated or mistreated in a given historical-cultural context." This is where the potential of faith-based communities to foster disability inclusion becomes apparent, where access – or inclusion more generally – in a religious context goes beyond "institutional accommodation and physical modification" to penetrate the "attitudinal orientation and participatory availability" of faith communities. (note 28) Schumm and Stoltzfus's work of analysing the social ramifications of perceptions of disability within religious and textual interpretations in Judaism, Christianity and

---

27. Schumm and Stoltzfus, **World Religions**, xi.

28. Schumm and Stoltzfus, **Religious Diversity**, xi. As the editors note further, "there is a notable difference between physical accessibility and socio-religious integration, between formal protection under the law and the advent for community, friendships, and group belongingness" in faith-based communities (xviii).

Islam points to the "real-life consequences" of religious constructions of disability. (note 29)

Yet to date, disability studies have not given religion the attention it requires, in spite of the fact that "in many parts of the world, particularly in the Global South, religion is central to how [many people] make sense of their lives." (note 30) The **Routledge Handbook of Disability Studies** (2020 edition), for example, is a 500-plus-page volume comprising thirty-five chapters of which none employ the lens of religion in relation to disability. The same is true of theology in African contexts: Bridget Hathaway and Flavian Kishekwa observe that there are few books that look at disability from a theological perspective within African contexts. (note 31)

Nokuzola Mndende has described religion as being "part of the fibre of society" across the African continent. (note 32) In fact, allegiance to a divine being is so fundamental to everyday life

---

29. Schumm and Stoltzfus, **Judaism, Christianity, and Islam**, xx.
30. Mugeere et al., "'Oh God!,'" 78.
31. Hathaway and Kishekwa, **Included and Valued**, 1.
32. Mndende, in Manganyi and Buitendag, "Critical Analysis," n.p.

that Anthony Mugeere et al. speak of a "reflex" response whereby the instinctive reaction to all that happens in life is to either praise or blame God. (note 33) Ancestors are another key element of African Traditional Religion. (note 34) Linda Woodhead notes that "conceptualisations of the ancestors play an important role in structuring religious experience and social life – so much so that African kin groups are sometimes described as communities of both the living and the dead." (note 35) All that happens within life, such as wealth, poverty, drought, rain, marriage, fertility, sterility and so forth, is often seen as the reward

---

33. Mugeere et al., "'Oh God!,'" 76.

34. There are differing perspectives regarding whether to speak of African Traditional Religions (plural) or African Traditional Religion (singular). We opt for the latter in this chapter, in line with several scholars – including theologian John Mbiti – who approach the debate with an "insider" perspective (Alolo and Connell, "Indigenous Religions," 146). Their argument is that while African Traditional Religion is expressed in countless ways, there is a shared basic belief system and worldview (Alolo and Connell, 146).

35. Woodhead in Mugeere et al., "'Oh God!,'" 65.

or sanction of human behaviour and actions by a supreme being acting through the ancestors, and disability is no exception. (note 36)

African Traditional Religion, African Christianity and Disability

The precise nature of the relationship between African Traditional Religion and African Christianity is complex and beyond the scope of this chapter. (note 37) What is clear is that religious dynamics at the intersection of interpretations of Jewish and Christian texts and African traditional religious beliefs can feed into the stereotyping of people with disabilities and become harmful. (note 38) This dynamic is fuelled by traditional beliefs about the evil origin of disability being paired with narratives from the Bible on the origin of disability as being associated with sin. (note 39) As a result, Eliot Tofa observes an "escalation" of negativity towards disabled people when misrepresentations of the teachings of Christianity are paired with misrepresentations

---

36. Ndlovu, "African Beliefs."
37. Maluleke, "Ten Theses," 375–76.
38. Machingura, "'Unholy Trinity,'" 212.
39. Machingura, 212.

of African traditional beliefs with negative connotations. (note 40)

Part of the reason why the relationship between African Traditional Religion and African Christianity is so complex is that, as noted by Hebron Ndlovu, instead of "absolute, binding, and categorical doctrines" on disability within African Traditional Religion, there are "direct and indirect teaching, attitudes, perspectives, insights, and principles that can be inferred from what particular African peoples do and say under the auspices of prayer, healing practices, magical rituals, festivals, ceremonies, moral teachings, sayings, proverbs, and normative behaviour." (note 41) Nevertheless, it is clear that African Traditional Religion impacts on theologies of disability within churches across Africa. As also highlighted by Selina Palm's chapter in this volume, one of the findings from Helen Ishola-Esan's study exploring the perceptions of 120 pastors – all postgraduates of the Nigerian Baptist Theological Seminary – towards ministry to people with disabilities was that 37 percent saw a connection between disability and witchcraft. (note 42)

---

40. Tofa, "Disabilities," 126.
41. Ndlovu, "African Beliefs," 32.
42. Palm, "One Body?," 10; Ishola-Esan, "Remnants of African Worldviews."

Francis Machingura notes that disability is "highly spiritualised" within African Traditional Religion, with beliefs on the causes of disability including the action of God, curses from ancestors, and witchcraft. (note 43) To reiterate, due to the superstition and misconceptions surrounding disability and its perceived association with evil, it is often viewed as something to be avoided. This has led to many of those living with disabilities losing the consideration and esteem of society, and, consequently, the protection that this affords. Further, disabled people are often perceived to be an additional unproductive burden and an entry point for the devil in the family. (note 44) Yet at the same time, and as noted above, there are also examples of those with disabilities being received with acceptance, kindness and

---

43. Machingura, "'Unholy Trinity,'" 212. Machingura explains that witches "are considered to be sources of evil that make use of extraordinary powers to afflict others."

44. The authors are using the terms "people with disabilities" and "disabled people" interchangeably in this chapter. For a discussion on the use of "identity first" and "person first" terminology, please see appendix 1.

protection. (note 45) As Senzokuhle Setume and Baamphatlha Dinama highlight, it is important not to only focus on negative perceptions of disability in African Traditional Religion, but to "present a balanced picture of African culture" in relation to disability inclusion: this is also important with regard to the curricula of theological education institutions concerning disability and church practice. (note 46) The next section focuses specifically on theology and practice within the church, highlighting important themes and areas of research for African contexts as well as challenges and opportunities for disability inclusion.

Major Themes in Disability Theology Emerging from the African Continent (note 47)
Disability, Purity and Sin

In their chapter on the complexities of the relationship between disability and religion, Juliana

---

45. Ingstad, "'Mpho ya Modimo'"; Machingura, "'Unholy Trinity'"; Ndlovu, "African Beliefs"; Nyangweso, "Disability in Africa."

46. Setume and Dinama, "African Traditional Religions," 25.

47. This section has been informed by a literature review commissioned by Tearfund in 2020 (Palm, "One Body?").

Claassens et al. highlight two interconnected themes that have had significant influence in the African continent: first, the representation of disability in the Bible in terms of "purity" and "wholeness," and second, the idea that sin and suffering are connected and "God is a God that is responsible for everything that happens." (note 48) The connection between sin and suffering, particularly as it relates to disability, finds resonance in the first of the "disabling" theological themes outlined by US-based scholar (note 49) Nancy Eiesland in **The Disabled God**, which concerns the conflation of disability and sin. (note 50) Eiesland's thinking, particularly her portrayal of the resurrected Christ in Luke 24 as the "disabled God," has been influential within theological reflection on disability in African contexts, and the book is referenced within much of the literature surveyed in this section. (note 51)

---

48. Claassens et al., "Engaging Disability and Religion," 151–52.
49. In this section, we will highlight the context of authors writing from outside Africa.
50. Eiesland, **Disabled God**.
51. Otieno, "Perspectives"; Machingura, "'Unholy Trinity'"; Mugeere et al., "'Oh God!'"; Kamchedzera, "Investigation."

In chapter 3 of this volume, Palm draws on Claassens et al. to show that the conversations on disability and sin, and purity and wholeness are connected and intersect with discussions on representation and interpretation in relation to the biblical text. Many scholars have problematized the negative representation of disability in the Bible. (note 52) In an article on the book of Job, Claassens highlights several examples, including that of Isaiah 56:10, where the words "blind" and "mute" are used metaphorically to signify negative characteristics. Claassens goes on to note instances such as Deuteronomy 28:28–29, where disability (blindness in this instance) is used in the form of a curse. (note 53) Other examples often highlighted include Old Testament laws such as Leviticus 21:16–23, which prohibits priests with a "blemish" from entering the most holy place in the temple, as well as passages

---

52. Githuku, "Biblical Perspectives"; Nkomazana, "'No One Who Has a Blemish Shall Draw Near'"; Kebaneilwe, "Disability as a Challenge." See also Saul Olyan's **Disability in the Hebrew Bible**, in which he examines "the ways in which the authors of [biblical] texts frequently stigmatize and seek to marginalize disabled persons through their representations, thereby contributing to social differentiation and inequality" (119).

53. Claassens, "Countering Stereotypes," 170–71.

from the New Testament where Jesus appears to associate disability with sin in the healing narratives. (note 54) When read literally and without knowledge of the wider context, texts such as these not only portray disability in a negative light, but could also be seen as either attributing disability to God or affirming its association with impurity and sin.

It is important to remember that biblical texts prohibiting priests with "blemishes" from entering the most holy place in the temple were written within the specific historical and cultural context of the temple period. (note 55) Consequently, as Machingura points out, these texts are to be understood "in a particular time period . . . linked to cultural ways of thinking." (note 56) The prohibitions described in the book of Leviticus emanated from wider cultural perceptions and understandings of purity, and, in this regard, it is important to reflect on the conceptualization of purity that shaped Jewish culture in ancient Israel. (note 57) Moral impurity was associated with

---

54. See, for example, John 5:14 and Luke 5:20.
55. Abrams, "Misconceptions."
56. Machingura, "'Unholy Trinity,'" 215.
57. In-depth engagement with the complete body of literature on "purity" and Judaism is beyond the scope of this chapter.

grave sins, such as murder and incest, while ritual impurity concerned contact with various natural substances related to birth, death, sex, disease and discharge (e.g. menstruation), a whole range of "impurities" which required purification. (note 58) Drawing on the work of British anthropologist Mary Douglas, Jerome Neyrey, writing in the context of the US, offers a helpful explanation of purity using the concept of "place": "'purity is a map of a social system which coordinates and classifies things according to their appropriate place." (note 59)
In Jewish culture, such maps existed for "things, places, persons and times," (note 60) and while what was in the appropriate place was considered "pure," what was not was considered a "pollution." (note 61) This is important because impurity is then not integral to the thing, place, person or time in question, but rather the result of it being in the "wrong **place** at the wrong **time**." (note 62)

---

58. Klawans, "Concepts of Purity," 1998. Contact with ritual impurity had serious religious consequences, rendering one temporarily unfit to enter sacred space.
59. Neyrey, "Idea of Purity," 94.
60. Neyrey, 95.
61. Neyrey, 91.
62. Neyrey, 92.

Turning to disability specifically and Leviticus 21:16–23, it is evident that in relation to persons, purity is represented by "physical wholeness." Priests not considered to be physically whole were not permitted to approach the altar, the most holy place in Jewish society at the time. On the basis of the understanding of purity outlined above, "wholeness" here must be understood as historically, culturally and spatially contingent, and therefore impurity cannot be unconditionally attached to the priests being categorized in this way. (note 63) Neyrey refers to several other biblical examples in this regard, including that of nudity – which is associated with impurity in Exodus 20:26, but not in Genesis 2:25 – and sexual intercourse. While sexual intercourse is not impure in and of itself, it is prohibited in relation to several places, persons and times; for instance, before offering a sacrifice (Lev 22:4). (note 64) Although this does not remove the troubling association of

---

63. As Christine Hayes explains, "ritual impurity is not a permanent or long-lasting stigma applied to certain groups selectively. The biblical system of ritual impurity is impermanent" ("Purity and Impurity," 749).

64. Neyrey, "Idea of Purity," 103–4. See Hannah Harrington's "Introduction" to **The Purity Texts** for further discussion on sexual intercourse as it relates to purity. Harrington notes that although

physical impairments with a lack of wholeness, this association needs to be understood in the context of how such impairments were perceived in Jewish society at the time. Further, what is important in relation to these passages is to understand the theological significance of ritual purity. As Ferdinand M'bwangi explains in relation to Leviticus 11, ritual purity was intended "for that particular period, to demonstrate the separateness (holiness) of the Israelites," who in their obedience to the rituals imitated God's holiness and distinctiveness in relation to the gods of other nations. (note 65)

In differing ways, much of the existing literature emerging from African contexts responds to the negative representation of disability within the Bible by referring to the person and work of Jesus Christ. (note 66) In light of the perspective on purity outlined above, this is an important line of thought. Jesus not only challenged the purity system, but also reformed it. In Neyrey's words, as "'the Holy One of God' and agent of

---

"the biblical laws are clear that celibacy is not the divine mandate on Israel, they are also clear that sexual intercourse causes impurity" (xxii).

65. M'bwangi, "Tribal Defilement," n.p.

66. See, for example, Githuku, "Biblical Perspectives."

God's reform: [Jesus] is authorized to cross lines and to blur classifications as a strategy for a reformed [and more inclusive] covenant community." (note 67) Strikingly, Jesus is often "out of place" in the gospels – yet instead of being a pollutant in relation to things, places, persons and times, he is a "source of purity." (note 68) This is also applicable to Jesus's resurrected body in Luke 24 that bears the marks of his crucifixion. Sinenhlanhla Chisale, whose work focuses specifically on women with disabilities, argues that purity must be "re-interpreted" for the sake of their inclusion within religious spaces:

> The purity myth suggests that God is accessible only to the pure and clean. . . . Jesus challenges this in the gospels as he becomes accessible to all, including those who are deemed religiously unclean, for example the healing of the haemorrhaging woman (Mk 5:25–34). This woman accesses a sacred space and touches the most sacred person in her condition of impurity, something that was forbidden by the

---

67. Neyrey, "Idea of Purity," 91.
68. Neyrey, 91, 115.

> Leviticus laws. This confirms that using the purity myth to deny women access to the sacred space of God is erroneous. (note 69)

In a similar vein, Sammy Githuku refers to the Christian understanding that Christ came as a perfect sacrifice **for all**, which revokes the earlier biblical prohibitions against people with disabilities. Unlike in an ancient temple context, in today's Christian church contexts "people with disabilities can therefore serve God in whatever area they choose." (note 70) Machingura highlights that the person of Jesus breaks all forms of traditional discrimination and purity taboos by associating with all people, including those excluded at the time: "from the gospel narratives we can see that [Jesus] was at great ease in embracing and interacting with women, the poor, refugees, disabled people and children. . . . For Jesus, there was no distinction between social restoration and physical healing." (note 71) In John 9, Jesus clearly dismisses the belief that disability is a result of sin. Although it is clear that the disciples "anticipated a connection between

---

69. Chisale, "Purity Myth," 9.
70. Githuku, "Biblical Perspectives," 93.
71. Machingura, "'Unholy Trinity,'" 220.

disability and sin," (note 72) Jesus explains that "there is no such cause–effect here" and instead encourages them to see the work of God within the situation. (note 73)

Disability, Normalcy and Healing

An important and connected area of research on disability within the varied contexts of Africa concerns physical healing. Grounded in the lived experience in the African context, as highlighted by Palm in chapter 3 of this volume, Claassens et al. note that "disabled persons are

---

72. Otieno, "Perspectives," n.p. See also Kabue, "Persons with disabilities in church and society," 12.

73. John 9:1–5 (Peterson, **The Message**). See also Ford, **Gospel of John**, 190. David Ford's commentary on another passage in John (John 5:1–9) indicates a conversation between Jesus and a paralysed man that respects dignity, freedom and the desires of the man, asking him, "Do you want [desire] to be made well?" Ford points out that this question by Jesus hints at the fact that a person's identity is often tied up with long-term illness. Ford refers back to the words of Jesus in John's first chapter, "What are you looking for?" (John 1:38), showing that Jesus interacts deeply with the desires, longings, motivations and hopes of the individuals he encounters (Ford, 125).

often excluded from worshipping communities [because] individuals who cannot be healed are a vivid reminder of being an expression of impurity or sin," an unhelpful consequence of theological misconceptions. (note 74) If not excluded from faith communities, people living with disabilities are often targeted by healing ministries. (note 75) As illustrated within Elizabeth Kamchedzera's research within Malawi, for example, when those with disabilities attend church it is often assumed to be because they are seeking healing, and it is clear from the official church statements regarding disability referenced in her paper that disabled people are often instrumentalized, used to demonstrate "[God's] power to heal or His power to use weakness to display His strength." (note 76) Several participants in Mugeere et al.'s study referenced "cases of pastors and other leaders who tend to exploit the plight of persons with disability in the name of performing healing miracles," single out those with disabilities as

---

74. Claassens et al., "Engaging Disability and Religion," 152. For further discussion on this, see Selina Palm's chapter in this volume.

75. Otieno, "Perspectives"; Möller, "Experiences"; Kamchedzera, "Investigation."

76. Kamchedzera, "Investigation," 5. For further discussion on this, see Selina Palm's chapter in this volume.

being testimony to God's punishment of the wicked, and "fake miracles of healing using people who are not living with disability." (note 77)

While the contributions in this volume are not making a case against healing per se, nor against the appropriateness of prayer for healing, they are challenging readers to think more holistically about the whole person, by reflecting critically on (often unintentional) harmful practices and theologies imposed on disabled people. This is from an insider perspective of authors who are faithfully part of the very congregations they observe. Within this context, the work of several African scholars emphasizing the holistic nature of the healing narratives in the Bible is noteworthy. (note 78) Emphasizing the

---

77. Mugeere et al., "'Oh God!,'" 75.
78. Holism has also been emphasized by a number of theologians whose insights echo the above on disability inclusion in the African church context. Reynolds, in **Vulnerable Communion**, raises the issue of unintended exclusion through implicit theologies in theodicy questions: "Under the banner of love, the allegedly benign intention to understand, accept, help and **heal** disabilities can ironically stymie the genuine welcome of disabled persons into our communities, signifying a deeper and perhaps more pernicious

importance of the societal dimension of healing and flourishing, Otieno notes that "Jesus primarily removes societal barriers in order to create accessible and accepting communities." (note 79) She argues for the need to differentiate between "healing and cure," redefining "healing from cure of the individual to the individual's restoration to a valued social role." (note 80) In a similar vein, Jessie Fubara-Manuel constructs a dialogue between the lived theologies of women with HIV

---

exclusion. Hence we must proceed with great caution and circumspection in the attempt to discern God's hand in human disability" (30; emphasis added). Theodicy is understood as "an attempt to vindicate divine providence with the realization of evil and suffering in the world" (192). In Otieno, "Perspectives," n.p., an overemphasis on "healing miracles" in churches can be accompanied by neglect of practical and social dimensions. In Mackenney-Jeffs's interviews with parents of severely disabled children in a UK church context, they expressed bewilderment with a strong emphasis on healing in charismatic church traditions, while practical support and understanding would have been more helpful (Mackenney-Jeffs, **Reconceptualising Disability**, 176).

79. Otieno, "Perspectives," n.p.
80. Otieno.

and disabilities and the work of the late Micheline Kamba, arguing that the women she interacted with through her research experienced holistic healing through personal relationship with Jesus Christ. This transformed their identities, increased their confidence and gave them the necessary tools to live with disability and counter stigma and exclusion. Expectation of physical healing was seen to be an important aspect of this process and relationship, but it was not their sole focus. (note 81)

To draw on theological reflection on this topic of healing from outside African contexts, the work of Australian theologians Shane Clifton and Greta Wells sheds light on the place of disability in Pentecostal theologies, and the possible implications of their focus on healing. (note 82) It is important to engage with Pentecostal perspectives due to their prevalence in African contexts. Clifton and Wells offer a critical and constructive discussion of the intersection between Pentecostal theology and disability studies, arguing that the Pentecostal movement with its emphasis on healing has potential both to reinforce the problem of disabling prejudice

---

81. Fubara-Manuel, "Interrogating Healing," 267.
82. Clifton and Wells, "Theology of Disability."

and to facilitate empowerment. (note 83) The healing narrative is a central motif in Pentecostal theology and practice which attracts many people to it, visible in the growth of the movement on the African continent. At the same time, as Malaysian-American Pentecostal theologian Amos Yong highlights, "complaints about Pentecostal-charismatic healing practices are legion in the disability literature." (note 84) Where disability – seen as illness – is associated with "unrepentant sin, a lack of faith, or demonic strongholds," unhelpful practices are shaped that can create confusion and shame. The main problem, according to Yong, is an "uncritical" application of these concepts in practice. (note 85)

An awareness of the danger of the medical model of disability is important in church contexts, including underlying assumptions that disability needs to be "fixed." On the contrary, people with disabilities can be valued as faithful agents of the Spirit – not just as bodies that need to be normalized through miraculous faith. Writing in the context of the US, Thomas Reynolds notes in regard to interpretations of scriptures that, when interpreted simplistically, selectively (even

---

83. Clifton and Wells, 347.
84. Yong, **Theology and Down Syndrome**, 242.
85. Yong, 241.

literally) and without a depth of contextual and historical understanding, scriptural passages can be appropriated in ways detrimental to people with disabilities, "unwittingly reproducing **normalcy** as hermeneutical vantage point" (emphasis added). (note 86) This feeds into the larger picture of ableism in Protestant theologies; and Reynolds identifies how "Protestantism and normalcy have colluded in ways that call for change." (note 87) We advocate for change to be embodied through moving the theological discourse away from a focus on "healing" – which is often underpinned by concepts of "normalcy" – towards an emphasis on "flourishing": towards theologies that are "life-giving" and have the potential to lead to "life in all its fullness." This resonates with Swinton's call for a move from an emphasis on health to the deep "shalom" found in the person of Jesus, and the experience of "wholeness, completeness and well-

---

86. Reynolds, "Protestant Christianity," 149. John Swinton, writing in the context of the UK, also highlights how the ways in which our understanding of normality, beauty, strength, intellect and reason is shaped have direct implications for the ways in which we understand and respond to disability (Swinton, "Who Is the God We Worship?," 277).

87. Reynolds, 147.

being" in restored relationship with God. (note 88) What is more, disability also challenges the assumptions of the health-and-wealth narrative in the so-called prosperity gospel. As British theologian Frances Mackenney-Jeffs has pointed out, prosperity gospel theology has difficulty accepting human suffering, and consequently people with disabilities can be regarded with suspicion. (note 89) At the same time, disability offers a profound challenge to ingrained assumptions and values, and disability theology confronts us with some of the less palatable facts of being human. (note 90) As such, disability can even help shape theologies towards a wholeness that does not merely focus on the "normative body" shaped by societal ideals, but instead looks to a redeeming interaction of that body with its faith community and society. (note 91) In this context, too, reconceiving "health and wealth" in terms of flourishing, and placing that flourishing

---

88. While the basic meaning of "shalom" is peace, the root meaning of the word is wholeness, completeness and well-being (Swinton, "From Health to Shalom," 233).
89. Mackenney-Jeffs, **Reconceptualising Disability**, 70.
90. Mackenney-Jeffs, 218.
91. Mackenney-Jeffs.

in the context of disability and illness, sets a holistic gospel within the context of our limits and vulnerabilities. (note 92)

Disability, Liberation and Dignity

There is no doubt that the theology and practice of the church has been a source of considerable harm for those living with disabilities in the African continent. Yet Claassens et al. highlight a tension between religion being "potentially complicit in the oppression of people with disabilities on the one hand and the lived reality of religion actually providing support, meaning, access, and opportunities on the other hand." (note 93) Although Claassens et al.'s comments are in relation to religion in general rather than Christianity in particular, Mugeere et al.'s research evidences a similar dynamic. Of the 103 people living with disabilities whom they interviewed across Kenya, Uganda and Zambia, although some referred to the "'disabling' effect" of religion, most attributed their success to "the grace of God." (note 94) Many scholars emphasize the importance of harnessing the Bible's liberative

---

92. Mackenney-Jeffs, 353.

93. Claassens et al., "Engaging Disability and Religion," 149.

94. Mugeere et al., "'Oh God.'"

potential, and this is an important theme within the existing literature. (note 95)

One example is Mmapula Diana Kebaneilwe, who notes that while the Bible is often perceived as "a resource for empowerment for the powerless . . . it has played a mixed role in the way [people with disabilities] have been and are being treated." (note 96) She provides "positive" and "negative" examples of biblical texts, pointing out that the Bible often portrays a "binary picture." Ultimately, however, Kebaneilwe places emphasis on Jesus as offering "a new paradigm" and a "liberative gospel." (note 97) Similarly, Machingura pleads for a "nuanced" and "liberative" hermeneutics for disability theology. (note 98)

Also notable here is the work of Ndlovu. Arguing that a theology of disability should in fact be a "theology of liberation," he suggests a "hermeneutics of suspicion" towards inherited biblical and theological views on disability, complemented by a "hermeneutics of critical endorsement" towards positive beliefs that can be

---

95. Machingura, "'Unholy Trinity'"; Möller, "Experiences"; Ndlovu, "African Beliefs."
96. Kebaneilwe, "Disability as a Challenge," 94.
97. Kebaneilwe, 93.
98. Machingura, "Disability and the Bible," 60.

"appropriated in the quest for the creation of more humane, just and inclusive societies." (note 99) Ndlovu is of the opinion that

> all African beliefs that espouse positive attitudes about persons with disabilities (such as the doctrine of **ubuntu/buntfu/botho**) should be appropriated and combined with Christian and philosophical ethical ideals that advocate for social equity. The purposeful appropriation of positive African ethical teachings drawn from African culture and experience is likely to give rise to a contextual African theology that, in the words of John Pobee, "the gospel can speak to Africans in the primordial symbols of African identity and existence." (note 100)

---

99. Ndlovu, "African Beliefs," 37.

100. Ndlovu, 29. Paul Leshota's research provides one such example of appropriation of this nature: two of the participants in his study "expressed a common sentiment regarding making the world more humane: **Re lokela ho ts'oaranang ka matsoho**, translated as 'We need to hold each other in arms,' although in Sesotho it is more than this and carries the nuance of equality: accepting each other with one's strength or contribution" (Leshota, "From Dependence to Interdependence,"

The quest for liberation is arguably rooted in a desire to respect the dignity and inherent worth of all people as created "B'tzelem Elohim," in the divine image. (note 101) Australian-Jewish disability rights activist and researcher Melinda Jones argues that "being made in God's image involves the inherent value and dignity of every person, and that the moral equivalence of people is to be reflected in every human action or endeavor." She concludes that "the full range of readings of Jewish theology support the human rights of people with disabilities." (note 102) The Hebrew Bible articulates a strong ethical imperative to treat people with disabilities fairly and to avoid exploiting them, alongside orphans, widows, strangers and so forth. (note 103) The topic of human dignity was one of the key focus areas of a theological conference hosted by Stellenbosch University in 2011. Titled "Theology, Disability and Human Dignity," the conference brought together a wide range of participants including academics spanning different disciplines, practitioners and those with lived experience

---

6). On this basis, and due to the foundational nature of community to African worldviews, Leshota proposes a theology of interdependence.

101. Watts Belser, "Judaism and Disability," 101.
102. Jones, "Human Rights," 128.
103. Watts Belser, "Judaism and Disability," 103.

of disability. Conference papers were published in the volume **Searching for Dignity**, which represents a contribution to the conference's goal to "reframe harmful theological ideas and to find new ways to talk about God and about human beings that respect their inherent dignity as unique individuals created in the image of God." (note 104) For example, Claassens uses the book of Job to respond to negative representations of disability within the biblical text by identifying counternarratives and placing them within a new theological framework rooted in "human dignity, inclusion and hospitality." (note 105)

Disability, Church Practice and Theological Education

A final important area of research encompasses attitudes and perceptions towards disability within Christian communities and among their leaders too. As reviewed in the introduction, three recent edited volumes by Samuel Kabue et al. focus on this theme and are intended for use as resource books on disability theology for theological

---

104. Claassens et al., "Introduction," 10.
105. Claassens, "Countering Stereotypes," 172.

education institutions. (note 106) Although the church has in many ways been a "pioneer in the care of [people with disabilities]," as Kabue argues, the church has also for the most part accepted the societal narrative that disabled people are "special and different from the rest of society." (note 107) Erna Möller's empirical research on accessibility in church practice shows that people with disabilities are excluded from faith communities not only because of the "inaccessibility of the physical structure of the church," but also on account of their experience of "others' ideas of disability and healing." (note 108) Louise Kretzschmar's **The Church and Disability in Southern Africa** is a notable contribution to the literature in this regard, offering an approach to disability inclusion that not only seeks to increase awareness of disability within the church, but also provides a resource that is both practical and accessible. However, more research on best practices for disability inclusion in African churches is needed. A final

---

106. Kabue, Mombo, Galgalo and Peter, **Disability, Society and Theology**; Kabue, Ishalo-Esan and Ayegboyin, **Perspectives on Disability**; Kabue, Kalengyo, Ndavula and Okala, **Changing Scenes of Disability**.

107. Kabue, "Persons with Disabilities in church and society," 15.

108. Möller, "Experiences," 130.

important work by disability activists Hathaway and Kishekwa, **Included and Valued: A Practical Theology of Disability**, argues that "in a continent where belief in the spirit world remains active, it is important to ensure that the Holy Spirit is the basis of our beliefs in the church." (note 109)

A connected key theme within the existing literature concerns the place of disability in theological education in Africa. South Africa-based researcher Seyram Amenyedzi's qualitative work on equity and access for persons with disabilities in theological education in Ghana evaluates the situation of blind persons, deaf persons and persons with physical disabilities. (note 110) Amenyedzi's aim is to explore the cultural dimensions of the stigmatization and exclusion they experience. In line with what we have called a cultural model, she constructs "the dialogue between the Ghanaian culture/traditional belief system and Christianity [as] a reflection of sociological-anthropological inculturation theology, which is an aspect of contextualization." (note 111) Her research finds that Ghanaian Christians tend to construct disability as a curse; in the church,

---

109. Hathaway and Kishekwa, **Included and Valued**, 1.
110. Amenyedzi, "Equity and Access."
111. Amenyedzi, 3.

disability is viewed in a similar manner to how it is constructed in Ghanaian culture itself. One consequence is constant pressure exerted on persons with disabilities to be healed by means of exorcism or through faith healing. In line with Reynolds's work (**Vulnerable Communion**), Amenyedzi concludes that "theological institutions need to realistically engage in dialogue from a disability theology and a theological hermeneutic of disability perspective . . . in order to integrate, include and embody persons with disability in their ministries and activities." (note 112)

On the basis of her empirical research in Malawi, Kamchedzera provides examples as to why many of those with disabilities do not want to attend church, and suggests that training for church leaders is needed. (note 113) Ishola-Esan's research clearly demonstrates this need: as mentioned above, 37 percent of the 120 pastors she interviewed – all postgraduates of the Nigerian Baptist Theological Seminary – saw a connection between disability and witchcraft; in addition, 42 percent saw disability as the result of possession by evil spirits, and 56 percent saw disability as

---

112. Amenyedzi, 3.
113. Kamchedzera, "Investigation," 15.

the result of God's will. (note 114) One of the findings from Nomatter Sande's empirical research within the Pentecostal church in Zimbabwe was that the subject of disability was entirely absent from the pastoral training curriculum at the church's seminary. (note 115) And in her research within ten theological institutions in southern Nigeria, Emiola Nihinlola found that only two institutions offered a course specifically on disability, both of which were bachelor-level courses – one on "special education" and the other on "religious education" – and that in a further two institutions, while disability did feature on the syllabus, it did not have its own course. (note 116) Considering the prevalence of misinterpretations and the experiences of disabled people within the church, some of which have been relayed in this chapter, it is clear that there is still a need to do more to ensure that disability is on the curriculum within theological education institutions.

Conclusion

This chapter has surveyed and discussed key pieces of work within the existing literature on

---

114. Ishola-Esan, "Remnants of African Worldviews," 109.
115. Sande, "Pastoral Ministry," n.p.
116. Nihinlola, "Disability Discourse."

disability and disability theology. While this body of work as a whole is vast, we have narrowed the scope of our study to scholarship that is particularly pertinent to the contexts of the African continent. A number of interconnected insights on the topic have emerged.

A survey on etiology has shown how cultural–religious beliefs surrounding causation can either lead to negative attitudes and discriminatory behaviours or, in contrast, foster positive engagement with disability. We have argued for a critical evaluation at the intersection of beliefs and theologies. In order to challenge and remove the barriers to genuine inclusion, it is crucial to engage critically, in a constructive way, with deeply ingrained beliefs and theologies around disability. We have therefore called for a careful engagement with biblical texts pertaining to disability. As Otieno rightly highlights on the basis of her research in Kenya, biblical representation and interpretation is one of the root causes of discrimination against those living with disabilities, and biblical texts "that have been interpreted in oppressive ways . . . continue to reinforce the marginalisation and exclusion of [people with disabilities]." (note 117) Given that interpreting biblical texts out of the contexts in which they were written can potentially

---

117. Otieno, "Perspectives," n.p.

harm people with disabilities in contemporary congregational contexts, this clearly highlights the importance of awareness and sensitivity in engaging with problematic key texts. (note 118)

A culture-sensitive approach to disability thus aims to read the Bible in a way that is sensitive to the cultural context it was written in, without directly translating it into one's own. North America-based scholars in religious studies and the Hebrew Bible Nyasha Junior and Jeremy Schipper describe the cultural model of disability as an approach that "analyzes how a culture's representations

---

118. Machingura, "'Unholy Trinity,'" 220. Applying a "redemptionist" reading of the Bible as a whole, and in context, could therefore be a valuable area of research for African faith communities in regards to disability. Redemptionism seeks to redeem a positive meaning and value in sacred texts by recontextualization, even when the text takes a negative stance on the condition described. Redemptionist approaches engage with how people with disabilities are represented in the texts and how contemporary scholars may reinterpret texts in the light of the insights from the disability studies literature. In Hector Avalos's words, the redemptionist approach seeks to "rescue the Bible from itself or from any modern misperception" (Avalos, "Redemptionism," 91).

and discussions of disability (and non-disability or able-bodiedness) help to articulate a range of values, ideals, or expectations that are important to that culture's organization and identity." (note 119) They point out that a cultural model of disability may help biblical readers in three ways: focusing on the cultural values associated with disability in the Hebrew Bible and the ancient Israelite societies that produced this literature; becoming aware of the contemporary cultural values that the reader assumes when interpreting biblical representations of disability; and determining whether interpretations of how disability operates in a given passage find sufficient support in the biblical text. (note 120)

Hermeneutics is therefore a critical area of research because it impacts all other areas, not least by influencing the perceptions and attitudes of church leaders and congregants towards those with disabilities, and therefore affecting the well-being of disabled people and their households. (note 121) Thus, we have argued that a nuanced and liberative hermeneutics is needed. Change can be effected only by addressing harmful beliefs and values with liberating holistic

---

119. Junior and Schipper, "Disability Studies," 35.
120. Junior and Schipper, 25.
121. Möller, "Experiences."

theologies from within faith communities, which can then lead to more inclusive actions and practices and movement towards the flourishing of all.

Bibliography

Abrams, Judith Z. "Misconceptions about Disabilities in the Hebrew Bible." In **Jewish Perspectives on Theology and the Human Experience of Disability**, edited by Judith Z. Abrams and William D. Gaventa, 73–99. New York: Haworth Pastoral, 2006.

Alolo, Namawu Alhassan, and James Astley Connell. "Indigenous Religions and Development: African Traditional Religion." In **Handbook of Research on Development and Religion**, edited by Matthew Clarke, 138–63. Cheltenham: Edward Elgar, 2013.

Amanze, James N. "The Attitudes of Six World Religions Towards People with Disabilities: A Critical Appraisal." In **Disability Is Not Inability: A Quest for Inclusion and Participation of People with Disability in Society**, edited by James N. Amanze and Jonathan S. Nkhoma, 45–63. Mzuzu: Muzuni, 2020.

Amenyedzi, Seyram. "Equity and Access for Persons with Disability in Theological Education, Ghana." PhD diss., University of Stellenbosch, 2016.

Avalos, Hector. "Redemptionism, Rejectionism, and Historicism as Emerging Approaches to Disability Studies." **Perspectives in Religious Studies** 34, no. 1 (2007): 91–100.

Chataika, Tsitsi. "Introduction: Critical Connections and Gaps in Disability and Development." In **The Routledge Handbook of Disability in Southern Africa**, edited by Tsitsi Chataika, 3–13. London: Routledge, 2019.

Chisale, Sinenhlanhla. "The Purity Myth: Feminist Disability Theology of Women's Sexuality and Implications for Pastoral Care." **Scriptura** 119, no. 1 (2020): 1–11.

Claassens, L. Juliana. "Countering Stereotypes: Job, Disability, and Human Dignity." **Journal of Religion, Disability & Health** 17, no. 2 (2013): 169–83.

Claassens, L. Juliana, Leslie Swartz and Len Hansen. "Introduction." In **Searching for Dignity: Conversations on Human Dignity, Theology and Disability**, edited by L. Juliana Claassens, Leslie Swartz and Len Hansen. Stellenbosch: Sun Media, 2013.

Claassens, L. Juliana, Sa'diyya Shaikh and Leslie Swartz. "Engaging Disability and Religion in the Global South." In **The Palgrave Handbook of Disability and Citizenship in the Global South**, edited by Brian Watermeyer, Judith McKenzie and Leslie Swartz, 147–64. Cham: Palgrave Macmillan, 2018.

Clifton, Shane, and Greta E. C. Wells. "Theology of Disability: The Spirit of Disabled Empowerment." In **The Routledge Handbook of Pentecostal Theology**, edited by Wolfgang Vondey, 346–56. London: Routledge, 2020.

Eide, Arne H., and Benedicte Ingstad. "Epilogue: Some Concluding Thoughts – The Way Ahead." In **Disability and Poverty**, edited by Arne H. Eide and Benedicte Ingstad, 225–31. Bristol: The Policy Press, 2011.

Eiesland, Nancy. **The Disabled God: Towards a Liberatory Theology of Disability**. Nashville: Abingdon, 1994.

Ford, David F. **The Gospel of John**. Grand Rapids: Baker Academic, 2021.

Fubara-Manuel, Jessie. "'Nothing Wey No Get Cure for This World': Interrogating Healing and the Miraculous for Women with Disabilities and HIV in Nigeria." In **Theologies and Practices of Inclusion**, edited by Nina Kurlberg and Madleina Daehnhardt, 252-71. London: SCM, 2021.

Githuku, Sammy. "Biblical Perspectives on Disability." In **Disability, Society, and Theology: Voices from Africa**, edited by Samuel Kabue, Esther Mombo, Joseph Galgalo and C. B. Peter, 79–93. Limuru: Zapf Chancery Publishers Africa, 2011.

Harrington, Hannah. **The Purity Texts.** London: Bloomsbury, 2007.

Harris-White, Barbara, and Devi Sridhar. "Disability and Development." In **The Elgar Companion to Development Studies**, edited by David A. Clark, 126–30. Cheltenham: Elgar, 2006.

Hathaway, Bridget, and Flavian Kishekwa. **Included and Valued: A Practical Theology of Disability**. Carlisle: Langham Global Library, 2019.

Hayes, Christine. "Purity and Impurity, Ritual." **Encyclopaedia Judaica** 16 (2007): 746–56.

Ingstad, Benedicte. "'Mpho ya Modimo – A Gift from God': Perspectives on 'Attitudes' Towards Disabled Persons." In **Disability and Culture**, edited by Benedicte Ingstad and Susan Reynolds Whyte, 246–63. Berkeley: University of California Press, 1995.

Ingstad, Benedicte, and Arne H. Eide. "Introduction: Disability and Poverty: A Global Challenge." In **Disability and Poverty**, edited by Arne H. Eide and Benedicte Ingstad, 1–14. Bristol: The Policy Press, 2011.

Ishola-Esan, Helen Olomu. "Impact of the Remnants of African Worldviews on Perception of Pastors Towards Ministering to Persons with Disabilities in Nigeria." **Journal of Disability & Religion** 20, no. 1–2 (2016): 103–18.

Jones, Melinda. "Judaism, Theology and the Human Rights of People with Disabilities." In **Jewish Perspectives on Theology and the Human Experience of Disability**, edited by Judith Z. Abrams and William D. Gaventa, 101–242. New York: Haworth Pastoral, 2006.

Junior, Nyasha, and Jeremy Schipper. "Disability Studies in the Bible." In **New Meanings for Ancient Texts: Recent Approaches to Biblical Criticisms and Their Applications**, edited by Steven L. McKenzie and John Kaltner, 21–37. Louisville: Westminster John Knox, 2013.

Kabue, Samuel. "Persons with Disabilities in Church and Society: A Historical and Sociological Perspective." In **Disability, Society, and Theology: Voices from Africa**, edited by Samuel Kabue, Esther Mombo, Joseph Galgalo and C. B. Peter, 3–25. Limuru: Zapf Chancery Publishers Africa, 2011.

Kabue, Samuel, Edison Kalengyo, John Ndavula and Anjeline Okala. **The Changing Scenes of Disability in Church and Society: A Resource Book for Theological and Religious Studies.** Nairobi: EDAN, 2021.

Kabue, Samuel, Esther Mombo, Joseph Galgalo and C. B. Peter. **Disability, Society, and Theology: Voices from Africa**. Limuru: Zapf Chancery Publishers Africa, 2011.

Kabue, Samuel, Helen Ishalo-Esan and Deji Ayegboyin. **Perspectives on Disability: A Resource Book for Theological and Religious Studies in Africa.** Nairobi: EDAN, 2016.

Kabue, Samuel, James Amanze and Christiana Landman. **Disability in Africa: A Resource Book for Theology and Religious Studies**. Nairobi: Acton, 2016.

Kamchedzera, Elizabeth T. "An Investigation Whether and How Christian Organizations Respond to the Practical Needs of Students with Disabilities: A Case of One College in Zomba." **Journal of Disability & Religion** 20, no. 1–2 (2016): 3–17.

Kebaneilwe, Mmapula Diana. "Disability as a Challenge and Not a Crisis: The Jesus Model." **Journal of Disability & Religion** 20, no. 1–2 (2016): 93–102.

Klawans, Jonathan. "Concepts of Purity in the Bible." In **The Jewish Study Bible**, edited by Adele Berlin and Marc Zvi Brettler, 1998–2005. Oxford: Oxford University Press, 2014.

Kretschmar, Louise. **The Church and Disability in Southern Africa**. Pietermaritzburg: Cluster Publications, 2019.

Kurlberg, Nina, and Madleina Daehnhardt, eds. **Theologies and Practices of Inclusion: Insights from a Faith-Based Relief, Development and Advocacy Organization**. London: SCM, 2021.

Leshota, Paul. "From Dependence to Interdependence: Towards a Practical Theology of Disability." **HTS Theological Studies** 71, no. 2 (2015): 1–9.

Machingura, Francis. "Disability and the Bible: The New Testament Narratives on Disability." In **Disability in Africa: A Resource Book for Theology and Religious Studies**, edited by Samuel Kabue, James Amanze and Christina Landman, 59–76. Nairobi: Acton, 2016.

———. "The 'Unholy Trinity' against Disabled People in Zimbabwe: Religion, Culture and the Bible." In **The Routledge Handbook of Disability in Southern Africa**, edited by Tsitsi Chataika, 211–23. London: Routledge, 2019.

Mackenney-Jeffs, Frances. **Reconceptualising Disability for the Contemporary Church**. London: SCM, 2021.

Maluleke, T. S. "Of Africanised Bees and Africanised Churches: Ten Theses on African Christianity." **Missionalia** 38, no. 3 (2010): 369–80.

Manganyi, J. S., and J. Buitendag. "A Critical Analysis on African Traditional Religion and the Trinity." **HTS Teologiese Studies/Theological Studies** 69, no. 1 (2013): Art. #1934.

M'bwangi, Ferdinand. "A Case of Tribal Defilement in a Kenyan Rural Village: A Narratological and Socio-Rhetorical Function of the Motifs of 'Hearing and Understanding' and 'Contrast' in Matthew 15:10–11 vis-à-vis Leviticus 11:1–4." **HTS Teologiese Studies/Theological Studies** 67, no. 3 (2011): Art. #427.

Möller, Erna. "The Experiences of People with Disabilities in Faith Communities and Suggestions to Enhance Their Inclusion." In **Searching for Dignity: Conversations on Human Dignity, Theology and Disability**, edited by L. Juliana Claassens, Leslie Swartz and Len Hansen, 129–41. Stellenbosch: Sun Media, 2013.

Mugeere, Anthony Buyinza, Julius Omona, Andrew Ellias State and Tom Shakespeare. "'Oh God! Why Did You Let Me Have This Disability?': Religion, Spirituality and Disability in Three African Countries." **Journal of Disability & Religion** 24, no. 1 (2020): 64–81.

Ndlovu, Hebron L. "African Beliefs Concerning People with Disabilities: Implications for Theological Education." **Journal of Disability & Religion** 20, no. 1–2 (2016): 29–39.

Neyrey, Jerome H. "The Idea of Purity in Mark's Gospel." **Semeia** 35 (1986): 91–128.

Nihinlola, Emiola. "Disability Discourse in the Curriculum of Nigerian Theological Institutions: Constraints, Possibilities and Recommendations." **Journal of Disability & Religion** 20, no. 1–2 (2016): 40–48.

Nkomazana, Fidelis. "'No One Who Has a Blemish Shall Draw Near': Pentecostals Rising above Disabling Hermeneutics." **Journal of Disability & Religion** 20, no. 1–2 (2016): 49–61.

Nyangweso, Mary. "Disability in Africa: A Cultural/Religious Perspective." In **Disability in Africa: Inclusion, Care, and the Ethics of Humanity**, edited by Toyin Falola and Nic Hamel, 115–36. Rochester: University of Rochester Press, 2021.

Olyan, Saul M. **Disability in the Hebrew Bible: Interpreting Mental and Physical Differences**. Cambridge: Cambridge University Press, 2008.

Omigbodun, Olayinka, Adebayo Odejide and Jide Morakinyo. "Highlights from the CAR study in Ibadan, Nigeria." In **Disability and Culture: Universalism and Diversity**, edited by T. Bedirhan Üstün et al., 185–94. Seattle: Hogrefe & Huber, 2001.

Otieno, Pauline A. "Biblical and Theological Perspectives on Disability: Implications on the Rights of Persons with Disability in Kenya." **Disability Studies Quarterly** 29, no. 4 (2009). https://doi.org/10.18061/dsq.v29i4.988.

Palm, Selina. "One Body? To Belong, We Have to Be Missed: Exploring Theologies of Disability from Southern Contexts." Internal Reflection Paper. Tearfund, 2020.

Peterson, Eugene H. **The Message: The Bible in Contemporary Language.** Colorado Springs: NavPress, 2002.

Rao, Shridevi. "Disability, Family Epistemologies and Resistance to Shame within the Indian Context." In **Disability in South Asia: Knowledge and Experience**, edited by Anita Ghai, 313–29. New Delhi: SAGE Publications India, 2018.

Reynolds, Thomas E. "Protestant Christianity and Disability." In **Disability and World Religions: An Introduction**, edited by Darla Y. Schumm and Michael Stoltzfus, 137–66. Waco: Baylor University, 2016.

———. **Vulnerable Communion: A Theology of Disability and Hospitality**. Grand Rapids: Brazos, 2008.

Room, Robin, Jürgen Rehm, Robert T. Trotter II, Angela Paglia and T. Bedirhan Üstün. "Cross-Cultural Views on Stigma, Valuation, Parity and Societal Values Towards Disability." In **Disability and Culture: Universalism and Diversity**, edited by T. Bedirhan Üstün et al., 247–91. Seattle: Hogrefe & Huber, 2001.

Sande, Nomatter. "Pastoral Ministry and Persons with Disabilities: The Case of the Apostolic Faith Mission in Zimbabwe." **African Journal of Disability** (Online) 8 (2019): a431.

Schumm, Darla Y., and Michael Stoltzfus, eds. **Disability and Religious Diversity: Cross-Cultural and Interreligious Perspectives**. New York: Palgrave, 2011.

———. **Disability and World Religions: An Introduction**. Waco: Baylor University, 2016.

———. **Disability in Judaism, Christianity, and Islam: Sacred Texts, Historical Traditions and Social Analysis**. New York: Palgrave, 2011.

Setume, Senzokuhle D., and Baamphatlha Dinama. "African Traditional Religions and Disabilities." In **Disability in Africa: A Resource Book for Theology and Religious Studies**, edited by Samuel Kabue, James Amanze and Christina Landman, 11–28. Nairobi: Acton, 2016.

Swinton, John. "From Health to Shalom: Why the Religion and Health Debate Needs Jesus." In **Healing to All Their Flesh: Essays in Spirituality,**

Theology, and Health, edited by Jeffrey Levin and Keith Meador, 219–41. Conshohocken: Templeton, 2012.

———. "Who Is the God We Worship? Theologies of Disability; Challenges and New Possibilities." **International Journal of Practical Theology** 14, no. 2 (2011): 273–307.

Tearfund Learn. "Interview: I Am Not Sick." 2019. https://learn.tearfund.org/en/resources/footsteps/footsteps-101-110/footsteps-108/interview-i-am-not-sick.

Tofa, Eliot. "Disabilities in the New Testament and African Religious Traditions." In **Disability in Africa: A Resource Book for Theology and Religious Studies**, edited by Samuel Kabue, James Amanze and Christiana Landman, 125–35. Nairobi: Acton, 2016.

Üstün, T. Bedirhan, Somnath Chatterji, Jerome E. Bickenback, Robert T. Trotter II and Shekhar Saxena. "Disability and Cultural Variation: The ICIDH-2 Cross-Cultural Applicability Research Study." In **Disability and Culture: Universalism and Diversity**, edited by T. Bedirhan Üstün et al., 3–19. Seattle: Hogrefe & Huber, 2001.

Watts Belser, Julia. "Judaism and Disability." In **Disability and World Religions: An Introduction**, edited by Darla Schumm and Michael Scholtzfus, 93–113. Waco: Baylor University, 2016.

Whyte, Susan Reynolds. "Disability between Discourse and Experience." In **Disability and Culture**, edited by Benedicte Ingstad and Susan Reynolds Whyte, 267–91. Berkeley: University of California Press, 1995.

World Council of Churches. "WCC Grieves Passing of Rev. Dr Micheline Kamba Kasongo." Oikoumene, 6 August 2020. https://www.oikoumene.org/news/wcc-grieves-passing-of-rev-dr-micheline-kamba-kasongo.

Yong, Amos. **Theology and Down Syndrome: Reimagining Disability in Late Modernity.** Waco: Baylor University Press, 2007.

2

Disability and the Bible

The Challenge of Reading Responsibly[1]

Grant Macaskill

> Your word is a lamp to my feet
>   and a light to my path.
> (Psalm 119:105) [2]

---

[1] This contribution is adapted from "Autism and the Bible: The Challenge of Reading Responsibly," in **Autism and the Church: Bible, Theology, Community**, by Grant Macaskill, 43–70. © 2019. Reprinted with the permission of Baylor University Press. All rights reserved.

[2] Unless otherwise noted, all quotations from the Bible are taken from the NRSV.

Introduction

This chapter outlines some principles that shape and constrain the responsible use of Scripture in relation to disability. These are not particular to African contexts, nor even to experiences of disability, but they do bear distinctively on these. Mostly, the principles that I outline here can be traced back to the earliest centuries of the church, when its centres of spiritual and intellectual leadership were particularly associated with northern Africa, Asia Minor and the Middle East. This is important to note because, in today's context, these rich principles of biblical reading have widely been replaced by interpretative practices that are popular in contemporary evangelicalism, the advocates of which consider themselves uniquely faithful to the Bible. Their interpretative approach is, however, much more affected by the values of the modern West than they typically recognize. The principles of interpretation developed by the early church provide us with accounts of reading the Bible faithfully that look quite different from these at key points and are pivotal to developing strong contextual interpretations of the Bible and disability.

In the paragraph above, I speak in the first place of "use" rather than "interpretation" or "exegesis." This reflects two acknowledgements and leads to a further caution that will then form the basis for the chapter that follows. First, Christians use or utilize Scripture in normative ways because we consider it to be distinctively authoritative for thought and practice, as the word of God. Most Christians will give such distinctive importance to the Bible, even if they disagree on how that importance should be conceived and related to other elements of authority, such as tradition. Confronted by any situation or reality, we will typically ask "What does it mean to think biblically about this?" This, though, means that the Bible can be an object of dangerous misuse, when its authority is claimed in support of a vicious position. The acknowledged status of the Bible within the Christian community places a burden on its readers to use it well, which is why the principles outlined here have such importance. Second, to speak of "use" highlights that our interpretation of Scripture can never be isolated from the situations into which it will speak and to which we apply it. We often approach Scripture precisely to find resources by which we can understand and engage with our circumstances. We need to acknowledge that it is proper to do so, but neither collapse the details of Scripture into our own circumstances – as if there are no differences to be negotiated – nor assume that there is something to be extracted from any given scripture that can straightforwardly be applied to those circumstances.

These two acknowledgements lead to my point of caution: in recognizing that we "use" Scripture, we must not allow ourselves to engage with it as if it is simply a "utility" or a "commodity." If Scripture is the word of God, then it is something that participates in God's communication with the church, something to which we listen and submit. But often our discourse about Scripture, and our methods of studying it, present it as something we possess and master, as if it were a commodity. And often our claimed mastery of it is another commodity, a means to status. Under the guise of "faithfulness," then, we can often commodify Scripture, and this is a particularly dangerous dynamic in our contexts of concern: the experience of disability in Africa.

The principles that I lay out here are drawn from some of my own recent work on Christian moral identity and on Christian intellectual humility, (note 3) both of which have been particularly attentive to how the Bible functions to shape the way that we think. They are also

---

3. Macaskill, **Intellectual Humility**; Macaskill, "Christian Scriptures," 243–52.

influenced by my involvement with discussions about the theology of disability. I currently teach at the University of Aberdeen, in my home country of Scotland. One of the distinctive features of our department is a particular interest in theology and disability, represented in the work of my wonderful colleagues John Swinton and Brian Brock, who have thought much longer and much harder than I have about disability (a word that we use out of necessity, rather than preference), and whose thinking has been shaped at the most basic levels by personal experience. To work within an academic community where disability is of central concern is a privilege, and it forces one to consider many of the interpretative values that we take for granted and ask whether they are problematic at a deep level. The principles I outline here have been shaped by this context, but they are not uniquely about disability. They are more basically about the ways in which we conceive the task of reading Scripture. Consequently, they may invite readers to reconsider their views on a whole range of issues beyond the current one.

Here, I simply offer a set of programmatic statements that take their own authority from the character of Scripture itself and from the interpretative principles that can be traced back to the earliest Christians, the church fathers who left us a legacy of christological and Trinitarian doctrine. The early church – with its centres in northern Africa, Asia Minor and the Middle East – developed a vital set of interpretative principles for the early church, which revolved around the question of how any given text is to be read within the context of the Bible as a whole, and in relation to the gospel of Jesus Christ. While these principles, which cohesively came to be known as "the rule of faith" (**regula fidei**), developed fluidly and without much explicit articulation, they were widely sustained. (note 4)

Before I consider these principles, though, I will consider three examples of thinking about a particular condition that is commonly categorized as a disability – autism – that I consider to be fundamentally flawed. Identifying the flaws in each will allow us to think a little more maturely about how the Bible should function properly in our theology in relation to a range of disabling conditions. Autism is not universally considered a disability; even autistic people who are themselves happy with that label will acknowledge that they are disabled only in or by specific circumstances. Hence, it exemplifies in important ways the intersection of social models of disability with medical ones. But it also illustrates the challenge

---

4. Bokedal, "Early Rule-of-Faith Pattern," 57–75.

of considering the range of disabilities recognized today, including those we call "hidden disabilities," in light of Scripture.

Misreading the Bible in Relation to Autism

The first example is, on one level, fairly innocuous, but it still opens up some important issues for us to reflect upon. In a 2010 article, S. K. Mathew and J. D. Pandian "diagnosed" a number of biblical characters as having what are known today to be neurological or psychiatric conditions. (note 5) Among the characters they diagnosed was Samson, whom they considered to be autistic; this "would precede the first known case of autism by centuries." (note 6) Without needing to rehearse any of the detail behind this proposed diagnosis, we can compare Mathew and Pandian's approach with the process of clinical diagnosis that would be experienced by a person with autism today. This involves lengthy interviews, both with the person (if he or she is able to communicate) and with family members. A detailed picture of the person's background and development is constructed, shaped (as far as possible) by the person's own testimony concerning his or her sensory and social

---

5. Mathew and Pandian, "Newer Insights," 164–66.
6. Mathew and Pandian, 164.

experiences. The process may take more than one day of interviews, and is regulated by very detailed, carefully developed questions of agreed diagnostic value. It is simply impossible to replicate this by relying on the limited third-person narrative detail of a biblical story contained in four short chapters of the Bible. (As an aside, I might note the parallels with the kind of "diagnosis" often passed by church members or pastors on other members of the congregation whom they consider to be "on the spectrum." This is usually a dismissive diagnosis, based, again, on an inadequate body of specific evidence.)

The approach also engages with the biblical story as a means to access a historical reality that lies behind the text and is obtainable through it; that is, the principal thing that the authors are seeking to obtain through their reading of the text is access to the historical reality of Samson's neurotype. Doing so neglects the real character, function and purpose of the narrative and the discourse, which is to communicate to its readers something that will shape their own lives in relation to God. This is not to question the historical veracity of the text – that is a debate for elsewhere – but to emphasize that the text is not principally intended as a vehicle for historical documentation, but rather for edification. As such, whatever historical details the text contains are rendered to us in a theological and educational narrative that is much more concerned with the demands of Yahwism and the dangers of idolatry than with the neurological health of its characters. (note 7) Put bluntly, Mathew and Pandian's approach to the text of the book of Judges is not appropriate to the character of the text.

To be clear, this is not to deny the possibility that some or many of the biblical characters were autistic, or neurodiverse in other ways. Even basic statistics indicate that many would have been. The point, rather, is that the narratives or their narrators may not be interested in giving us the historical data that would suggest this and may be motivated in their characterizations of characters by other concerns. As autistic or neurodiverse readers, we may identify with those characters, and this is fine, but we need to be careful not to make assumptions about the historical detail of their lives based on texts that are not reducible to historical reports.

---
7. "Yahwism" designates the worship of the God whose name is disclosed in the Tetragrammaton, YHWH. The name is usually translated as "the Lord" in the Old Testament, reflecting the reverence with which the name was treated: readers would substitute the word for "Lord" in the place of the name itself.

The second example is dramatically more disturbing, to the extent that I feel the need to issue a trigger warning to any parents of autistic children that what follows may be upsetting. I am also sufficiently disturbed by it that I do not want to publish a link to the relevant website, since I do not want to promote it in any sense. In the course of my research, I came across a website that compared the symptoms of autism to the biblical accounts of demon possession. Mutism, fits, spasms, destructive behaviour and so on: these were represented as significant parallels between the descriptions in the gospels of people who had demons driven from them and the behaviours seen in autistic children. The conclusion reached was that what is seen as an epidemic of autism today is actually evidence of demon possession. The correct way to treat this, therefore, is with prayers for deliverance or exorcism. As disturbing as this claim was in itself, it was overshadowed by the comments that readers had posted to the website about their own experience as parents. They affirmed the identification of autism with demon possession and, in many cases, spoke about their own experience of praying (unsuccessfully) for their own children to be delivered from the demons that possessed them.

Multiple responses could be made to this; these will be reprised in the positive proposals outlined below. For one thing, stories of demonic possession within the Bible are actually relatively uncommon and are particularly clustered within the Synoptic Gospels and Acts. There are only a few stories outside these. That fact has some bearing on the proportional significance of the demonic within the Bible and relates to one of the proposals below, namely, that we need to allow biblical proportions to play some role in our biblical interpretation, to respect the shape of the Bible as a whole. Second, the association of a demonic presence with a nonverbal ("mute") person is really confined to two stories (Matt 9:32–3 / Luke 11:14; Matt 12:22); only by conflating these stories with others involving demons and violence (Matt 8:28–33) can one construct something that shares superficial characteristics with autism. Third, "mutism" or "nonverbalism" is more commonly represented in the Bible simply as a physical disability, listed alongside lameness and blindness as people come to Jesus for healing (about which we will say more below), as in Matthew 15:30–31. The final point is perhaps the most important: the problem with this approach is that it does not take seriously the need to understand what we are bringing back to the Bible to be understood in its light. It ignores the evidence that autism is associated with genetic factors and with demonstrably different neurological features; it does not take seriously enough that these are necessarily part of what the condition is and involves. Those who contributed to the website mentioned above might accuse me here of putting modern science "before" the Bible, but it is actually a basic principle of biblical truthfulness that we expect to see a coherence between the physical world that science investigates and the world as it is rendered to us in Scripture. The two involve different identifications and therefore different principles of investigation, (note 8) and they cannot be collapsed into each other, but we expect to see some kind of coherence, of a kind that means we cannot ignore the physical dimension of autism (genetics, neurology, etc.) by labelling it as demon possession. I will say more below on how we negotiate the technological present in relation to the pre-technological past, but at this point the main problem with this

---

8. Torrance, **Theological Science**, 9–10, makes the point in relation to theology that the mode of scientific investigation must be determined by the nature of the object of study, a principle that prohibits the simple transfer of scientific methodologies to the study of God. This point can be applied to Scripture, too, although with the important caveat that Scripture participates in the creaturely world of things in history.

approach can be expressed in these terms: its advocates do not take seriously the evidence for the physical causal factors known to be associated with autism. (note 9)

The third problematic use of the Bible is more subtly wrong, although it may be nearly as disturbing as the one just considered. For some, autism and similar conditions are problems to be "healed." This view takes its warrant from the various stories of healing that we find in the Bible, particularly in the New Testament, and most extensively within the context of the gospels and Acts. In some cases, it can be married to what is sometimes referred to as a "health and prosperity" understanding of the gospel, where those who have true faith in God enjoy a flood of blessings that ought typically to include the healing of illnesses and the provision of material prosperity. Sometimes this is traced to a view of sickness and suffering that links them very closely to the problem of sin: where sin is properly dealt with, healing and prosperity should follow. For reasons that I will outline below, this approach should be seen as highly problematic. In other cases, though,

---

9. As a contrastive example of how the biblical material can be read in relation to issues of mental health, see Stuckenbruck, "Demonic Invasion," 94–119.

the view of where healing and blessing fit into Christian experience may be less sweeping and less thoroughly problematic: they may be affirmed as things that often, but not always, accompany God's life-giving presence, to be prayed for and hoped for, but not considered to be routine.

Any reflection on this must affirm that the Bible includes stories of healing, sometimes involving people who are disabled in some sense. It must also recognize that some of those healings appear to have a programmatic significance, representing the decisive change that has taken place with the coming of Jesus and closely linked to the realization of his work of deliverance from sin. In Matthew 11, for example, Jesus responds to John's question about whether he is indeed the Messiah in part by referring to his work of healing:

> When John heard in prison what the Messiah was doing, he sent word by his disciples and said to him, "Are you the one who is to come, or are we to wait for another?" Jesus answered them, "Go and tell John what you hear and see: the blind receive their sight, the lame walk, the lepers are cleansed, the deaf hear, the dead are raised, and the poor have good news brought to them. And blessed is anyone who takes no offence at me." (Matt 11:2–6)

The references to those who are healed are generally understood to evoke the expectations of the prophet Isaiah about the figure of the Servant, so that their function is not to indicate that healing will now be the new normal, but rather to demonstrate that Jesus is, indeed, the messianic Servant. This is in line with other parts of Matthew that similarly link the revelation of the Davidic king with particular acts of healing. (note 10)

Nevertheless, the healings are described as real events, and we should take this seriously. We must also acknowledge that there are points in the Bible, notably in the Psalms, (note 11) where the language of sickness and affliction is used by people who are burdened by a sense of their own sin, and who identify their suffering as some kind of divine chastening.

These observations mean that we cannot ignore the apparent biblical warrant for the view that autism, like any other disabling condition, might be (or even "should be") healed. But the same can be said of every view that, through the centuries, the church has come to consider wrong or even heretical: all can point to particular scriptural texts for warrant. The proper response to these

---

10. Novakovic, **Messiah**.
11. See, for example, Ps 51:8.

must always be to highlight that other parts of the canon of Scripture contain important corrective or balancing truths that must be brought to bear on such assertions. In relation to healing in general, it needs to be noted that the stories of healing, as with those concerning exorcism, are particularly clustered within the gospels and Acts, where they continue to have an exceptional significance. The miracles of Jesus continued to be "miraculous" and not commonplace; they are exceptional interventions, rather than the norm. The same is true of the miracles in Acts: only a small number of healing stories are recounted, which must be considered exceptionally significant. James, certainly, speaks of the prayer offered in faith that will make the sick person well (5:15), and does so in a way that suggests he is speaking about regular practices of prayer, but his words need to be read alongside the passages in Paul's writings that speak of suffering and sickness as things that continue to be present in the life of the believer and that are vital to our manifestation of divine grace.

> But we have this treasure in clay jars, so that it may be made clear that this extraordinary power belongs to God and does not come from us. We are afflicted in every way, but not crushed; perplexed, but not driven to despair; persecuted, but not

forsaken; struck down, but not destroyed; always carrying in the body the death of Jesus, so that the life of Jesus may also be made visible in our bodies. (2 Cor 4:7–10)

This leads towards one of the core principles that must inform the use of Scripture, which simply recognizes that any given text or passage needs to be considered within the wider context of the Bible as a whole. One of the most basic problems in contemporary Christian uses of Scripture is a tendency to move immediately from the exegesis of an isolated text (or even a small set of texts) to making a moral or theological claim that is asserted as "biblical." This problem becomes visible quickly when we seek to deal with an issue like autism, but it affects our moral and theological reasoning much more broadly. As we will see below, such an approach fails to show proper respect or reverence to the character of Scripture as a complex work of divine communication.

One further point can be made on the topic of healing and on the use of Scripture in relation to it. Readers in the Global North need to be sensitive to the ways in which our basic assumptions are coloured by the social and intellectual context of late modernity, and we need to allow Scripture to challenge those assumptions. Readers in an African context, meanwhile, need to be aware that such assumptions often underlie the values they encounter in literature that originates in the Global North, and in missionary and health care organizations based in those areas.

One of the subtle issues that we face concerns our perception of what it means to be healthy and whole. Within the context of the Global North – which cherishes the idea of the self-contained, self-reliant, autonomous individual (note 12) – we tend to think of health and well-being in individualist terms, assuming that the healthy individual is one who needs no care and who can live a productive and constructive life. We may even map the need for care and support onto a theology in which the image of God has been compromised and damaged by sin. (note 13)

Without necessarily dismissing this view, we need to be open to the possibility that we are refracting the biblical material through a distinctively modern account of being human, which neglects the possibility that one can live a joyful life of flourishing while being entirely

---

12. Taylor, **Sources of the Self**; MacIntyre, **After Virtue**, 30–34.
13. See the discussion of the image of God in Macaskill, **Autism and the Church**, chapter 3.

dependent on the caregiving of others. (note 14) Often this accompanies a particular conception of the image of God (**imago Dei**), one that links it to the possession and manifestation of certain properties or capacities by the individual. Such an understanding can be traced back to pre-modern theology, but it becomes radically more dominant in the modern era, in the wake of the Enlightenment and the influence of humanism. At this stage, I am seeking not to offer an alternative way of thinking about the **imago Dei**, but simply to alert readers to the possibility that they (or those who influence them) may be working with a set of very modern assumptions about what it means to be a flourishing human being. Under the influences of the intellectual discourse of the urbanized Global North, we may think of healing (and, for that matter, our ultimately destined condition) in ways that are shaped by this individualist account of the **imago Dei**.

The problems with the last two of these three approaches – the identification of autism as demonic and the expectation that it should be healed – are complex, but generally emerge from a tendency to read certain biblical passages without due consideration for the teaching of the wider

---

14. This is a key principle in Swinton, "From Inclusion to Belonging," 172–90.

Bible, rather than from misreading the passages in themselves. The principles offered in what follows will, I hope, provide helpful correctives to this.

Principle 1: We Read the Bible in a Way That Is Governed by the Person and Story of Jesus Christ

To read the Bible "Christianly" means to read all of the Bible in a way that is informed and governed by the identity of Jesus Christ, "the mystery that has been hidden throughout the ages and generations but has now been revealed to his saints" (Col 1:26). He is the Word that became flesh (John 1:14), and John's identification of him in such terms is suggestive of the fact that the meaning of Scripture must always be approached through his particular embodiment of it; for, as John continues, "no one has ever seen God; it is God the Only Begotten, who is in the Father's heart, who has made him known" (John 1:18, my translation).

To say this should be fairly uncontroversial to any Christian reader, but its importance can be attenuated by ways of conceiving "Christ-centredness" that fall short of the way it is rendered in the New Testament. It is not simply that Jesus is the great exemplar of Christian morality, whose behaviour is to be emulated and whose lead is to be followed; neither is it simply the case that Jesus is now identified as the God to whom obedience is rendered. In the first, Christ-centredness is a matter of imitation (exemplified in the "What would Jesus do?" slogan), while in the second it is a matter of worshipful obedience to the king. Both of these are good and important elements of Christ-centredness, but taken by themselves they fall short of the way that the New Testament writers speak of Christ, not just as one by whom obedience is modelled, or to whom it is rendered, but as the one in whom salvation and goodness are constituted, and apart from whom they do not exist. This language is ubiquitous in Paul's writing, but it is found widely through the New Testament. The words of Jesus that are reported in John's gospel communicate the significance of the incorporative grammar most effectively: "Those who abide in me and I in them bear much fruit, because apart from me you can do nothing" (John 15:5).

Importantly, at several points in the New Testament, this kind of language is used both of salvation and of creation, or even of God's providential care for the cosmos. In Colossians 1:15–20, for example, Paul writes, (note 15)

---

15. The authorship of Colossians is a matter of debate among scholars. For an overview, see Foster, **Colossians**.

> He is the image of the invisible God, the firstborn of all creation; for in him all things in heaven and on earth were created, things visible and invisible, whether thrones or dominions or rulers or powers – all things have been created through him and for him. He himself is before all things, and in him all things hold together. He is the head of the body, the church; he is the beginning, the firstborn from the dead, so that he might come to have first place in everything. For in him all the fullness of God was pleased to dwell, and through him God was pleased to reconcile to himself all things, whether on earth or in heaven, by making peace through the blood of his cross.

Here it is not only salvation that is "in Christ," as it is often represented in Paul's writings, but everything in creation, from before time and into eternity. They are not, of course, all "in" him in the same way, (note 16) but the text is particularly concerned to highlight the corresponding senses in which creation, providence and redemption are constituted in and through the person of Jesus Christ. When the text goes on to speak of him as the mystery that had been hidden through the

---

16. Macaskill, "Way the One God Works," 112–25.

ages but has now been revealed (Col 1:26), this is more than just a reference to the importance of the events narrated in the gospel as part of God's unfolding plan of redemption: it is, instead, an articulation of the new perception that the entirety of God's dealings with the cosmos throughout its existence has been done "in Christ." The reading of any text of the Old Testament, then, must now be conditioned for the Christian by the knowledge of who Jesus Christ is.

This is illustrated by what we see in the opening of John's gospel, where Jesus (represented as "the Word") is described as the one who made all things and in whom the light that gives life to all things exists: "All things came into being through him, and without him not one thing came into being. What has come into being in him was life, and the life was the light of all people" (John 1:3–4).

This is often read as if John is simply using creation imagery to render the identity of Jesus; he is doing this, but he is also retelling the story of creation in christological terms. The imagery in John 1 draws upon both the account of Genesis 1 and the description of Wisdom in Proverbs 8, but the force of the appropriation is to recast both creation and the enjoyment of God's life-giving presence as inseparable from the person of Jesus Christ. When, later in the gospel, Jesus tells his disciples that "apart from me you can do nothing" (John 15:5), he is not speaking principally as a moral exemplar, but as the source of goodness itself.

Grappling with this involves some reflection on notions of "participation." If these passages are taken seriously, then all goodness involves some kind of participation in the life of God through Jesus Christ, even if we necessarily distinguish the kind of participation that is experienced by the believer from the kind that might be embodied by any person or creature that does or enjoys good. This was one of the key themes in the writings of the early church fathers, who recognized that all goodness is derived from the presence of Jesus Christ, but were also concerned to affirm the special kind of participation that is involved in salvation, and that is enjoyed by those who believe and partake of the sacraments. (note 17)

This is important because it presses back on a way of reading the Bible that reduces the gospel to a "fix" for the problem of sin, a correction of the damage introduced by the fall. Instead, it demands that we read all of the Bible as "evangelically

---

17. Russell, **Doctrine of Deification**; Macaskill, **Union with Christ**, 42–76.

conditioned" and oriented towards a particular kind of flourishing, when God will be all in all (1 Cor 15:28) and will bring each creature to its telos.

Principle 2: We Read the Bible as a Complex Whole

The Bible, considered as holy Scripture, is normative for the thought and life of the Christian church, but it exercises this normativity as a genetically diverse collection or even as a library. This is simply a matter of observing and acknowledging that our sacred Scriptures contain poems, proverbs, stories, songs, sayings, prophecies, letters and some commandments. Certain parts of the collection may have a particular programmatic significance for other parts (the gospel narratives, most obviously), but one of the problems that needs to be challenged is the tendency to think of "biblical authority" in a way that is reduced to one or two of the genres. The point has been made by David Kelsey and reiterated by Kevin Vanhoozer, and it is worth pausing to reflect on the observations that they have made. (note 18)

---

18. Kelsey, **Uses of Scripture**, 125–58; Vanhoozer, **First Theology**, 125–58.

When we think of "biblical authority," we tend to allow one or two particular concepts to govern our ways of thinking, most commonly that of the commandment that should be obeyed or of the reliable account of salvation history within which we understand ourselves. Importantly, those concepts tend to be accompanied by a particular governing metaphor about God's relationship to us: he is seen as the legislator (or king) who, through the biblical salvation history, creates the world and then brings it back into order when sin makes it go wrong by the breaking of his commandments. This feeds into our understanding of gospel and atonement, which are principally conceived in terms of a kind of debt collection for our failure to keep the commandments. (note 19) As a result, we often think of the Bible as a "manual for life" and conceive its authority in ways that reflect this, while reducing salvation to the notion that commandment-breakers are delivered from the punishment that they deserve.

This concept of authority, however, struggles to accommodate many of the genres of Scripture and the way they operate. It is not easy to apply it to the mode of normativity exercised by the book of Proverbs, which rattles off saying after

---

19. The same observation is made by Hauerwas, **Character and the Christian Life**.

saying informed by the kind of wisdom that comes from long observation of the world, from lessons learned by watching ants work and vicious people plot. Neither does it easily accommodate the normativity of a psalm, or even, for that matter, of a short story that does not obviously or significantly take forward the grand scheme of salvation history. It may not deal meaningfully with the storied character of the gospels and Acts, the way that they shape our thinking as narratives, (note 20) and may squeeze their material into an account of "the gospel" or "salvation history" that is actually abstracted from much of the detail.

We need to recognize that Scripture norms and regulates our life and thought as a wild and unruly collection of works. (note 21) This involves a certain humility, an acknowledgement that we will never master or own it, but will instead subject ourselves to its abrasion, by reading it and allowing its wordplay to affect us as readers. Like all literature, it does this by engaging us holistically,

---

20. By this, I mean that it is not just the story that is important, but the way the story is told.
21. Macaskill, **Intellectual Humility**, 207–38.

by shaping our affections and sympathies as much as our propositional beliefs. It shapes us as a library. (note 22)

Recognizing this prevents us from approaching scriptural authority as something that can be reduced to proof texts for a particular position. All texts need to be evaluated within the context of the collection as a whole, which involves thinking about how other generic parts of the Bible might inform, correct or nuance what is suggested by the text in front of us. If this sounds worryingly open and unresolved, it should: we should be unnerved by our reading of Scripture; our assumptions should be challenged by it. (note 23) There are certainly truths that can be seen as necessary to Christian faith, but even these have generally been distilled into doctrines that take seriously the whole of Scripture; there are no proof texts for the Trinity, but trinitarianism is the correct doctrinal formulation of what the Bible, as a whole, teaches us about God.

---

22. The designation of the Bible as a library is widely found through the traditions of the church. It is an important and suggestive image of the diverse modes of biblical authority.

23. Macaskill, **Intellectual Humility**, 207–38.

In relation to disability, the point is vital, and it takes us back to the misuses of Scripture discussed above. These focus on a particular set of texts that speak about demonic realities or healings, but do not frame these in relation to the biblical texts that represent sickness or weakness as conditions in which grace can truly flourish, as necessary elements of our participation in the witness of Jesus Christ. Instead, this approach directs us towards a reflection on broader principles that can be traced across the genres of Scripture and that emerge in the complex moral account reflected in the Old Testament, both in the law and in the wisdom writings. These have a scope and a level of practical detail that is not seen in the New Testament, but is arguably assumed by the various writers. The law regulates religious life and the festival calendar, but it also regulates agricultural and architectural principles; it bears on worship, but it also bears on social justice and wealth distribution. It bears on the way a society values its members, both human and animal, especially those who are vulnerable. This is the kind of detailed picture in which we can begin to think about disability and Christian community.

Principle 3: We Respect the Historical Particularities of the Bible

This third principle is worded with special care. Most biblical scholars recognize the importance of engaging with the biblical texts as historical documents, so that some engagement with their historical context or background is necessary to their interpretation. To a significant extent, however, this part of the biblical scholarly task has come to dominate the conception of the task as a whole, so that the majority of serious biblical scholars now effectively work as historians rather than theologians. This is one of the reasons why so little has been done to address the question of how we should think biblically about disabilities that are not encountered in ancient biblical texts: if biblical scholars cannot find historical data in the text or its background that correspond to a contemporary topic, they will have nothing to say to it. In relation to autism, the only way we can escape this is by recovering a properly theological vision for the task. Reading the Bible properly summons us to speak rightly of God, and speaking rightly of God forces us to speak differently about everything else.

But it remains the case that the biblical texts are historically particular and took their form through the organic agency of historically located persons, (note 24) even if these persons were inspired by the Spirit to communicative acts that continue to speak throughout the ages. It is necessary to acknowledge this in our attempts to read the Bible, and to remind ourselves constantly that we read the texts as "cultural foreigners" to the worlds in which they were written. (note 25) The danger that attends us is always that we see something in the text that is not there (or, conversely, that we fail to see something that is there). If we read the Bible carefully, sensitive to this, then the world of the text can reach forward to ours, absorbing and reshaping it, investing it with fresh value. If we read it carelessly, we will absorb the world of the text to ours, smothering its radical qualities with our conventional ones.

An example of this is found in the issue of gender roles. In the Global North, we live in a world that has dramatically reordered the respective status of males and females. Many Christians, of course, consider this to be a rejection of biblical gender

---

24. The word "organic" is particularly associated with the Reformed tradition, but what it labels is broadly recognized: the Bible is the word of God, but its composition involves the agency of real, historically located human beings.

25. For this idea, see Malina, **New Testament World**, 1–6.

roles and rail against it. That very reaction, though, often reflects a lack of recognition of just how radical the cultural shift is that has taken place within the New Testament Christian community, and how far it has already gone towards reordering perceptions of the value and role of women. Many Christians today will understand the Bible to reflect their own ecclesial situation, in which men and women play different roles and functionally have different value; they will point to texts in the New Testament that seem to reflect this complementarian structure. (note 26) They will generally, though, not recognize the historical sociological significance attached to the fact that a church meets in the home of a woman –

---

26. Most obviously, the guidance to wives and husbands in Eph 5:21–33. The translation of this passage is not as straightforward as often assumed, since the imperative "submit" is not found in 5:21 in the earliest manuscripts nor in the earliest patristic quotations of the verse. Neither is there a finite form of the verb "submit" applied to wives in verse 24. In both cases, where these early manuscripts are concerned, the language of submission must be carried forward from the participle in verse 20, "submitting to one another." That participle is masculine plural in form, and must therefore be understood to designate the group as a whole.

which would assign her a position of leadership and oversight – or the fact that Paul, departing spectacularly from the conventions of the day, will direct his commendations and greetings to named women within the church in Rome. Those familiar with the culture of the day and the way it ascribed honour and status according to gender are right to see something quite subversive in Romans 16:

> I commend to you our sister Phoebe, a deacon of the church at Cenchreae, so that you may welcome her in the Lord as is fitting for the saints, and help her in whatever she may require from you, for she has been a benefactor of many and of myself as well.
>
> Greet Prisca and Aquila, who work with me in Christ Jesus, and who risked their necks for my life, to whom not only I give thanks, but also all the churches of the Gentiles. Greet also the church in their house. Greet my beloved Epaenetus, who was the first convert in Asia for Christ. Greet Mary, who has worked very hard among you. Greet Andronicus and Junia, my relatives who were in prison with me; they are prominent among the apostles, and they were in Christ before I was. (Rom 16:1–7)

The reason for citing this passage is simply that its shocking force is appreciated only if the reader knows something about the cultural conventions of the day and the sociological significance of its departures from these. To describe Phoebe as a benefactor (or "patron") is to label her as a person of power, to ascribe honour and authority to her. To describe the church as meeting in the house of Prisca and Aquila is to assign ownership of the house to both of them, a fundamentally anti-patriarchal move.

That said, an important corollary of respecting the historical particularity of the text is that we recognize the extent to which the authors might have thought about disability or impairments in ways that we find difficult or even unacceptable. We need to accept that the Bible is full of stories that reflect the social stigmatization of persons with disabilities of various kinds and that the authors may have regarded these in ways that were woven into their culture. (note 27) We should not try to minimize or downplay the significance of such elements, but we should also recognize that they reflect the organic inspiration of Scripture and the involvement of human writers whose own contributions are transformed by the canonical context into which they are assembled. Again, the

---

27. Olyan, **Disability in the Hebrew Bible**.

recognition that we read the whole canon in the light of what has been disclosed in the person of Jesus Christ is absolutely pivotal to the right handling of such observations: now that we know this truth, we cannot consider any of the parts of the Bible apart from it. The canonical context is thus a transformational context.

Principle 4: We Read the Bible within the Communion of the Church

There is an irreducibly social dimension to life governed by scriptural authority. Scripture is directed towards reading communities who engage with the material in the context of communal practice and life. In fact, for most believers until relatively recently (and still for many in Africa), the only way that Scripture could be encountered was socially, because most Christians were illiterate and were therefore reliant on others to read it to (or with) them. Some may have been fortunate to have had literate household members, but most would encounter Scripture primarily in the context of worship, where it was read within the performance of praise and sacrament.

Where literacy rates are high and where (as we have already noted), a certain individualism is basically assumed, this social dimension can be undervalued or neglected. Reading and listening to the Bible can be "privatized" into something that individuals do within their personal walk of faith, even if they associate themselves with a church community. I ask what moral burden the text lays on me, rather than on us, and the social or corporate dimension of the church follows this, as an obligation that devolves first upon me. I align myself with a particular church community because it holds views to which I subscribe. Even the notion of church unity becomes a function of the collective agreement of a group of individuals to a set of beliefs or practices; it is defined in voluntarist terms.

Ironically, our personal reading can actually be very heavily conditioned by the way the Bible is understood within our community. Without realizing it, we are often governed by the dynamics of social identity, adopting interpretations that position us as insiders within a group and rejecting ones that position us as outsiders. The various individual "helps" and tools that are used in discipleship – daily Bible-reading notes, or Bible study guidelines – contribute to this, however well intended they may be. They reinforce the conviction that, as an evangelical, for example, I ought to read this verse in a particular way. Where the need to read the Bible within the communion of the saints is acknowledged, such influence can be negotiated properly. But when we work with a basic model in which each of us reads the Bible independently, such influences become dangerous: we assume that a particular reading is "just what the Bible says," without recognizing and reflecting upon the extent to which we have received our interpretation from our subcultures.

Both Testaments have, as the addressees of the divine word, communities of faith. While, at points, particular messages may have come to particular figures, these were for the building up (and sometimes the tearing down) of the community, whether Israel, Judah or the church. The corporate dimension is essential, even to the representation of individuals. God's covenant with Israel may, at points, focus on an individual like David, but it is still a covenant with the nation, and his word to that people is covenantal in character. The church is the body of Christ, and its status as a community is a function of the union of each believer to Christ and thereby to every other member. None of this is intended to minimize personal responsibility or the place of personal reading of Scripture, but rather to say that each individual who reads Scripture as the word of God is already identified corporately as part of the communion of saints.

This matters because disability is a reality that is necessarily owned and faced by the community, and not just by persons with autism themselves or their caregivers. The starting point for considering disability as it affects persons within the church is that it is already a reality within the body of Christ, and that the proper response to it must be made by the body. To weave this principle back into our first one: we approach disability as something that has been united to Christ and his body. Such an acknowledgement immediately highlights the problem of those who have been asked to leave churches because of difficult behaviours, and, as we will see, it will underpin the kinds of attitudes that should be expected within the church.

Principle 5: We Read the Bible Humbly as a Fallible Community

It is important to our framing of the communal dimension of reading the Bible that the Scriptures we read are often directed against their readers, representing them as in dire need of correction. This is true throughout the Old Testament, and continues to be true in the New Testament. It is sobering that such criticisms and castigations are directed towards people who are nevertheless affirmed as being in Christ and filled with the Spirit. To speak of the Bible being read by the communion of saints, or the body of the church, does not make Scripture something that is owned by the church, but rather something that speaks prophetically within it.

This is important, because it prevents us from assuming that the church will automatically be a morally good, and therefore safe, environment for disabled people or their families. Quite the opposite: we should assume that the church will be the battleground of good and evil and that those who come into the church can expect to see both lovely and ugly values at work.

To press this further, it also means that we should expect our experience of disability to expose some of those values, and to incur an obligation that we reconsider them. An important element of this involves the recognition that much of what is represented as vicious within the people of God in the Bible – what is linked to the constitutional corruption of their "flesh" – involves religious thought and practice. Throughout the Bible, the people of God (and not just those outside that people) are castigated for thinking wrongly about God and how they should act. This criticism is levelled as sharply at Spirit-filled people in the New Testament church as it is at those living under the old covenant; it is levelled at those who think the performance of evangelical identity necessarily involves doing a certain set of things as much as it is levelled at those who make a golden calf or commit adultery. In the case of Paul's writings, what is most striking is that he sees the problem as running so deep that those who need to be castigated are convinced within themselves that they are being faithful.

Crucially, such criticisms are levelled at people who possess the word of God and define themselves by their commitment to it. That comment may shock some readers, but it is important to recognize the truth behind it. The Pharisees, for example, were basically a renewal movement: they read their Bibles literally and called for their fellow Jews to renew their commitments to the divine commandments, to living in purity, to standing out from the wider immorality and impurity of the world – all so that they would see blessing restored to the people of God. This is a long way from the caricature of the Pharisees that is commonly deployed, which represents them as mere legalists. (note 28) But Jesus describes the Pharisee who proselytizes others to his viewpoint as a "child of hell" (Matt 23:15 NIV; literally, "son of Gehenna"); he regards the Pharisees' purity as that of a whitewashed tomb (Matt 23:27). When this is seen not as a dismissal of legalism (and far less as a criticism of

---

28. Sievers and Levine, **Pharisees**.

Judaism as such) but as a more pointed statement about particular views on purity and justice, directed to those who share many commitments with contemporary evangelicals, the real significance of the statement emerges.

Many of the things we consider to be good or necessary expressions of Christian thought and practice are actually products of our evangelical culture. In some cases, these may not be problematic until they are elevated into the position of idols, functioning as surrogates for the real presence of God, which disturbs and disrupts even as it enriches. Like all such surrogates, they are incapable of genuinely generating love and life and end up enslaving us to violence. They will never meet the distinctive needs of those affected by disabilities any more than they will meet our own needs truly; but the presence of the disabled may call attention to the emptiness and awfulness of those cultural idols. Provided, that is, that we are humble enough to exercise repentance. (note 29)

Where churches have asked families affected by disabilities such as autism not to attend because their behaviour compromises the performance of the worship service, something is functioning as an

---

29. Macaskill, **Intellectual Humility**, 207–38.

idol. Where Christians undervalue others because they do not fit a certain expectation of what a believer will look and sound like, something is functioning as an idol.

Principle 6: We Read the Bible with the Spirit Who Illumines

If we are so sinful, even when we hold the word of God, how can we ever be led to truth? The answer for the New Testament writers, developed most fully (though not exclusively) by John and by Paul, is that the Holy Spirit dwells within us. He unites us to Jesus Christ, who is made actually present within us and whose mind we come to have (1 Cor 2:14). This effect of the Spirit is not represented as an instantaneous transformation that definitively eradicates sin within the church or individual Christian. Rather, we are transformed by the renewing of our minds (Rom 12:2) as the Spirit wars with our flesh (Gal 5:16–17). This is why, as I have noted above, the church must be seen as the battleground, and we must expect to encounter sin within it, even at the level of its structures.

Reading the Bible "spiritually" most obviously entails reading prayerfully, but in a way that acknowledges particularly our need for illumination, and our instinctive preference to remain in darkness. It is striking that one of the lengthiest expositions of the Spirit's ministry in the New Testament – Romans 8 – centres on the experience of prayer by those who are beset by the world and continue to live within the limits of their sinful flesh. It is structurally important that this account is preceded by the description in Romans 7 of Paul's struggling with the continuing presence of sin in his life. (note 30) The representation of prayer in Romans 8 suggests that the believer's life is not one of easy triumph and success, but one of struggle and weakness. When that prayerfulness is brought to the reading of Scripture, it is powerfully liberating.

Reading spiritually also means reading in community. Just as we can privatize our relationship with the Bible, so we can think of the Spirit as something that illumines us individually. Consistently, however, the Spirit is represented as someone who indwells us collectively, even if that collective residing necessarily devolves to the level of the individual. His collective indwelling of us

---

30. The relationship between Rom 7 and the chapters that flank it, particularly in terms of the assumed identity of the writer, has been the subject of much debate in scholarship. The core question concerns whether Paul writes as a Christian struggling with sin, or whether he here writes from the standpoint of his pre-Christian life.

generates the unity of the church: "For in the one Spirit we were all baptized into one body – Jews or Greeks, slaves or free – and we were all made to drink of one Spirit" (1 Cor 12:13).

The giving of the Spirit to each of us, moreover, is represented as being for the common good (1 Cor 12:7). This imagery is used in the context of the depiction of the church as the body of Christ, and points to the idea that the Spirit's ministry of edification is realized through the interaction of the various members, just as the flourishing of a body is realized through its parts working well together. Dynamically, this involves the kind of exchange that is represented in Colossians 3:16, interestingly also rendered in terms of indwelling: "Let the word of Christ dwell in you richly; teach and admonish one another in all wisdom; and with gratitude in your hearts sing psalms, hymns, and spiritual songs to God."

This verse also leads us to the last point, which closes the loop with the first of our principles. The "word" is identified with Christ, with the language of singing psalms suggestive of the fact that the Old Testament continues to be prominently in view. And this word dwells within the body of Christ: the Spirit's indwelling work does not reidentify the body in a way that is separable from the identity of Christ, but rather realizes its identification with him. What this verse calls us to is a thoroughgoing expression of Christian identity: living in the body of Christ and allowing his voice to speak richly among us, as we speak to each other (sometimes correctively) about what is written in the whole of his word, in the Old and New Testaments.

The point is an important one because, as with the other distortions we have noted, we can consider the Spirit-filled community to be a place of victory and triumph. We can think about the Spirit in terms that are primarily about power. But he is "the Spirit of the Son" (Gal 4:6), (note 31) and we should expect him to manifest the Son's identity in ways that are consistent with the gospel story itself. We should expect him to be present in the kind of victory over sin that is cruciform, (note 32) that looks weak and fragile and unimpressive. (note 33) This is precisely how Paul describes the life of the church in 2 Corinthians 4, where he describes us as having "treasure in clay jars." It is not simply that these bodies are

---

31. Properly, he is the Spirit of "his" Son (as in NRSV), which takes the identification further into the inner relations of the Trinity.

32. M. Gorman, **Cruciformity.** Note, however, Nijay Gupta's recent reflections on cruciformity in Gupta, "Cruciform Onesimus?"

33. Cf. 2 Cor 4.

ugly shells for the indwelling glorious Spirit, but that they are vessels that continue to carry the death of Jesus within their own constitution, as a necessary part of their participation in his life (1 Cor 4:10). Within a community marked by that kind of Spirituality, the needs of the disabled, and the blessings that they can bring with their presence, can be met and realized.

Conclusion

In this chapter, I have sought to establish an interpretative framework in which we can read the Bible constructively with a view to "thinking biblically" about disability. The principles that I have laid out are not specific to a disability-oriented reading of the Bible, or to an African one, but bear on all interpretation of Scripture. To a significant extent, they simply reflect the "rule of faith" that governed the interpretative practices of the early church. The distinctive challenges posed by disability, however, bring the need for such principles to be observed into the foreground. As the example of autism has shown, if these principles are not observed or recognized, any attempt to read the Bible in relation to disability will be unsuccessful, or even counterproductive.

What the reassertion of the principles in relation to disability highlights is that a serious effort to think properly about disability brings with it a body of further blessings for the church. If we learn to think better about disability, we will learn to think better about everything else, too.

Bibliography

Bokedal, Tomas. "The Early Rule-of-Faith Pattern as Emergent Biblical Theology." **Theofilos** 7 (2015): 57–75.

Foster, Paul. **Colossians**. Black's New Testament Commentaries. London: Bloomsbury, 2016.

Gorman, Michael J. **Cruciformity: Paul's Narrative Spirituality of the Cross.** Grand Rapids: Eerdmans, 2001.

Gupta, Nijay. "Cruciform Onesimus? Considering How a Slave Would Respond to Paul's Call for a Cross-Shaped Lifestyle." **Expository Times** 133, no. 8 (2022): 325–33 (published online ahead of print release).

Hauerwas, Stanley. **Character and the Christian Life.** San Antonio: Trinity University Press, 1975.

Kelsey, David. **Eccentric Existence: A Theological Anthropology**. Vol. 2. Louisville: Westminster John Knox, 2009.

———. **The Uses of Scripture in Recent Theology**. Minneapolis: Fortress, 1975.

Macaskill, Grant. **Autism and the Church: Bible, Theology, Community**. Waco: Baylor University Press, 2019.

———. "Christian Scriptures and the Formation of Intellectual Humility." **Journal of Psychology and Theology** 46 (2018): 243–52.

———. **The New Testament and Intellectual Humility**. Oxford: Oxford University Press, 2018.

———. **Union with Christ in the New Testament**. Oxford: Oxford University Press, 2013.

———. "The Way the One God Works: Covenant and Ethics in 1 Corinthians." In **One God, One People, One Future: Essays in Honour of N. T. Wright**, edited by John Dunne and Eric Llewellyn, 112–25. London: SPCK, 2018.

MacIntyre, Alasdair. **After Virtue: A Study in Moral Theory**. Notre Dame: University of Notre Dame Press, 1981.

Malina, Bruce. **The New Testament World: Insights from Cultural Anthropology.** Louisville: John Knox, 2001.

Mathew, Stephen K., and Jeyaraj D. Pandian. "Newer Insights to the Neurological Diseases among Biblical Characters of Old Testament." **Annals of Indian Academy of Neurology** 13 (2010): 164–66.

Novakovic, Lidija. **Messiah, the Healer of the Sick: A Study of Jesus as the Son of David in the Gospel of Matthew**. WUNT II: 170. Tübingen: Mohr Siebeck, 2003.

Olyan, Saul. **Disability in the Hebrew Bible: Interpreting Mental and Physical Differences**. Cambridge: Cambridge University Press, 2008.

Russell, Norman. **The Doctrine of Deification in the Greek Patristic Tradition**. Oxford: Oxford University Press, 2004.

Sievers, Joseph, and Amy-Jill Levine, eds. **The Pharisees.** Grand Rapids: Eerdmans, 2021.

Stuckenbruck, Loren. "The Human Being and Demonic Invasion." In **Spirituality, Theology, and Mental Health**, edited by C. Cook, 94–119. London: SCM, 2013.

Swinton, John. "From Inclusion to Belonging: A Practical Theology of Community, Disability and Humanness." **Journal of Religion, Disability and Health** 16 (2012): 172–90.

Taylor, Charles. **The Sources of the Self: The Making of Modern Identity**. Cambridge: Cambridge University Press, 1992.

Torrance, Thomas F. **Theological Science**. Oxford: Oxford University Press, 1969.

Vanhoozer, Kevin. **First Theology**. Leicester: IVP Academic, 2002.

3

Am I Being Punished?

Reimagining Sin Alongside People with Disabilities in Southern Africa

Selina Palm

Introduction

Michelle grew up in South Africa with a degenerative eye disease. Through her life, she was surrounded by Christian pastors seeking to cure her of her "blindness." For years as a child, she was dragged from church to church by her well-meaning parents in vain attempts to reverse her increasingly disabling difficulties with her sight. She also began to bargain with God to heal her, but slowly realized that the underlying theological framing of seeking healing, and trying to find the spiritual roots of her disability, was damaging for her own process of learning to live with her condition, and for her own relationship with God. (note 1)

Many people with disabilities, and often their families too, quietly exit the church for reasons similar to Michelle's. As a result, their stories and their needs remain invisible to pastors and wider church congregations. One father of a son living with a disability in the Western Cape explained, "I have failed to find the right church to handle my son's disability. Now he stays home crying because he can't go to church yet all his friends at school do. [His] friends think he is not church material because of his condition." (note 2)

Recent empirical studies among hundreds of families of people with disabilities across Southern Africa demonstrate that this experience is common within the region. One respondent living with a disability noted, "Although it is called 'the church of God,' some [people with disabilities] are continually shut out because they are different.

---

1. Nell, "On Her Blindness," 161–66.
2. Mduli, "Disability in South Africa," 40.

They are viewed as burdens draining the limited resources, yet these are God's resources provided for all mankind to be used communally." (note 3)

Research among 103 people with disabilities across Zambia, Uganda and Kenya showed their experienced reality of religious-related stigma that could attribute blame to them for their conditions by, for example, seeing them as failing in their faith, being punished by God or as needing miraculous healing. (note 4) If these damaging practices are to change, churches' understandings of disability must be re-examined at their theological roots. The exclusion and stigmatization of people with disabilities are frequently based on harmful theological scripts around disability that can also reflect a complex entanglement of religion and culture. (note 5) Until these scripts are challenged and changed, it is unlikely that more positive practices will be embedded. For many people with disabilities, belonging to a faith community is about more than access and participation, although these are important. People with disabilities want to be in an environment that is free from negative attitudes and perceptions

---

3. Mduli, 40.
4. Mugeere et al., "Oh God!," 65, 75.
5. Lowe, "Disability and Sin," 185–94.

towards them, especially when those attitudes are justified by theological assumptions. (note 6) This chapter will seek to contribute to this task.

Disability and Churches

According to the World Health Organization, an estimated 15 percent of people in the world today live with some form of disability, and this encompasses intellectual, psychosocial, physical, sensory and invisible types. (note 7) That translates to over 28 million people within Southern Africa alone. (note 8) However, while the majority of people with disabilities live in the Global South, much of the work on disability theology has been carried out in the Global North and may not resonate with the practices, epistemologies or contexts of the South. (note 9) Malaysian theologian Amos Yong insists that a post-colonial theological lens on disability is required. (note 10) Disability must also be understood intersectionally in relation to issues such as race, class and gender, without merely becoming a footnote to a long list

---

6. Mduli, "Disability in South Africa," 40–49.
7. WHO and the World Bank, **World Report on Disability**, 29.
8. Kretzschmar, **Church and Disability**, 1–15.
9. Palm, **One Body?**, 2–3.
10. Hittenberger, "Receiving God's Gift," 145.

of other oppressions. Theological questions require specific attention if the gap is to be bridged in practice between an increased focus on disability being seen in global settings, and the many local churches that may cling to ancient interpretations and where disability stigma often remains prevalent. Southern Africa has been shaped by a nexus of colonial histories, Christian missionary theology and African traditional beliefs, and all three of these elements can entangle to reinforce disability stigma. (note 11) The context of Southern Africa is the focus of this chapter as it is where the author lives and practices theology, although these ideas may apply to other contexts. (note 12)

Across Southern Africa, many church theologies still connect sin and disability in harmful ways that can exclude, and even demonize, people living with disabilities, and some also continue to use language about disabilities that stigmatizes. The Bible and its stories of healing can be unwittingly misused to exclude and shame people living with disabilities. As a result, problematic theologies of healing and exorcism often remain embedded, especially, but not only, in Pentecostal spaces. Fewer than 5–10 percent of all people living with disabilities worldwide are estimated to be involved

---

11. Ndlovu, "African Beliefs," 29–39.
12. Avalos, "Disability Studies," 343–54.

in churches, and they have been referred to by various theologians as "missing people." (note 13) At the same time, a number of theologians of disability across the African continent are developing promising alternative theological approaches that seek to centre the voices of people living with disabilities. (note 14) However, these alternatives often still hover abstractly above the lived realities of many people with disabilities within local churches. (note 15)

At the heart of many of these problematic theologies remains a tenacious connection between people with disabilities and theologies of evil, demonic infiltration, curses, sin and punishment. In the Southern African context, this attitude has been strongly entangled with Christian beliefs. (note 16) The long colonial history that exists across Southern Africa has led to much Christian mission theology becoming complicit with colonial cultural norms that perpetuated hierarchies of value and segregationist policies. During the period of colonialism, the absolute

---

13. Kretzschmar, **Church and Disability**, 1–15; Calder, "To Belong," 262–86.
14. Kretzschmar, 1–15. Kabue et al., **Changing Scenes**; Palm, "Doing Theologies of Disability," 1–39.
15. Mugeere et al., "Oh God!," 64–81.
16. Longchar, "Sin, Suffering, and Disability," 47–58.

unquestionable sovereignty of God (and thus the absolute sovereignty of colonial rulers) was strongly reinforced. This in turn reinforced a tendency to see disability as God-ordained, and created theological hierarchies of value that placed some people closer to God than others and played a social role in moralizing disability as imperfection and abnormality. Associated cultural connotations of stigma, shame and ugliness combined with these beliefs to exclude and marginalize many people with disabilities from church spaces rather than creating forms of belonging as full participants. While some Christian missions did reach out to assist people with disabilities, a paternalistic charity lens typically predominated over a justice lens, as the Ecumenical Disability Action Network (EDAN) of the World Council of Churches has noted. (note 17) This could lead to unnecessary segregation, or even the institutionalizing of people with disabilities. This approach of segregation and institutionalization has been challenged by the contemporary disability rights movement in South Africa, as theologian Louise Kretzschmar, among others, has detailed. (note 18)

---

17. World Council of Churches, **Gift of Being**, 245.
18. Kretzschmar, **Church and Disability**, 10, 89.

Untangling Harmful Theologies of Disabilities

Contemporary theological engagement with disabilities must start with the lived realities of people living with diverse disabilities. A see–judge–act theological framework, used to explore different kinds of social oppression in Southern African contexts, has been deployed in recent years by some South African theologians as a methodology for engaging disability theologically. (note 19) Here, the harm and exclusion that many people with disabilities encounter in practice becomes the starting point for disrupting and reimagining the Christian story if new life-giving stories are to be found and told alongside them.

However, this requires all people of Christian faith to ask themselves hard questions. Why has the church so often failed people with disabilities? What does Scripture say about disability? Nigerian theologian Emiola Nihinlola notes that "disability raises fundamental questions about the goodness and sovereignty of God." (note 20) Nihinlola insists that a practical theology of care, ministry and action that can make sense in contemporary African contexts is still urgently needed. Malaysian

---

19. Kretzschmar, 10, 89.
20. Nihinlola, "Disability Discourse," 41.

theologian Amos Yong, whose theology has been shaped by growing up with a brother living with Down's syndrome, challenges the entire Christian project as ableist and asks provocative questions such as "How can we learn from disability advocates, who have increasingly challenged assumptions of ableism? What might a redemptive and biblically-sound understanding of disability look like?" (note 21)

A persistent thread within Christian tradition has been that disability signifies a "special" relationship with God and that the person is either divinely blessed or damned. (note 22) Instead, Yong asks how embracing the spiritual gifts of a person with special needs can help us all to better receive the kingdom of God. (note 23) If churches are to unlearn their theological scripts on disability, they must grapple with these difficult questions and resist the temptation to offer simple, dogmatic answers. Acknowledging the complicity of many church beliefs in disability oppression must be the starting point for a more liberating theological journey by churches alongside people with disabilities to renounce what Yong

---

21. Hittenberger, "Receiving God's Gift," 141.
22. Claassens, Shaikh and Swartz, "Engaging Disability and Religion," 147–64.
23. Hittenberger, "Receiving God's Gift," 141–60.

names as a problematic theological ableism in Christianity. (note 24) This thread is entrenched across Southern Africa in part due to an embedded legacy of colonial Christian missions with a strong Calvinist predestination lens which insists that God is sovereign and disability God-ordained. Southern Africa, due to Protestant missionary influence, still places a strong emphasis on literal interpretations of the Bible which often leads to problematic assertations about disability as disability scholars have documented in this context. (note 25) At the same time, African traditional religious and cultural beliefs also remain influential in this region, shaping a resurgence in African Initiated Churches where religion and culture can entangle in ways that reinforce disability stigma, especially around issues such as "albinism." (note 26) A strong belief in God's sovereignty and in Jesus as a healer, both of which are prevalent ideas in Southern Africa, can have a dark side for people with disabilities if they are then depicted as being sick and in need of healing. This is a main reason why many people with disabilities leave churches, especially in Southern African contexts: "Many faithful persons with impairments have testified that the healing narratives and their interpretations have been a

---

24. Yong, **Theology and Down Syndrome**, 41.
25. Githuku, "Biblical Perspectives," 79–93.
26. Mugeere et al., "Oh God!," 64–81.

reason to turn away from the church. These stories have been used to treat people with disabilities and their families as objects of pity who need to be cured and forgiven." (note 27)

Two different ways of connecting disability and sin underlie many of these healing narratives and their associated harmful beliefs and practices, and it is to these that this chapter will now turn.

First, there is a prominent theological tendency to see disability as an act of God and even as a punishment from God for sin committed by the person, the family or their ancestors: (note 28) "according to one of the primary forms of moral and/or religious models of disability, disability should be regarded as a punishment from God for a particular sin or sins that may have been committed by the person with disability." (note 29) This view has a significant impact on much church preaching and Bible interpretation within Southern Africa and can lead to the exclusion from church participation of persons with disabilities and/or their family. Other research in the region shows that this religious–moral theory of disability often

---

27. World Council of Churches, **Gift of Being**, 246.
28. Chataika, "Cultural and Religious Explanations," 117–28.
29. Retief and Letšosa, "Models of Disability," 2.

leads to many people with disabilities experiencing discrimination by Christians based on the premise of parental sins being visited on children with disabilities. (note 30) This distorted doctrine of sin must be urgently reformulated in the light of a disability-aware understanding if Christians are to avoid causing harm by conflating sin, curse and punishment with disability. The total providence of God remains an influential belief across much of Southern Africa. (note 31) It also shapes how disability is portrayed in the Bible by making a link between sin and suffering whereby God is responsible for everything that happens, including health, life, healing and misfortune. Biblical texts such as Deuteronomy 32:39 and Isaiah 45:7 as well as "blessing and curse" texts attributed to God such as Deuteronomy 27–28 have been used to offer a cause-and-effect logic that connects obedience to God with blessing, health and flourishing in life. Based on this interpretation of these texts, suffering, poverty, barrenness and disabilities are then seen as a deserved punishment from God. (note 32)

---

30. Mugeere et al., "Oh God!," 64–81.
31. Claassens, Shaikh and Swartz, "Engaging Disability and Religion," 147–64.
32. World Council of Churches, **Gift of Being**, 246.

A second harmful way of connecting sin and disability is the belief that disability is caused by evil spirits, the devil's curse or even as a form of witchcraft or demonic infiltration, especially in the case of intellectual or psychosocial disabilities. In this understanding, God is not perceived to cause or desire disability but a different form of stigma still rebounds on the person with a disability as he or she becomes a symbol of evil forces and viewed as in need of special prayer, healing and exorcisms. (note 33) Fears can escalate within church communities that this spiritual disease might be "contagious" and its "carriers" should be feared or avoided. (note 34) Healing then carries deeply moral and spiritual connotations, as does a so-called "failure" by individuals to be healed. Julie Claassens and her colleagues suggest that the reason why people living with disabilities are often excluded from worshipping communities is the belief that individuals who cannot be healed are a reminder of expressions of impurity, evil or sin that needs to be cleansed from their midst. (note 35)

---

33. Mugeere et al., "Oh God!," 64–81.
34. Chataika, "Cultural and Religious Explanations," 117–28.
35. Claassens, Shaikh and Swartz, "Engaging Disability and Religion," 147–64.

Samuel Kabue, a Kenyan theologian, who has been blind from the age of sixteen, notes,

> The presence of people with disabilities in such churches is viewed as a failure by the church to combat the devil. It is therefore seen as a challenge to the church that calls for constantly invoking Christ's power to heal, and when this does not happen the concerned person with disability is blamed for lack of faith. This is the surest way of telling the person that he or she does not belong. (note 36)

Nigerian scholar Helen Olomu Ishola-Esan also notes that in many African societies today,

> [people with disabilities] are still categorized as invalid, inadequate or inferior according to social understandings of perfection. They are positioned as hopeless and helpless, to be pitied or the symbol of a curse and shame to the whole family and community and this leads to their rejection. At the other extreme they can be seen as

---

36. Kabue, quoted in Claassens, Shaikh and Swartz, 153.

superhuman, wielding mystical powers that can harm or benefit the community and are feared and avoided. (note 37)

In her 2016 study of 120 Christian pastors in Nigeria, Ishola-Esan found that 37 percent of pastors still connected disability and witchcraft, 42 percent connected disability and evil spirit possession, and 56 percent saw disability as God's will and as necessary punishment from God for sins committed. (note 38) This shows that people with disabilities are still seen as "deviants" within many African societies, with a strong link made between disability and evil in ways that influence new Christian leaders. This has damaging practical consequences across the continent. For example, in Zimbabwe, women with disabilities are often excluded from becoming wives and mothers as they are viewed as being under an ancestral curse. (note 39)

While the two theologies above may seem to be at odds with each other – one from God and one from the devil – they in fact form two poles in a sacred binary of disability. Both emphasize

---

37. Ishola-Esan, "Remnants of African Worldviews," 105.
38. Ishola-Esan, 103–18.
39. Chisale, "Disabled Motherhood," 1–9.

the individual moral character of the person with a disability and sacralize disability by focusing on spiritual causes. Pastors may feel obligated to give an answer to questions raised by people with disabilities around why this has happened to them. They tie their answers into the existing doctrinal system of creation and fall, regardless of the harmful impact of the answers on the person concerned, who can feel excluded from God's original blessing, positioned as a direct symbol of the fall into sin, or reduced to an object to be healed. Anthony Buyinza Mugeere and his colleagues highlight numerous experiences of people with disabilities across Southern and East Africa who have had pastors exploit them in the name of performing healing miracles, even enacting fake physical disabilities from which miraculous healing is then proclaimed. (note 40) "I really detest these pastors and other preachers who preach that persons with disability are cursed by God because of the sins committed by their ancestors. It's worse when some of them fake miracles of healing using people who are not living with disability. . . . It's so disappointing" (polio survivor, Zambia). (note 41)

---

40. Mugeere et al., "Oh God!," 64–81.
41. Mugeere et al., 64–81.

If God is seen as the sovereign cause of disability, then a cluster of harmful theologies can emerge. Disability must either be patiently accepted or the person or his or her family must have done something bad to deserve this punishment. In other theologies, the devil and evil spirits are seen as possessing that person and need to be cast out. All these responses assume a spiritual cause for disability and then look for someone to blame. (note 42) Since God is inevitably perceived as blameless, the blame is often pushed back onto the person with a disability. He or she may be expected to model virtuous suffering, by viewing the disability as a "glorified thorn in the flesh" or even as a supernatural power to be feared by others, or the person may be seen as excluded from the original blessing of the goodness of all creation and in some way flawed or defective. (note 43)

An increasing tendency is also emerging across many parts of the African continent to view disability, and therefore people with disabilities, as a means by which to display God's healing power. Malawian theologian Elizabeth Kamchedzera points out that many Pentecostal churches

---

42. Chataika, "Cultural and Religious Explanations," 117–28.
43. Mugeere et al., "Oh God!," 64–81.

treat people with disabilities as "platforms for the demonstration of God's power to heal or to use their perceived weakness to display God's strength." (note 44) As a result, people with disabilities are viewed as coming to church merely "in search of healing." (note 45) A resurgence has been identified within Southern Africa of many churches commodifying disability for a performative spectacle of spiritual healing power with people with disabilities as key players in dramatic healing rituals where pastors claim to possess miraculous cures. (note 46) Many African Pentecostals believe that the work of Christ on the cross delivers believers from all generational curses including disability. (note 47) This belief, combined with the earlier ideas discussed, can lead to a refusal to take seriously the ongoing human challenges that people living with disabilities may face. It also creates expectations of miraculous healing that disempowers many people who are living with disabilities and emphasizes only a triumphalist Christology.

---

44. Kamchedzera, "Investigation," 5.
45. Kamchedzera, 14.
46. Claassens, Shaikh and Swartz, "Engaging Disability and Religion," 148.
47. Nkomazana, "'No One Who Has a Blemish,'" 49–61.

As a result, many interpretations of the Bible are caught up in these entanglements of disability as sin, curse, demonic or punishment. (note 48) Botswanan Pentecostal theologian Fidelis Nkomazana shows that the Bible itself often attributes disability to God, and that this often poses challenges for literalist readers. (note 49) To reiterate, literal biblical interpretation is a common approach to the Bible across Southern Africa, due in part to a legacy of Protestant missionaries. Nkomazana notes that the Old Testament does suggest in some places that God brings disability as punishment for sin, as an expression of God's anger over people's disobedience or as a curse due to non-belief. (note 50) The Bible itself then becomes a contested site of struggle which contains both positive and negative potential scripts for disability.

Towards Redemptive Biblical Interpretations of Disability

Old Testament scholars within South Africa are increasingly showing that the Bible's human authors often take for granted the ancient idea

---

48. Kretzschmar, **Church and Disability**, 10.
49. Nkomazana, "'No One Who Has a Blemish,'" 49–61.
50. Nkomazana, 49–61.

that disability is caused by God. (note 51) As a result, these scholars insist there is a need to read various Bible stories more deeply and "against the grain" to find disability-informed counter-readings. This takes a number of forms. First, specific Bible passages such as Leviticus 21 are still often used to justify the exclusion of people with disabilities from certain roles within church spaces, such as the priesthood. A strong holiness and purity tradition is found within the Old Testament in particular. This was designed to enable the Jewish people to distinguish themselves culturally and religiously from the surrounding peoples with whom they coexisted, but it was also influenced by other religions that either saw the body negatively or glorified the "perfect" body. These passages exist in tension with other biblical commitments to inclusive justice and compassion, creating sites of struggle within the biblical text that South African scholars such as Gerald West have probed. (note 52) Misuse of these verses, without disability-informed engagement and contextual Bible reading strategies, can justify disability-exclusive theologies, according to Amos Yong. (note 53) Deeper engagement with these theological traditions is needed to "do no harm."

---

51. Claassens, "Job, Theology and Disability," 55–66.
52. West, **Stolen Bible.**
53. Yong, **Bible, Disability**, 2–4.

The Bible often also describes central theological ideas of sin and forgiveness metaphorically by using disability-related terms such as blindness, brokenness, weakness, sickness and lameness, thereby creating a perceived wider negative moral and spiritual understanding of disability. The contributions of people living with disabilities to God's plans within the Bible are often ignored or silenced within traditional interpretations of these texts. For example, many prophets and leaders chosen by God had weaknesses or disabilities, such as Moses, Elijah and Paul, but these aspects are often erased from their stories or used merely to emphasize God's triumph over disability. Southern Africa has developed vital post-colonial contextual resources for rereading the Bible in the struggle against apartheid and colonization. (note 54) As with other oppressions, such as race, gender and slavery, the Bible has many of these beliefs embedded within its texts and careful reinterpretation of these difficult texts in church congregations is essential.

Over many centuries, the Bible has frequently been read and interpreted through an ableist lens. For example, Yong points to legal passages in Deuteronomy and healing stories by Jesus, both of which are still interpreted through a normate

---

54. Kretzschmar, **Church and Disability**, 10.

lens (which perceives only the abled body as the normal body) in most churches. (note 55) Acknowledging this problematic reality is a critical first step to developing alternative forms of redemptive re-engagement with the Bible through a disability hermeneutic in practical ways that churches can embed more sensitively in their services and practices. This approach decentres abled experience from its position as theologically normative, as Indian theologian Manohar Pradeep notes: "Because church and society are dominated by able bodied people, disability theology should start from a struggling community of the disabled. . . . perceiving how God is present with people with disabilities and unmasking ways in which theological inquiry has further instituted able-bodied experience as the theological norm." (note 56)

These Bible texts require careful christological readings alongside local communities in the light of Christ's own broken body to expose their normate biases and to resist a focus on a perfect body. (note 57) Rereading the Bible contextually from the unique perspectives of people with diverse disabilities, who are present in many of

---

55. Yong, **Bible, Disability**, 2–4.
56. Pradeep, "Disabled God."
57. Yong, **Bible, Disability**, 50.

its stories, can be productively juxtaposed with similar stories of experiences of disability exclusion and stigma today. (note 58) These people in the Bible include figures such as Jacob (Gen 32:25–32), Moses (Exod 4:10–12), Ehud (Judg 3:15–26), Samson (Judg 16:21–30), Leah (Gen 29:17) and Mephibosheth (2 Sam 9). South African biblical scholar Claassens' disability reading of the story of Job is just one example of a counter-reading that can help to shape new theological ideas on disability that are rooted in human dignity, inclusion and hospitality. It challenges the religious stereotypes of disability within the story as Job moves from abled privilege to disability through disease. (note 59) Theological imagery shapes the underpinning assumptions with which the text is read and has often led to a narrow "curative imaginary" in many churches in ways that do harm to those whose bodies or minds are then labelled as disabled or "invalid." Connecting sin, curse and disability can lead to the stigmatization and manipulation of people with disabilities as overburdened containers for wider human suffering and the fears of abled people. Many people with disabilities in Southern Africa feel reduced to their disability alone, with their own agency and needs ignored, for an agenda that drags them up to the

---

58. Lees, "Lazarus, Come Out!," 97–110.
59. Claassens, "Job, Theology and Disability," 57.

front of the church to be prayed for. These harmful approaches place the spiritual burden with the individuals and not with wider society to adapt and support them. To reimagine sin alongside people with disabilities in Southern Africa, these underlying theological roots that still oppressively sacralize disability must be surfaced and tackled.

Liberating Theologies of Disabilities in Southern Africa

A new generation of disability theologians is also emerging across the African continent. This includes Samuel Kabue in Kenya and Micheline Kamba in the Democratic Republic of Congo (who sadly passed away in 2020). The All African Council of Churches has played an important role in supporting the Ecumenical Disability Advocates Network's (EDAN) engagement with the World Council of Churches, placing a much-needed emphasis on transforming theological education. (note 60) Significant practical progress has been made in the last decade; however, harmful theological scripts on sin often persist in church practice, and must be reimagined alongside people with disabilities to see sin as exclusion, oppression and a refusal to recognize the image

---

60. Amanze and Kabue, "Disability, Religion and Theology," 1–2.

of God within the spectrum of human diversity, including not excluding people with disabilities. Only if sin is recalibrated will the links between disability and sin that shape the misuse of the Triune God as sovereign Father, Jesus as healer and Spirit as exorcist, be broken.

What Yong terms "disenchanting disability" remains an essential task in Southern Africa if this problematic framing of sin is to be refuted. Instead, disability must be connected to the wider reality of a world which contains many different kinds of suffering, as noted by Botswanan theologian Mmapula Kebaneilwe. (note 61) Disability needs intentional engagement but does not need to be exceptionalized. For Yong, disability is a human variation and a product of evolutionary processes and should not be treated as a special form of suffering that needs a separate theology of creation or fall. (note 62) Rather, it is linked to diverse forms of human suffering in a limited world, as Marno Retief and Rantoa Letšosa also emphasize in the Southern Africa context. (note 63) Yong points to the need for Christians to commit to "do no harm" with

---

61. Kebaneilwe, "Disability as a Challenge," 93–102. Also Hittenberger, "Receiving God's Gift," 154.
62. Yong, **Bible, Disability**, 110–15.
63. Retief and Letšosa, "Models of Disability," 1–8.

their beliefs, emphasizing that God does not split people into categories but desires all to be saved and valued. (note 64) He argues that Christians must resist inherited tendencies to sacralize disability or focus on divine causes. This is critical for Southern Africa, which has often inherited a blueprint model of sovereignty. Theologians here may benefit from Amos Yong's eschatological orientation to disability which offers a redemptive thrust focused on what God is doing in the light of disability, (note 65) moving "from the idea of divine omnipotence causing all events to the idea of divine omni-compassion redeeming all events." (note 66) Sin then becomes a refusal to accept human limits, including our attempts to avoid human vulnerability and even the tendency to push this vulnerability only onto people with disabilities. Sin is then manifested socially in requiring a sameness that ignores differences and centralizes what is often perceived to be "normal" in a way that then represses lived experiences of human diversity. It is these social, structural sins of exclusion against people with disabilities that defile and pollute the people of God and need exposure, and not the so-called sins of people with disability or their families. To imagine God venting

---

64. Hittenberger, "Receiving God's Gift," 168.
65. Yong, "Gifts of the Spirit," 87.
66. Hittenberger, "Receiving God's Gift," 155.

punishment on individuals through disability makes God a monster. We are all entangled in brokenness as part of the wider human condition and people with disabilities should never be singled out as under a special curse.

Drawing on omni-compassion as embodied in Jesus (note 67) can offer an image of God that embraces disabilities and refuses to assume that all disability is either tragic loss or requires curing. Many people with disabilities have unique perspectives to add to the church and temporarily-abled people must learn from these as well as give up their often-distorted quest for control and the perfection of human bodies. The theme of "valuable diversity without division" runs through the World Council of Churches document on disability. (note 68) It resists entrenched and often Western-infused religious and social norms of perfection against which many people living with disabilities feel they are constantly judged and found wanting. Yong points to a choice for Christian churches between the winner ethos, epitomized by the church at Corinth, which leaves some behind in a false striving for perfectionism, and the theology of weakness that

---

67. Kebaneilwe, "Disability as a Challenge," 93–102.
68. World Council of Churches, **Gift of Being**, 235–49.

he sees embodied by both Paul and Jesus and which offers a different theological approach to disabilities. (note 69)

If this reorientation of sin is taken seriously, it becomes a sin for churches to exclude people with disabilities from the original blessing of being created in the image of God. This is reinforced in the 2016 World Council of Churches document **The Gift of Being: Called to Be a Church of All and for All**, which envisions church as a place where everyone is of value to God and where either lumping "the disabled" together as one homogeneous group or setting them apart from all others as special or segregated is unacceptable. (note 70) Agency is given to all humans at creation to tell their own story with an insistence that all creation is good, and that creational equality is not based on ability. Disabilities are not framed as the consequence of a person's sin, lack of faith or unwillingness to be healed. It requires a fresh understanding of the image of God to reclaim this insight, as people with disabilities have insisted upon:

---

69. Yong, "Running the (Special) Race," 209–25.
70. World Council of Churches, **Gift of Being**, 235–49.

Understanding that I was created by God enables me to say well, "I have no problem with my disability. Maybe other people who see me struggle to climb the stairs in a wheelchair do, but I don't. And I have no problem saying that I'm a person with a disability because God had a purpose in creating me and there is no such thing as a disability but just different abilities" (Zambian male physically impaired participant). (note 71)

The motif of the image of God is also increasingly being connected to human dignity in specific relation to disability and is gaining traction across Southern Africa. (note 72) Southern African scholars suggest this theological theme can also resonate with important African religious values that build on the principle of **ubuntu** (humanness through connection to an inclusive community) and require the opening of hospitable space for all. (note 73) This can help challenge existing stigmatizing disability language in many African contexts that still connects disability to negative

---

71. Mugeere et al., "Oh God!," 72.
72. Claassens, "Job, Theology and Disability," 55–66.
73. Chataika, "Cultural and Religious Explanations," 117–28.

qualities of inability, dependence and evil, and instead shift towards the positive language and rituals of mutual interdependence.

If disenchanting disability is to become more fully embodied in the church, the Bible needs to be read in more liberating ways with close attention to how sin is being framed. (note 74) Southern African scholars have unique insights to offer here due to their post-colonial theological history of reinterpreting the biblical texts misused to justify colonial oppression. (note 75) Decolonizing disability theologically and disrupting ableism within the Bible text must be a communal enterprise which is done alongside people with disabilities, if it is not to remain an elite academic project. Contextual Bible study methods can offer ways to help readers disconnect sin and disability in these ancient texts, which are often harmfully internalized by Christian people with disabilities like Michelle (see introduction to this chapter). (note 76) Contextual Bible study can also allow readers to reclaim the positive stories of people with disabilities who are used by God

---

74. Avalos, "Disability Studies," 343–54.
75. Dube, "Post-colonial Feminist Interpretation," 89–102.
76. Mugeere et al., "Oh God!," 64–81. See also Lowe, "Disability Theologies," 185–94.

in the Bible, in order to make their agency and action more visible and to challenge the ableism that shapes many prominent Bible metaphors in the light of a disability hermeneutic. Together, these offer newly redemptive ways of reading Bible stories with a disability hermeneutic. (note 77) A christological lens is needed here; not by viewing Christ as the perfect superman who triumphantly conquers and heals all disabilities and diseases, as is still present in many African Pentecostal churches, but by embracing a solidarity Christology that aligns with a disabled God. This sees Jesus not primarily as powerful exorcist and healer, but as vulnerable, disfigured, tortured and even disabled himself and yet still a reflection of God, with the marks of his wounds remaining in his resurrected body offering signs that God bears the scars of life with us all. Claassens and colleagues insist that these kinds of disability-informed Bible readings can unsettle the currently excluded position of disability and underpin a potentially liberating new politics of disability for Southern Africa. (note 78)

---

77. Yong, **Theology and Down Syndrome**, 150.
78. Claassens, Shaikh and Swartz, "Engaging Disability and Religion," 147–64.

The Church as a Spirit-Filled Ecclesial Community of Embrace

The Pentecostal possibilities in birthing an ecclesial community of one body with many members, as imagined by Yong, can resonate with Southern African realities. (note 79) African themes of **ubuntu** and interconnectedness must look beyond the narrow curative imaginaries that still shape the distorted theologies of much miracle healing in churches, to instead remap the kingdom of God as a space of full belonging for all people with diverse disabilities. Those at the margins of society can then become the centre of a new vision of mutual embrace. This requires a decisive shift from charity models of disability to transformative patterns of social justice, reimagining the Spirit as an advocate for, and with, those whose voices and bodies are often made invisible, enabling people with disabilities to become assets and gifts to, and in, their churches. Southern Africa can benefit from adapting Yong's liberating pneumatology, shaped by a faith commitment to one baptism, one body and one Spirit, which challenges all social divisions, including a problematic abled/disabled binary. Engaging disabilities theologically also reshapes how church and ministry can be understood and practiced in Southern Africa, in light of the gifts of

---

79. Yong, **Bible, Disability**, 110–15.

God that people with diverse disabilities can be to the church and the world:

> People with profound disabilities are not agents of ministry in the normal senses of that notion, but they are conduits of the revelatory and transformative gifts of God's Spirit for those who will slow down enough to befriend them, to see, hear, and touch in faith, and to receive God's presence into their own lives. What will happen if local congregations become known as communities constituted by friendships with people with profound disabilities? (note 80)

If this theological counter-vision is embraced, churches can also move beyond questions of access alone to deeper themes of belonging, recognition of practices of exclusion, and the need to let go of harmful interpretations. This involves first recognizing, and then reimagining, inherited embedded and problematic theological narratives around healing of people with disabilities. It requires more attention to the disabling attitudes of many Christians within congregations who may still use theology to stigmatize and marginalize people with disabilities. Churches will need to be

---

80. Yong, 114.

supported by their leaders to embrace a Pauline theology of weakness (1 Cor 12:22) that offers a biblical reminder of the church as one body with many members, with a liberating mission not only to people with disabilities but also with and from them. [81] Pentecost offers a vision of the many-tongued, multisensory realities of church communities and the diverse gifts of all, where people with disabilities can play an important role in constituting the church as an upside-down kingdom of justice. Some Southern African churches have begun this important journey. For example, in 2016, the KwaZulu Natal Christian Council (KZNCC), which works closely with disability organizations in their context, suggested that Paul's "thorn" (2 Cor 12:7) might make him the first disability theologian. [82] Despite these promising initial reflections, there is a long road ahead if all churches are to become places of theological safety that do no harm to those who are living with disabilities.

Nkomazana points to two contrasting understandings of healing in African Pentecostal churches: one focused on forgiveness as healing, and as the driving out of sin and demons,

---

81. Kretzschmar, **Church and Disability**, 89.
82. KwaZulu Natal Christian Council, "Theology of Disability."

reflecting a disabling hermeneutic; and one emphasizing inclusion as healing within the one body where all have a place and a contribution to make. (note 83) This second resonates with reimagining sin as exclusion and with Yong's pneumatological imagination. Where "many tongues" creates space for people with disabilities, diversity is honoured with an ethic of hospitality within an interconnected body:

> It is the responsibility of the whole body to put a stop to the stigmatization and marginalization of people with disabilities [PWDs]. . . . Because the church is to be a community of the weak and not of the strong, PWDs are at the centre and not the margins of understanding what it means to be the people of God. . . . Each person with disability, no matter how serious, severe, or even profound, contributes something essential to and for the body, through the presence and activity of the Spirit. People with disabilities become the paradigm for what it means to live in the power of God and to manifest the divine glory. (note 84)

---

83. Nkomazana, "'No One Who Has a Blemish,'" 54.
84. Yong, "Gifts of the Spirit," 88.

Churches are, as a result, called into a mission of mutual accompaniment alongside (and not primarily to) people with disabilities. (note 85) Jesus welcomed people with many diverse kinds of disabilities into the kingdom of God, though they would have been excluded under his Jewish tradition (Matt 4:23; 15:30). (note 86) The image of restoration has been used in South Africa as an invitation to "make room" for all, including people with disabilities, and includes not only the care of the most vulnerable as the entry condition for the kingdom or community of God but also their empowerment as active, unique contributors who will be first in the kingdom. (note 87) This offers space for what Yong sees as the deep understanding of, and contributions to, God's kingdom offered by those with profound disabilities. (note 88) For Yong, we are only at the start of interpreting the languages of others into tongues we can all understand, and this remains the ongoing miracle of Pentecost. (note 89) An inclusive ecclesiology

---

85. Kamba, "Mission as a Movement," 91–94.
86. Kamchedzera, "Investigation," 3–17.
87. KwaZulu Natal Christian Council, "Theology of Disability."
88. Hittenberger, "Receiving God's Gift," 159.
89. Yong, "Disability and the Gifts of the Spirit," 80.

reimagines the church away from an elite set of all-powerful pastors who miraculously heal, towards a non-hierarchical charismatic fellowship whose mission is empowered by the Holy Spirit as the champion of the weak, which encourages participatory rituals for the inclusion of people with disabilities. Yong emphasizes that the gifts of people with disabilities offers a rich resource to both renew church life and to reinterpret its theology and teachings in ways that are too deep to be contained by "normality." (note 90) Likewise, Paul Leshota from Lesotho reflects theologically on being interconnected as one body to see inclusive communities as foundational to many African worldviews. He notes the need to hold to the African proverb "we need to hold each other in arms" if people with disabilities are to be accepted as fellow participants in deep solidarity, with church rituals of inclusion in which all have the right to participate. **Ubuntu** offers ways for African churches to create identity through community where difference leads to welcome in a Eucharistic meal of hospitality around the table. (note 91)

---

90. Hittenberger, 144.
91. Leshota, "Dependence to Interdependence," 1–9.

Finally, Malawian theologian Joseph Thipa's work on kingdom theology and its implications for people living with disability resonates with Yong's insistence that the promise of the "kingdom" highlights that people with disabilities will be present in Zion as part of a wider restoration. (note 92) In Southern Africa, the KZNCC notes similarly that "the inclusivity of people with disability is seen in God's plan for the restoration of the Israelites. . . . In the restoration God ensured that all [people with disabilities] would also be brought back. God did not want the blind and the lame left behind but to be restored." (note 93) Yong asks all Christians to reflect more deeply on the question, "How can embracing the spiritual gifts of a person with special needs help us to receive the kingdom of God?" He offers a reminder that to be "able" is not to be "normal" and God's kingdom may in fact turn ableism upside down. (note 94) The Bible offers hints that the eschatological reign of God will include people with disabilities with the marks of their impairments apparent not erased, as seen in the resurrected body of Jesus. While some theologians assume that the inclusion in the

---

92. Thipa, "Doctrine of the Kingdom," 77–83.
93. KwaZulu Natal Christian Council, "Theology of Disability."
94. Hittenberger, "Receiving God's Gift," 141–60.

kingdom of God of people with disabilities means their cure, both Yong and Thipa instead focus on the transformation of human prejudices which cause such pain to those living with disabilities.

Conclusion

There remains much for churches in Southern Africa and beyond to recognize and wrestle with. Entrenched ideologies of disability exclusion remain prevalent in many Christian doctrines, traditions and sacred texts and need critical recognition and radical reinterpretation. But there is also reason to hope. Disability informed voices are emerging from Southern Africa and beyond to reimagine Christianity's core doctrines of creational equality, sin, Pentecost, a boundary-crossing Jesus, healing narratives, and the shared task of the church to be a just home where all are welcomed and belong, and to better equip emerging faith leaders who are studying theology and religious studies to engage differently. (note 95) However, the disability/sin/curse nexus must be tackled at its roots within local congregations. It has led to distorted forms of healing and prayer in many churches, despite the harm these patterns cause in the lives of people with disabilities who

---

95. Kabue et al., **Changing Scenes**; Palm, **One Body?**, 1–35.

may not experience or even seek to experience physical "healing." To ignore these beliefs is to remain complicit with how these heresies remain embedded in Christian traditions and communities and get entangled with pre-existing cultural myths. It is an important theological task to re-engage these ideas contextually and redemptively. Reimagining sin must take seriously the social lived aspects of exclusion in the day-to-day lives of many people with disabilities and criticize the entrenched hierarchies of normalcy and ableism in the Bible and many of its traditional interpretations. Churches must openly recognize and confess their patterns of exclusion, stigma and ableism, and instead draw on the image of a Spirit-filled united body with many gifts. A liberating pneumatology can help churches be reimagined as communities of shared vulnerability where all participate, belong and have gifts to offer, and where people living with disabilities are placed first, and not last, in the celebratory feast which Christians aim to embody.

Bibliography

Amanze, James N., and Samuel Kabue. "Disability, Religion and Theology: African Perspectives." **Journal of Disability and Religion** 20 (2016): 1–2.

Avalos, Hector. "Disability Studies and Biblical Studies: Retrospectives and Prospects." **Interpretation: A Journal of Bible and Theology** 73, no. 4 (2019): 343–54.

Calder, Andy. "To Belong, I Need to Be Missed." **Journal of Religion, Disability & Health** 16, no. 3 (2012): 262–86.

Chataika, Tsitsi. "Cultural and Religious Explanations of Disability and Promoting Inclusive Communities in Southern Africa." In **Searching for Dignity: Conversations on Theology, Disability and Human Dignity**, edited by Juliana Claassens, Leslie Swartz and Len Hansen, 117–28. Stellenbosch: Sun Media, 2013.

Chisale, Sinenhlanhla. "Disabled Motherhood in an African Community: Towards an African Women Theology of Disability." **Die Skriflig/In Luce Verbi** 52 (2018): 1–9.

Claassens, Juliana. "Job, Theology and Disability: Moving Towards a New Kind of Speech." In **Searching for Dignity: Conversations on Theology, Disability and Human Dignity**, edited by Juliana Claassens, Leslie Swartz and Len Hansen, 55–66. Stellenbosch: Sun Media, 2013.

Claassens, Juliana, Shaheen Shaikh and Leslie Swartz. "Engaging Disability and Religion in the Global South." In **The Palgrave Handbook of Disability and Citizenship in the Global South**, edited by Brian Watermeyer, Judith McKenzie and Leslie Swartz, 147–64. Cham: Palgrave Macmillan, 2018.

Dube, Musa W. "Towards a Post-colonial Feminist Interpretation of the Bible." In **Hope Abundant: Third World Theology and Indigenous Women's Theology**, edited by Kwok Pui-lan, 89–102. New York: Orbis, 2010.

Githuku, Sammy. "Biblical Perspectives on Disability." In **Disability, Society, and Theology: Voices from Africa**, edited by Samuel Kabue, Esther Mombo, Joseph Galgalo and C. B. Peter, 79–93. Limuru: Zapf Chancery Publishers Africa, 2011.

Hittenberger, Jeff. "Receiving God's Gift of a Person with Special Needs: Amos Yong's Theology of Disability." In **The Theology of Amos Yong and the New Face of Pentecostal Scholarship Passion for the Spirit,** edited by Wolfgang Vondey and Martin Mittelstadt, 141–60. Leiden: Boston, 2013.

Ishola-Esan, Helen Olomu. "Impact of the Remnants of African Worldviews on Perception of Pastors Towards Ministering to Persons with Disabilities in Nigeria." **Journal of Disability & Religion** 20, no. 1–2 (2016): 103–18.

Kabue, Samuel, Edison Kalengyo, John Ndavula and Anjeline Okola. **The Changing Scenes of Disability in Church and Society: A Resource Book for Theological and Religious Studies**. Kenya: World Council of Churches, 2021.

Kamba, Micheline. "Mission as a Movement 'Together Towards Life.'" In **Moving in the Spirit: Report of the World Council of Churches**

Conference on World Mission and Evangelism**, edited by Risto Jukko and Jooseop Keum, 1–94. Geneva: World Council of Churches, 2019.

Kamchedzera, Elizabeth. "An Investigation Whether and How Christian Organizations Respond to the Practical Needs of Students with Disabilities: A Case of One College in Zomba." **Journal of Disability & Religion** 20, no. 1–2 (2016): 3–17.

Kebaneilwe, Mmapula D. "Disability as a Challenge and Not a Crisis: The Jesus Model." **Journal of Disability & Religion** 20, no. 1–2 (2016): 93–102.

Kretschmar, Louise. **The Church and Disability in Southern Africa: Inclusion and Participation**. Pietermaritzburg: Cluster Publications, 2018.

KwaZulu Natal Christian Council. "KZNCC on Theology of Disability: Texts of Promise and Wellness." 2016. Accessed 6 June 2020. Unpublished.

Lees, Janet. "Lazarus, Come Out! How Contextual Bible Study Can Empower the Disabled." In **Disability, Society, and Theology: Voices from Africa**, edited by Samuel Kabue, Esther Mombo, Joseph Galgalo and C. B. Peter, 97–110. Limuru: Zapf Chancery Publishers Africa, 2011.

Leshota, Paul. "From Dependence to Interdependence: Towards a Practical Theology of Disability." **HTS Theological Studies** 71, no. 2 (2012): 1–9.

Longchar, Wati. "Sin, Suffering, and Disability in God's World." In **Disability, Society, and Theology: Voices from Africa**, edited by Samuel Kabue, Esther Mombo, Joseph Galgalo and C. B. Peter, 47–58. Limuru: Zapf Chancery Publishers Africa, 2011.

Lowe, Mary Elise. "'Rabbi, Who Sinned?' Disability Theologies and Sin." **Dialog: A Journal of Theology** 51, no. 3 (2012): 185–94.

Mduli, Patrick. "Disability in South Africa: A Theological and Socio-economic Perspective." Master's thesis, Stellenbosch University, 2012.

Moller, Erna. "The Experiences of People with Disabilities in Faith Communities and Suggestions to Enhance Their Inclusion." In **Searching for Dignity: Conversations on Theology, Disability and Human Dignity**, edited by Juliana Claassens, Leslie Swartz and Len Hansen, 129–44. Stellenbosch: Sun Media, 2013.

Mugeere, Anthony B., Julius Omona, Andrew E. State and Tom Shakespeare. "Oh God! Why Did You Let Me Have This Disability? Religion, Spirituality and Disability in Three African Countries." **Journal of Disability & Religion** 24, no. 1 (2020): 64–81.

Ndlovu, Hebron L. "African Beliefs Concerning People with Disabilities: Implications for Theological Education." **Journal of Disability & Religion** 20, no. 1–2 (2016): 29–39.

Nell, Michelle. "On Her Blindness: Reflections on Being Blind in the World and Associated Issues of Faith." In **Searching for Dignity: Conversations on Theology, Disability and Human Dignity**, edited by Juliana Claassens, Leslie Swartz and Len Hansen, 161–66. Stellenbosch: Sun Media, 2013.

Nihinlola, Emiola. "Disability Discourse in the Curriculum of Nigerian Theological Institutions: Constraints, Possibilities and Recommendations." **Journal of Disability & Religion** 20, no. 1–2 (2016): 40–48.

Nkomazana, Fidelis. "'No One Who Has a Blemish Shall Draw Near': Pentecostals Rising above Disabling Hermeneutics." **Journal of Disability & Religion** 20, no. 1–2 (2016): 49–61.

Palm, Selina. "Doing Theologies of Disability in South Africa." **Journal of Systematic Theology** 2, no. 3 (2023): 1–39.

———. **One Body? To Belong, We Have to Be Missed: Exploring Theologies of Disability from Southern Contexts.** Internal Report. Tearfund UK, 2020. Unpublished.

Pradeep, S. Manohar. "Disabled God: Disability Ethics Research Paper." Disabled World, 6 June 2018. Accessed 6 June 2020. https://www.disabled-world.com/news/asia/india/imago-dei.php.

Retief, Marno, and Rantoa Letšosa. "Models of Disability: A Brief Overview." **HTS Theological Studies** 74, no. 1 (2018): 1–8.

Thipa, Joseph A. "Implications of the Doctrine of the Kingdom of God for Building a Better Life for People with Disability in Africa: A Case Study of Malawi." **Journal of Disability & Religion** 20, no. 1–2 (2016): 77–83.

West, Gerald. **The Stolen Bible: From Tool of Imperialism to African Icon.** Leiden: Brill, 2016.

World Council of Churches. **The Gift of Being: Called to Be a Church of All and for All**. 2016.

Yong, Amos. **The Bible, Disability, and the Church**. Grand Rapids: Eerdmans, 2011.

———. "Disability and the Gifts of the Spirit: Pentecost and the Renewal of the Church." **Journal of Pentecostal Theology** 19, no. 1 (2010): 76–93.

———. "Disability and the Gospel: How God Uses Our Brokenness to Display His Grace." **Journal of Disability & Religion** 19, no. 1 (2015): 85–95.

———. "Running the (Special) Race: New (Pauline) Perspectives on Disability and Theology of Sport." **Journal of Disability & Religion** 18, no. 2 (2014): 209–25.

———. **Theology and Down Syndrome: Reimagining Disability in Late Modernity.** Studies in Religion, Theology, and Disability. Waco: Baylor University Press, 2007.

Zulu, Edwin. "WatipaLeza: A Critical Re-engagement of Nsenga (African) Religious Values and Disability." **Journal of Disability & Religion** 20, no. 1–2 (2016): 84–92.

4

Holistic Healing in Acts 3:1–10

A Transformative Church for All People (note 1)

Micheline Kamba

Introduction

Our understanding of healing focuses on Acts 3:1–10. The rereading of this text, with its picture of

---

1. This chapter is a republished version of "Holistic Healing in Acts 3:1–10: A Transformative Church for All People" by Micheline Kamba published by John Wiley and Sons in **International Review of Mission** 105, no. 2 (2016): 268–79. Copyright © (2016) World Council of Churches. Reprinted with the permission of John Wiley and Sons. All rights reserved.

healing, will lead to an understanding of inclusive healing, in the sense that marginalized people are included in the healing. This means that the healing is holistic, rather than focusing on either physical or spiritual healing alone. The research on which this chapter is based sought to explore the issue of holistic healing for a transformative church. The chapter brings into perspective the following questions: What is entailed in Jesus's healing of people with disabilities? And how can the issue of healing be opened up to the possibility of building a community of love, justice, peace and diversity? In an attempt to answer these questions, this chapter has two parts. In the first section, I focus on my personal rereading in view of my own disability experience and my experience with Bible study participants, using narrative interpretation of the existing literature and interpreting from a psychospiritual perspective framed by a liberation theology of disability. In the second section, I engage a dialogue between biblical scholars and others on the different perspectives on healing. My overall objective in this chapter is to offer a new biblical understanding of the text and, at the same time, a theological reflection on healing to assist church leaders and Christians to understand that people with disabilities, like all human beings, deserve to be in fellowship with God and with other people for the sake of social transformation.

Introducing the Text: Acts 3:1–10

The text of Acts 3:1–10 is the first miraculous story recorded by Luke in the book of Acts. It is connected with the preceding text, Acts 2:43, which states, "Many wonders and signs were being done by the apostles" (NRSV). The heart of this story is that these wonders and miracles were done "in the name of Jesus Christ of Nazareth" (3:6): hence, the Lord saves human beings through Jesus. Salvation is thus the principal theme of Acts, its narrative being centrally concerned with the realization of God's purpose to bring salvation in all its fullness to all people. (note 2) God so loved the world that he sent his only beloved Son into the world, so that "whoever believes in him shall not perish but have eternal life" (John 3:16). This links to the programmatic speech of Jesus: the Kingdom of God [has] come to the earth, so that those who are poor, marginalized, prisoners and oppressed must be free and recover the light of joy (see Luke 4:18–19). Jesus encountered people with disabilities through his healing and miracles, because he preferred to "spend time with the 'least' rather than with people of wealth, influence, power or even those in the religious hierarchy" (John 9; Mark 2:17). (note 3)

---

2. Martin and Davids, "Salvation," 19; Farmer, "Cure of the Lame Man," 1514.
3. Tada, "Christ's Compassion."

Therefore, the book of Acts is a continuation of Jesus's action through and by the power of the Holy Spirit. The connection between Acts 2:43 and Joel's prophecy (Joel 2:28–32) demonstrates "the outpouring of the Holy Spirit on Jesus's disciples and announces the Good News with healing and miracles." (note 4) In other words, the healings and miracles in the gospels and in the book of Acts show how the excluded have been integrated into society by Jesus's ministry, emulated by the apostles. (note 5)

This chapter is in two parts. The first part deals with my own rereading of the text, which I have called "autobiographical criticism" and in which I imply my disability experience, which is explicated in my doctoral thesis, "Developing a Holistic Educational Programme through Contextual Bible Study with People with Disabilities in Kinshasa, Democratic Republic of Congo: IMAN'ENDA as Case Study," through the lens of social transformation. The second part presents the dialogue in which I engage with Bible study participants' responses

---

4. Brown et al., "Acts 3, 1–11," 735.
5. Matt Edmonds states that the "divine healings" are commonplace in the Old and New Testaments, and the gospels record over forty healing miracles in the ministry of Jesus (Edmonds, **Theological Diagnosis**, 141).

to the scholarly points of view on the text. I interpret the verses according to the way they are interlinked.

Autobiographical Criticism

As stated above, this first part focuses on my personal rereading in view of my own disability experience and my experience with participants of a Bible study that I conducted with church leaders and some persons with disabilities. I use narrative interpretation of existing literature, and interpret from a psychospiritual perspective framed by a liberation theology of disability.

The text is a healing story of a traditional type and shows that healings and miracles are an essential part of the gospel message. (note 6) However, the aim of this section is to explore aspects of healing other than those that become apparent in an initial reading of the text. I will broaden the concept of healing for the sake of social transformation of people with disabilities.

The first two verses (vv. 1–2) introduce the characters of the story. These are Peter and John, known as Jesus's apostles (Peter is the famous

---

6. Pervo, **Acts**, 98; Schmidt, **Yes, You Are Healed**, ix; Willimon, **Acts Interpretation**, 42.

apostle who took the lead in addressing the crowd on the day of Pentecost, in Acts 2:14–28). The story begins with information about Peter and John, and about the prayers in the temple. As for the man who has a physical impairment, he is unnamed, and is identified only by his "handicap."

The anonymity of people with disabilities in the gospels reveals that people with disabilities were ignored and stereotyped. To name people is a sign of identification and recognition in their homes, communities or society, but people with disabilities are commonly excluded from such identification and recognition.

Verse 2 portrays the unnamed physically impaired man as a man of great infirmity, a useless man. The description of the man being carried by other unknown (unidentified) people emphasizes the hopelessness of his situation. As Fontaine says, "concepts of purity, [the] divine origin [of] disability, and objectification [of people with disabilities] for theological and literary purposes all work together to paint a negative picture of the possibilities and the powers of the disabled." (note 7)

---

7. C. R. Fontaine, quoted in Bruce, "Daughter of Abraham," 3.

Verse 2b says the man was "carried to the temple gate called Beautiful." The "Beautiful gate" was likely the Corinthian Gate, which led from the Court of the Gentiles to the Court of Women. (note 8) According to the rules safeguarding the holiness of the temple, people with disabilities were separated and kept apart because they were impure and hence forbidden to enter (Lev 21:18; 2 Sam 5:8).

The mention of the "time of prayer" indicates that there were several times for prayer at the Jerusalem temple (in the morning at 9 a.m.; at 12:00; in the afternoon at 3 p.m.; and in the evening). (note 9) It may be that the afternoon service was crowded; this could mean that the "lame beggar" was being carried to the temple because of the density of the crowds. In any case, the "giving of alms was an important part of the Jewish faith and so beggars found it profitable to be near the temple." (note 10)

In dealing with verses 3 to 7, we see that the man saw Peter and John enter the temple and asked for money, but Peter and John stopped and shared with him what they had found to be a far

---

8. Parsons, "Character of the Lame Man," 295–312.
9. Richards, **Bible Reader's Companion**.
10. Wiersbe, **Bible Exposition Commentary**, 412.

more precious thing: "the name of Jesus Christ of Nazareth." The name of Jesus Christ was the focal point that the apostles wanted to raise up and glorify to the people of Israel (Acts 3:11–20).

I see in this text that silver and gold are a temporary help, meeting a short-term need. Introducing Jesus into the life of this man was a timeless gift, and an unexpected one.

The words of verse 3, "when he saw Peter and John . . . he asked them for money," indicate that this man was taught to beg for money so he could buy food at the end of the day. He could do nothing to support himself except beg. He was helpless from the moment he was born, and he was made to believe that people with disabilities could not go anywhere or do anything without external help: all his life he had had to rely on someone. This leads to an understanding of why this man did not ask to be healed. He had likely heard of the apostles' healing miracles, but he did not ask to be healed – he asked for money instead. The temporary assistance of money was preferred over the permanent help of healing, revealing his acceptance of his hopeless situation. This picture reveals the portrayal of the man as stereotypical and foregrounds many of the problems faced by people with disabilities.

The words "rise up and walk" (ESV) are an order, a command to change position, to upgrade his condition. The man had always been seated outside the temple, unable to walk. These words were aimed at transforming his situation.

The act of "taking him by the right hand" and the way they "helped him up" are linked with Peter and John's command that the man should stand and walk. This suggests that the healing process should be an achievement that requires words and action to be tied together. (note 11)

Verses 8 and 9 show that the fact that the man with a disability "jumped to his feet," "began to walk" and was able to go with them "into the temple" represented a miracle of healing. The man experienced a complete transformation in his life. The two verses give an overview of the holistic healing that occurred.

First, there is emotional healing. Verse 5 shows the "crippled beggar" expecting to receive money from Peter and John. Yet, while Peter and John might have had money for him, a greater gift was about to be given to the man: the gift of being able to stand up and walk in the name of Jesus Christ.

---

11. Pervo, **Acts**, 100.

Here, silver and gold provide only temporary help, since everyone who receives this will soon be needy again. Whereas "the name of Jesus Christ" is a permanent help: whoever receives it will never need to ask again (John 4:13–14).

The expression "rise up and walk" (ESV) contrasts with the man's lifetime spent sitting and being carried, signs of his uselessness and hopelessness. When Peter (and John) told him to stand and walk, this gave him a sense of hope and the strength to restart his life, to be independent and free. Hence for this man, before he could receive physical healing, his soul and mind had to be healed.

Second, there is social healing, which verse 8 refers to when it says that once the man was cured, he entered the temple. This means he joined other people; he joined his community in the temple.

The text informs us that the man had been carried all the time, but that during prayers he was left outside alone. He was a beggar, a poor man, an impure man, excluded from activities such as prayer in the temple. He may have been a beggar for a long time, because those who went into the temple for worship knew and recognized him (v. 10). This means that the way they saw him when he was sitting was different from how they saw him when he was standing and walking. Therefore, this healing changed the minds of people who had stereotyped and discriminated against him.

Third, there is physical healing, referred to in the phrase "in the name of Jesus Christ of Nazareth, walk" (vv. 6–7) and the fact that "he jumped to his feet" (v. 8). This shows that through this name the power did flow, the "cripple's" feet and ankles were strengthened, and the man walked and leaped, living proof of the power of Jesus. The healing was instantaneous (a miracle), with no further treatment needed. Here I would highlight the paradigm shift, the change of position of the man: he used to sit, unable to stand and walk; but with words and actions he was able to stand up and walk, even to jump. This was a visible change experienced by the man. The fact that he moved forward to his life made his life story different.

From a disability perspective, the physical healing is not only that supernatural miracle, but the ability to act and do things differently.

Fourth, then, is the spiritual healing described in verse 8, which highlights that the first thing this healed man did was to enter the temple, approach the throne of God and give thanks. The text seems to imply that this man might have been taught that he had to sit outside the temple – not to pray, but to have access to people so he could beg. He might also have been taught that he was impure, separated from God, and that only once healed could he enter the temple. Thus, when he felt strengthened in his feet and ankles, he entered the temple, "walking and jumping, and praising God" (v. 8b).

Verse 10 starts with the fact that the people "recognised him" as the same man who had been sitting outside and begging for alms, and "they were filled with wonder and amazement." This reveals that even the people in the temple received the "miracle-healing" (vv. 10–11), in the sense that their minds were opened to know that before God, everything is possible, and that there is no place for discrimination or stereotyping.

Summary of Personal Reflections

My particular reading of this text of Acts 3:1–11 is an auto-critical reflection of the situation that people with disabilities experience in their daily lives.

As a person with a disability who has experienced failed physical healing, (note 12) I have

---

12. "My experience as a young lady with a disability influenced most of my spiritual life and my calling into the ministry. It was so difficult to be accepted as God's creation. During my teenage years, I was wondering about my physical state. I attempted many times to commit suicide. One day my sister knew that and she came to me and said 'My dear sister, what you want to do is not a solution to your problems. Pray and ask your God what life means to you as a young lady with disability. And ask God why He wants you to remain like this.' These words from my sister were very powerful and made me conscious of my situation. As Victor Frankl says, 'to be conscious, take action and be responsible.' I prayed, cried, implored God to teach me the meaning of my life. My sister and I devoted three days to fasting and praying to God to help me. That time was really a healing time. Since that time I have never prayed God to heal me physically, because I know, as Paul recognized, that 'God's grace is sufficient for you, His strength is made perfect in weakness' (2 Corinthians 12:10). Then I took courage and I believed in what my sister told me; she was inspired by the Holy Spirit. From that time I accepted myself as a woman with a disability and I knew that God had a good plan for me. That was in 1984. Today, I

demonstrated in my reflection that physical healing is not the only form of healing in this text – though initially, these stories in the book of Acts present the many signs and miracles performed by the apostles. There are other forms of healing (emotional, social and psychospiritual) that, as stated above, challenge people with disabilities as well as leaders of the Christian church, who think that when a person with a disability is not healed, he or she is being denied fellowship with God and with other people.

From this text I have argued that before this man was physically healed, Peter and John took time to talk with him to show him that silver or gold could not limit his life. He must move on and see further in his life. I noted that it was not the fact that this man could stand and walk which amazed people. Instead, it was the way he scaled to another, new life. I do not deny the supernatural healing,

---

understand my vocation as that of encouraging people with disabilities to 'rise up and walk' spiritually so that they can be independent in their quest for transformation of their situation, both in Church and Society." Micheline Kamba's testimony in "Toward a Theological Programme of Disability Studies in Africa – with special focus on DRC," in **African Theological Education Handbook** (forthcoming).

because I do know that God is all-powerful. Yet from my disability experience I recognize another form of physical healing that I call "visible change" which people with disabilities experience in their lives. (note 13) This is manifested through their abilities to do things differently.

My understanding of physical healing here is seeing the person shift to another level that was not expected, because many people with disabilities have been alienated by the culture and tradition of their context so that they cannot do anything in their lives because they are disabled. Therefore, my statement to church leaders through liberative education could empower people with disabilities to revive hope and a new life.

My reading of this text is that of a church leader for the effective awareness of the integration of people with disabilities in church. I recognize

---

13. I unfold this in the section on healing in chapter 7 of my thesis. My understanding of "visible change" from a liberation theology of disability is the improvement of the abilities. Therefore, I state that this can be possible only when a person has experienced an emotional and spiritual healing.

that they need assistance to discover their real identities so they can take up leadership in their respective communities.

People with Disabilities in Dialogue with Scholars

In this second part, I foreground, on the one hand, the contribution made by participants of the Bible study group and my own contribution in regard to disability in ancient Jewish and Greek society and modern times, in the Bible study on Acts 3:1–11. On the other hand, the dialogue involves the discovery of different types of healing, in contrast to the scholarly material which adheres to a narrow definition of healing in the Bible, specifically in the text of Acts.

The participants raised two points: the location where the man was placed in relation to the temple, and the attribution by Jews of impurity to disability, which was a social construct. The location, the Beautiful gate, was open to all comers, including all kinds of people of lower standing, such as cattle dealers and money-changers; at the gate would lie the beggars (mostly people with disabilities) (Luke 16:20; John 9:8). It was associated with the image of Jewish society, as opposed to the Court of the Gentiles, which housed the impure people with disabilities.

Thus, this court was called the "outer" (meaning lower) court. (note 14) This highlights that "the social construction of disability posits that if negative meanings are associated with people with disabilities, [then] behaviors, objects, and language associated with people with disabilities will be negative." (note 15)

Scholars have interpreted a "handicap" or disability as punishment for sins, committed either by the persons with disabilities themselves or by their relatives in earlier generations, referring to the Bible to support their interpretations (Lev 26:16; Deut 28:22; John 9:2). (note 16) Therefore, disability has been understood as signifying the absence of God.

Participants in the Bible study went beyond this and found that the text they studied did not portray disability as linked to impurity or pity alone. They pointed out that this text had two kinds of responses to people with disabilities: first, society's attitude, and second, God's view of disability, as revealed through the apostles.

---

14. Bible History Online, "Court of the Women."
15. McNair and Sanchez, "Christian Social Constructions," 35–50.
16. See further explanation in McNair and Sanchez, 36; Fritzson and Kabue, **Interpreting Disability**, 11.

This approach reveals that people with disabilities do not need pity or mercy, but rather compassionate understanding and opportunities to develop their self-confidence, realize their possibilities and abilities, and follow their vocation.

The apostles' approach presents a challenge to those who claim that they stand by vulnerable persons. First, Peter and John stopped and approached the place where the man was sitting, showing that they knew that, as followers of Jesus, their mission was to be with those who were unwell. Second, Peter and John took time to talk with the man. In the context of disability, dialogue and interaction are important in a profound sense: people with disabilities are recognized as individuals with needs, aspirations and strengths, the same as able-bodied people. Third, they took him by the right hand, which was a sign of love, welcome, support, encouragement and integration. The apostles "take sides with the victims of stigma and discrimination against the institutions and their leaders who promulgate stigmatization and discrimination forms of theology." (note 17) This leads to the second part of this section: the discovering of different ways of healing by the participants in the Bible study.

---

17. West and Zengele, "Reading Job 'Positively,'" 112–24.

Different Ways of Healing

Healing and miracles in the New Testament, especially in the book of Acts, served as a sign of the Holy Spirit to the apostolic company (2 Cor 12:12) to confirm the new message they were preaching (Heb 2:3–4). (note 18)

The rereading of this text from the perspective of disability shows that there is more than one way of healing in this story.

Scholars argue that a person with a disability was excluded from society because of his or her physical condition. Disability was seen as a consequence of sin or of the disabled person's parents' sin. For these reasons, the laws aimed to separate such people from others who were seen as pure. Only the person who was healed was invited into the community to pray in the temple. (note 19)

Healing in this text concerns the inclusion of and respect for a human being: treating him or her with equality. Reinders says, "Every human being has an interest in being treated with equal respect,

---

18. Biblical Studies Online, "Gift of Miracles."
19. Bruce, "John 5, 1–8," 40; Albl, "'Whenever I Am Weak,'" 148.

including the mentally disabled, inasmuch as everyone has an interest in being included as a respected member of society." (note 20)

However, the healing recorded in this passage was unexpected. This man had not asked to be healed, meaning that he had no faith and was resigned to his situation. Peter and John did not set out to heal or to do miracles: they healed not "by might nor by power," but by God's Spirit and will. (note 21)

---

20. Reinders, **Future of the Disabled**, 73.

21. I have compared this story with that of Paul, who was not healed of his "thorn in the flesh" (2 Cor 12:7–10); also, Trophimus was not healed of his illness (2 Tim 4:20). Timothy, too, was not cured of his stomach problem. This is to point out to those who today are called divine healers, and who state that when a person with a disability is not healed it is because of a lack of faith, that, on the contrary, "faith on the part of the one healed was not a requirement or condition. Faith was often rewarded, but it was never stated to be a condition of a person's healing, nor was it ever used as an excuse for a failed attempt to heal." Therefore, theologically, a miracle is God's sign through the Holy Spirit. Biblical Studies Online, "Gift of Miracles"; Pache, "Miracle," 498.

A "Western scientific world-view might argue that the medical conditions described in the biblical narrative could not be physiologically cured by divine intervention. Some theologians would even argue that the dispensation of such types of healing ended with the advent of Western scientific medicine." (note 22) Despite these opinions, the gospel healing of Jesus includes restoration and integration into the physical as well as the spiritual realm in the community. As the participants of the Bible study expressed, healing in this text is holistic: emotional, physical, social and spiritual.

In today's context, people with disabilities have felt hurt by events in church or during the healing prayers in crusades. Theo Schmidt says, "We have a healing ministry and not a hurting ministry." (note 23) The use of a wheelchair, white cane, or walker to campaign and attract people to attend healing services or crusades is a humiliation of and disrespect for people with disabilities. (note 24) A Lausanne Occasional Paper

---

22. Fritzson and Kabue, **Interpreting Disability**, 20–21.
23. Schmidt, **Yes, You Are Healed**, 7.
24. EDAN Newsletter (July–September 2005), 2; Lausanne Committee for World Evangelization, "Hidden and Forgotten."

notes, "People with disabilities become deeply disappointed over having been denied healing by God or being abandoned by Him to intervene in their pain, loss and disability. As a result, a root of bitterness and scepticism about the Christian faith often takes hold." (note 25)

The challenge posed by the text of Acts 3:1–11, then, is to reconstruct the relationship between people with disabilities and God by developing their awareness of the love of God in their lives, whatever their physical condition, and effecting spiritual healing. The text highlights that healing is also emotional and social in nature, since it involves people with disabilities experiencing the compassion, empowering support and love of others, and also inclusion in their community as full and productive members of society.

Matt Edmonds argues, from the same perspective, "when healing is not treated foremost as an act of inclusion, a diagnosis can quite easily appear to be a more general attitude of negativity towards difference. This, of course, is further isolating for the person who already feels that they exist on the

---

25. Lausanne Committee for World Evangelization, 16.

margins of society." (note 26) Therefore, a theology of healing from a disability perspective must involve social inclusion and mutual acceptance.

Many people with disabilities have been hurt and have lost their trust in their relationship with God because, in the healing ministry, they were made to expect that healing would be spectacular and instantaneous. Healing, however, is under God's management, as Schmidt says: "The healing may be what we prayed for, but on the other hand it may not be what we prayed for. The person is not rejected, but begins a journey of discovery of healing." (note 27) This concurs with my comments above on Acts 3:6:

> The expression "rise up and walk" (ESV) contrasts with the man's lifetime of sitting and being carried, signs of his uselessness and hopelessness. When Peter (and John) told him to stand and walk, this gave him a sense of hope and the strength to restart his life, to be independent and free. Hence for this man, before he could receive physical healing, his soul and mind had to be healed.

---

26. Edmonds, **Theological Diagnosis**, 160.
27. Schmidt, **Yes, You are Healed**, 9.

Conclusion

The text of Acts 3:1–10 was at the centre of a Bible study with church leaders. I view this text as a picture of holistic healing because it reveals different ways of healing: emotional, social, physical and spiritual. The text challenges the church to deal with the issue of disability holistically.

The Bible study participants who were church leaders came to understand their attitudes towards people with disabilities, and through the Bible study they opted for change. Their propositions reflected that the church needs to adopt the stance of holistic healing to become a church of all and for all, which is what I mean by "a transformative church."

The rereading of the text focused on a reconstructed view of people with disabilities to be realized with the support of church leaders. This support is understood as involving education, which will serve as a source of empowerment and as the means of liberation for people with disabilities.

Bibliography

Albl, Martin. "'For Whenever I Am Weak, Then I Am Strong': Disability in Paul's Epistles." In **This Abled Body: Rethinking Disabilities in Biblical**

Studies, edited by Hector Avalos, Sarah J. Melcher and Jeremy Schipper, 145–58. Atlanta: Society of Biblical Literature, 2007.

Bible History Online. "The Court of the Women in the Temple." 2012. https://bible-history.com/court-of-women.

Biblical Studies Online. "The Gift of Miracles and Healing Today." http://www.biblicalstudies.com/bstudy/spiritualgift/ch 17.html.

Brown, Raymond E., Joseph Fitzmyer and Roland Murphy, eds. "Acts 3, 1–11." In **The New Jerome Biblical Commentary**, 735. London: Geoffrey Chapman, 1948.

Bruce, Patricia Frances. "'A Daughter of Abraham': Luke 13:10–17 and the Inclusion of People with Disabilities." **Journal of Constructive Theology** 11, no. 1 (2005): 3–27.

———. "John 5, 1–8: The Healing at the Pool – Some Narrative, Socio-Historical and Ethical Issues." **Neotestamentica** 39, no. 1 (2005): 39–56.

EDAN (Ecumenical Disability Advocates Network) Newsletter July–September 2005.

Edmonds, Matt. **A Theological Diagnosis: A New Direction on Genetic Therapy, "Disability" and the Ethics of Healing.** Philadelphia: Jessica Kingsley, 2011.

Farmer, William R., ed. "Acts 3.1–11: The Cure of the Lame Man." In **The International Bible Commentary: A Catholic and Ecumenical Commentary for the Twenty-First Century**, 1514. Collegeville: Liturgical, 1998.

Fritzson, Arne, and Samuel Kabue. **Interpreting Disability: A Church of All and for All.** Geneva: WCC, 2003.

Kamba, Micheline. "A Church of All and for All: An Invitation to a Round Table, Acts 3, 1–10." Unpublished paper presented at the Methodist Church of Southern Africa's Annual Conference, 2011, at Lesotho Sun, Maseru.

———. "Developing a Holistic Educational Programme through Contextual Bible Study with People with Disabilities in Kinshasa, Democratic Republic of Congo: IMAN'ENDA as Case Study." PhD thesis, UKZN, 2013. Published under the title **Holistic Education through Bible Study**. Atlanta: Scholars, 2014.

Lausanne Committee for World Evangelization. "Hidden and Forgotten People Ministry among People with Disabilities." Lausanne Occasional Paper No. 35 B. 2004. https://lausanne.org/wp-content/uploads/2007/06/LOP35B_IG6B.pdf.

Martin, Ralph P., and Peter H. Davids, eds. "Salvation." In **Dictionary of the Later New Testament and Its Developments**, 19. Downers Grove: InterVarsity Press, 1997.

McNair, Jeff, and Michelle Sanchez. "Christian Social Construction on Disability: Church Leaders." **Journal of Religion, Disability & Health** 11, no. 4 (2007): 35–50.

Pache, René, ed. "Miracle." In **Nouveau dictionnaire biblique**, 498. Saint-Légier sur Vevey: Éditions Emmaüs, 1961.

Parsons, Mikeal C. "The Character of the Lame Man in Acts 3–4." **Journal of Biblical Literature** 124, no. 2 (2005): 295–312.

Pervo, Richard L. **Acts: A Commentary**. Minneapolis: Fortress, 2009.

Reinders, Hans S. **The Future of the Disabled in Liberal Society: An Ethical Analysis.** Notre Dame: University of Notre Dame Press, 2000.

Richards, Larry. **The Bible Reader's Companion**. Wheaton: Victor, 1991.

Schmidt, Theo. **Yes, You Are Healed: A Journey of Healing.** Parkhurst: Christ Healing Fellowship, 2007.

Tada, Joni Eareckson. "Christ's Compassion for 'The Least' and People with Disabilities." **Lausanne World Pulse** 9 (2007). https://lausanneworldpulse.com/themedarticles-php/811/09-2007.

West, Gerald, and Bongi Zengele. "Reading Job 'Positively' in the Context of HIV/AIDS in South Africa." **Concilium** 4 (2004): 112–24.

Wiersbe, Warren W. **The Bible Exposition Commentary**. Wheaton: Victor, 1991.

Willimon, William H. **Acts Interpretation: A Bible Commentary for Teaching and Preaching**. Atlanta: John Knox Press, 1998.

Part 2

Different Perspectives on Disability: Transforming Church and Institutional Practice

Part B

5

An African Community Perspective in Positive Dialogue with Disability and Christianity

Edwin Zulu

Introduction

In African contexts, disability provokes a wide range of reactions and responses. Some see it in a negative light due to prejudices informed by religion or culture. There is a general belief that there is a cause to everything that happens – good and bad. Consequently, any bad conditions are considered to be the result of an evil spirit and good things, the result of a good spirit. As Mangany and Buitendag note, "the reality of life for an African is that there is never a separation of physical from spiritual. To the traditional

African there is no coincidence or accident. Nothing happens by chance." (note 1) In addition to this, there is a dominant and unhelpful view that physical impairment is the consequence of sin, which is taught in some Christian churches. Negative narratives such as this are often connected to the interpretation of Scriptures such as Leviticus 21, which equates physical impairments with ceremonial uncleanness. Furthermore, persons with disabilities are often considered burdensome, due to the belief that they cannot contribute to the well-being of the community. These negative perceptions have contributed to stigma against people living with disabilities. This stigma has, in some instances, led to neglect and segregation. In other cases, persons with disabilities have been denied space to live their lives to the full.

In this chapter, I make a case for rethinking these views theologically and practically due to the conviction that a person living with a disability is just like any other human being, created in the image of God and deserving of dignity. Since all persons are God's creation, their inherent dignity cannot be removed in any way, no matter what form they are born in or what they have attained in their lives. As South African theologian Nico

---

1. Mangany and Buitendag, "Critical Analysis," 11.

Koopman points out, our dignity resides in the loving act of God, the Creator, who summons us into being and gives us life. Koopman further states that

> human dignity as a created dignity means that we receive our dignity from the creator. Our dignity is inalienable because it is given by the creator. It is inalienable because it does not come from humans, but it comes from the creator. It is inalienable because it is not dependent upon the recognition of dignity by the frail and unreliable hearts, minds and actions of humans, but it is dependent upon the living God. (note 2)

The main argument I put forward in this chapter is that reading the Bible closely with an African perspective of community in mind can assist in some way to deconstruct negative perceptions of and prejudices against people living with disabilities. Further, it can enable us to appreciate the wonderful art of God in every person, including people living with disabilities. This is because the Bible should be a tool of emancipation for everyone to see God at work in his creation, rather than a tool to demean God's work and creativity. This position is enhanced by the African view of life that accommodates every person

---

2. Koopman, "Men and Women," 20.

as a creation of God in diversity (**chilengedwe cha mulungu**), (note 3) regardless of one's looks, colour, form or shape.

In an African community, everyone is part of the community at all times of their existence. Furthermore, there is an understanding that all children of the community come from God and are a gift from God. This honoured gift of children is received as a gift for the community, despite the fact that children are born into particular families. In addition, there is a general understanding that no one can question God about the timing, nature and composition of a gift; it is just graciously received. The Creator (God) designs all persons differently and no one can argue with the Creator. In African communities God is generally described in relation to his attributes, and as "the One who originates things, builds, moulds, shapes, and constructs them, producing finished end

---

3. This is the Chewa language. Chewa is spoken in Malawi, Mozambique, Zimbabwe and Zambia. In Zambia, the Chewas are found in the Eastern Province of Zambia, though a variation of Chewa (Nyanja) is widely spoken in most parts of Zambia. This phrase is translated as "creation of God" or "God's creation."

products." (note 4) This view of humanity in African communities urges us to see that diversity is God's design for all his creation.

In this chapter, I first outline four perspectives on disability that are common in Africa. Following this, I discuss the importance of religion and Christianity in African communities. I also introduce an African perspective on community, outlining some of its key values and concepts. Finally, I make a case for the need to engage in a dialogue between the Bible and African perspectives of community in a quest to objectively address the misinterpretations and consequent negative perceptions held regarding disability in some African contexts today. (note 5)

Methodologically, the chapter undertakes a critical analysis of secondary documents on disability in an African context and the Bible in order to engage in a meaningful dialogue on disability. The literature is primarily drawn from Southern and East African experiences. However, there is also reference to literature from a wide biblical scholarship on the subject matter. The references to literature from Asia are due to the fact that Asia, like Africa, has also been wrestling with issues surrounding

---

4. Mbiti, **Concepts of God**, 93.
5. The perspective of this chapter is African and specifically from a Zambian context.

disability. The Association for Theological Education in Southeast Asia (ATESEA) has promoted this, and it interfaces with the Ecumenical Disability Advocates Network (EDAN), which is a project of the World Council of Churches (WCC) in which some African voices on disability have been given a forum.

African Perspectives on Disability

Disability is described in a number of ways in African communities. Four important perspectives will be introduced in this section. Although not the only views on disability in the context of Africa, they have been selected because they are important for the ensuing dialogue.

Disability as a Curse

Disability is often seen as a punishment from God or curse because of sin within the family. As Shiriko notes,

> In most African communities, there is a strong belief that nothing just happens. Everything is caused by a variable – whether figuratively, real or imagined. The belief in especially the forces of "our gods" and "unseen" has remained particularly very

strong. This belief system has been passed on from generation to generation and is firmly embedded in society. (note 6)

According to Kealotswe, there is a general belief in Botswana that the main reason for disability is that it is a curse from an angry ancestor. (note 7) For this reason, disability is generally viewed in a negative light, and this is well put by one African activist:

> In the majority of African Cultures, disability is viewed as a curse to the extent that the family within which a person with disability is born experience rejection in the community. Families with disabled people tend to hide the "source of their shame" from the eyes of the community from whom they seek acceptance. (note 8)

This is why, in the past, children born with a disability were abandoned or simply killed. However, despite the fact that today children who are born with a disability are not abandoned, the mindset that considers disability a curse persists. As Longchar points out, "a dominant

---

6. Shiriko, "Disability: Social Challenges," 170.
7. Kealotswe, "Attitudes towards Disability," 43.
8. Muigai, "Disability and Sexuality," 199.

Christian view of physical impairment is that it is the consequence of sin. Even today, the majority of Christians believe that it is the consequence of sin, punishment from God or a curse to the family." (note 9)

The curse narrative is so embedded in people's minds that persons with disability face exclusion from full participation in church and theological education. In some instances, they are abused by being subjected to inhumane actions in the name of healing. Amenyedzi rightly states that "if persons with disability are valued for who they are, the focus in these churches would not be on healing. . . . Efforts would rather be geared towards accessibility leading to inclusion and integration." (note 10) This is so because persons with disability are a creation of God in his own image (**imago Dei**). For this reason, as a community or church, we have no reason at all to deny them this God-given right and space.

It is important to emphasize that a number of biblical texts, within both the Old and the New Testament, do not support this negative view of disability. According to Hathaway and Kishekwa,

---

9. Longchar, "Culture, Sin, Suffering and Disability," 216.

10. Amenyedzi, "Disability and Healing," 3.

Jesus's emphatic response in John 9:3 is a clear indication that this view is misplaced: "'Neither this man nor his parents sinned,' said Jesus, 'but this happened so that the works of God might be displayed in him.'" (note 11) Hathaway and Kishekwa also note that the general perception that disability is a consequence of sin cannot be sustained since we all have sinned and were born in sin yet we do not all have a disability. For this reason, "theologically, it makes no sense to say that God sends a disability as a punishment in an arbitrary fashion." (note 12)

Disability as Inability

Disability can also be seen as an inability to perform certain tasks. The perception is that a person with a disability is unable to perform certain tasks that are basic for human survival in community, such as to fend for oneself or undertake specific tasks in relation to one's livelihood. There is a general perception that when a person is disabled, he or she has inadequacies with regard to making a meaningful living and contributing to the community. Writing in the context of Tanzania, Rutachwamagyo explains that

---

11. Hathaway and Kishekwa, **Included and Valued**, 66.
12. Hathaway and Kishekwa, 66.

people with disabilities in Tanzania tend to be viewed as "defective, infirm, invalid, unable, unfit and freakish." (note 13)

We need to also point out an observation made by Kealotswe concerning attitudes to disability in Botswana, namely, that in the past,

> able bodied people were important because they could work on the land and in cattle posts since subsistence farming required much manual labour. Thus, disabled people were not considered worthy members of the community. However, Botswana vision 2016 under the title **A Just and Caring Society** maintains that no persons should be disadvantaged because of disability or misfortune. (note 14)

Disability as a Gift from God

Although not a dominant societal perspective, there is a view that a disability is a gift of God and that any person born with a disability should be seen as a gift from God. This position is described in various ways in African folklore and idioms, and

---

13. Rutachwamagyo, "Profile of Tanzanians," 364.
14. Kealotswe, "Attitudes towards Disability," 50.

in the accounts of early anthropologists. (note 15) Ingstad's work in Botswana, for example, shows how claiming that a child was a gift from God was a way to avoid a stigmatizing label for a disability. Several children in her study sample who were born with visible disabilities had been given the name **mpho ya modima** (meaning "a gift from God"). This is in line with the Tswana tradition of giving children a name that is meaningful for the life situation they are born into. According to Ingstad's account, the Tswana god Modimo, and even the Christian counterpart carrying the same name, was associated with omnipotent power demonstrated by entrusting human beings with special challenges, such as a child with a disability. (note 16)

Many Africans believe that God gives gifts to people and God makes the choice, and as his creation, our role is to receive. This is the reasoning behind some of the names given to persons born with disability: **Talandila** (We have received), **Chakupa leza** (Given by God). These names seek to portray that a child is born in the

---

15. In a similar vein, Chisale notes that the dignity and inclusion of people with disabilities "was always promoted through folktales that were told to children" ("Purity Myth," 2).

16. Ingstad, "Mpho ya Modimo," 253.

community and is part of the community; this is why the whole community celebrates a birth and it is not only a family affair. A child born with a disability is also received as a "gift" to the community. This general acceptance in the community is due to the understanding that God gives different and unique gifts to various people, "since God is unique." (note 17) Furthermore, child-bearing is considered sacred, irrespective of whether the child has a disability or not.

Disability as Being Differently Abled

A fourth view is the general perception that all human beings are made by God, who has made people in various shapes and designs for reasons known only to God himself. Mbiti notes that the Nuer people believe that God is the one who creates humans: "it was God who created them, making some dark, and others pink, some fast in running, and others slow, some strong and others weak." (note 18) The reality is that one person may be able to do something which another person is not able to do. Everyone was created differently. This implies that while a person may be disabled, he or she may possess skills and abilities that are unique to him or her,

---

17. Idowu, **African Traditional Religion**, 153.
18. Mbiti, **Concepts of God**, 277.

thereby enabling that person to contribute in a unique manner to the community. In other words, disability is not necessarily lacking abilities. This is because everyone is moulded differently by the moulder (God): "According to the Lodagaa, God evidently created all mankind as a potter does his pots." (note 19) For this reason, it is argued that one is abled uniquely to function in the community. This is why, in most instances when disability is described in certain African communities, it is descriptive of the disability one has. For example, **wolemara manja** and **wolemera mendo** (note 20) imply that one has a disability in one area, but that does not necessarily mean one has an impairment in one's whole person. One can still function effectively without any impediment in other areas. Therefore, "disability" in African contexts does not relate only to physical aspects, but may refer to a number of things. It can also be used metaphorically, to refer to personality, abilities, and even failures.

---

19. Mbiti, 275.
20. **Wolemara manja** – a disability of the hand; **wolemara mendo** – a disability of the legs.

The Importance of Religion in African Communities

African communities are deeply religious. Religion is found in all areas of human life and the values and morals of individuals and communities are based on this religiousness. (note 21) There is belief in a creator God who made the earth and all that is in it, including humans. (note 22) This God, who is known by various names and attributes, instils values that regulate communities in order to imitate God's ideals. He made everything according to his likeness, and this entails that all humans are God's creation without any distinction or segregation. As a result, religion plays a significant role in shaping community values. In other words, religion is a vehicle through which culture is expressed. In his discussion of religion and culture in Ancient Israel, Dearman puts this view in perspective stating: "religion, therefore, is not just part of culture, but it is inseparable from it, providing symbols for the interpretation and legitimation of culture and also for its criticism. The two are symbiotically related, although a culture may be host to more than one religion with which it is intertwined." (note 23)

---

21. Mbiti, **Introduction**, 10.
22. Mbiti, **Concepts of God**, 105.
23. Dearman, **Religion and Culture**, 3.

An African Community Perspective

Mbiti, one of the most pronounced scholars on African religion, brings in a perspective worth noting in connection with notions of community:

> African religion functions more on a communal than an individual basis. For example, its beliefs are held by the community; therefore it does not matter much whether or not the individual accepts all these beliefs. The ceremonies are performed mainly in or by a group of the family, by relatives, by the whole population of one area or by those engaged in a common occupation. (note 24)

The religious nature of African communities compels people to adjust their culture and customs to their interpretation and application of the Bible in their context. An example from the Ngoni people in 1900 helps us to see the cultural adjustments that resulted from the influence of the Bible and Christianity. Christianity was introduced to the Ngoni people in 1900. (note 25) As with many African cultures, before the missionaries came the Ngoni people had their own

---

24. Mbiti, **Introduction**, 10.
25. Zulu, "Interpreting the Exodus," 365.

beliefs about God, **Unkulunkhulu**. (note 26) This God was the creator of everything and resided in heaven. To superintend the affairs of his people he worked through the ancestors as intermediaries. (note 27) Therefore, the ancestors needed to be venerated, but not worshipped. (note 28) To remind themselves about their origins and their God, the Ngoni people would pay homage to their God through the annual **N'cwala** ceremony, and this has continued to the present day. (note 29) Many Ngoni people converted to the Christian faith and it became

---

26. Since the Ngoni people of this region originated from Zululand in South Africa, this term has Zulu origins. It refers to God as a self-originating deity and is often used as a name of praise for God. The Zulu of South Africa also use the term **Mvelinqangi** to refer to God.

27. Zulu, **Ancestors, Religion and Worldviews**, 23–24.

28. We need to mention that there is a big debate in African biblical scholarship as to whether Africans worship or venerate their ancestors. We do not need to enter into that debate here, as it is not part of the scope of this chapter.

29. This is a ceremony that is commemorated every year in Zambia by the Ngoni people of Eastern Province. The Ngoni celebrate the first harvest as a blessing from God and celebrate

a vehicle through which the Ngoni of Zambia expressed their religious life. This is because their own religious ideals were able to accommodate Christian ideals, which consequently became part of their enlarged worldview. Today, the Bible remains significant and has influenced them in many aspects of their lives. It enhances their own views of God and the morality that God projects among them. We want to believe that just as has happened among the Ngoni people, a similar process has occurred in many other African communities today.

African Christianity and Community

African communities have been impacted and influenced by Christianity for a long time. Since communities are not static, this influence has over time resulted in the emergence of various blends of African Christianity with traditional beliefs. Yet just as Christianity has influenced African communities, the opposite is also true, and elements of African cultures have consciously or unconsciously influenced Christianity in Africa. One example of how African beliefs and ideals have been integrated into African blends of Christianity

---

their identity through dance and dress. This ritual ceremony is held on the last Saturday of February each year.

is the African view of humans as a creation of God who is considered to be a moulder. As pointed out by Mbiti, the idea of God moulding people into shapes blends well with the creation story in the book of Genesis 1:27 and 2:7. (note 30) In the Genesis story, we see how God created Adam and Eve from clay. This text also indicates that the Creator decided how one is created, male and female. This explains why the interpretation is well accepted among the African communities that have been influenced by Christianity.

Thus, diverse forms of African Christianity are growing rapidly and in dynamic ways, creating a complex African Christianity. As Galgalo states, "We have multiple appropriations of the gospel and numerous forms of faith expression that exist side by side." (note 31) Galgalo goes on to explain that "the plural nature of African Christianity cannot be overemphasized. The number of adherents grows by the day and so do the cults and diverse denominations that they follow." (note 32)

African Christianity is dynamic, complex and evolving. This is because any worldview can be enlarged through an encounter with other

---

30. Mbiti, **Introduction**, 84.
31. Galgalo, **African Christianity**, 81.
32. Galgalo, 82.

worldviews as time passes by, to such an extent that it grows and does not remain fixed: "This worldview is never static, it is dynamic, just as the society in which it is expressed is dynamic, always being enlarged in its encounter with other worldviews. It is a lifelong process, so to speak." (note 33) Thus, despite Christianity's influence for centuries among African communities, there are still African values that have remained and have been integrated into a blend of Christianity displayed in Africa.

An African Community Perspective

Many African communities are built around values that bind them together. An ideal community is one into which every individual is integrated without regard to any status or condition but simply because they are human. This is propelled by the view that human beings belong to each other in a unique way. As a result, it is considered honourable to ensure that everyone is included in the community, and shameful when people are excluded. In this section, we introduce an African perspective of community, outlining some of its important values and concepts: namely, communality, **ubuntu** and honour/shame.

---

33. Zulu, **Ancestors, Religion and Worldviews**, 7.

Communality, *Ubuntu* and Honour/Shame

African communities are often well-knit entities made up of ideals and values unique to each community. Everyone is connected to the others through lineage or kinship, and great importance is placed on this, as described by Thorpe: "Kinship is reckoned to be a result of both birth and marriage. It controls social relationships between people, governs marital customs and regulations and determines acceptable interpersonal behaviour." (note 34)

As a result, there is an inherent solidarity and unity created through this connection. Consequently, no one lives as an individual; the community becomes the arena for human interactions, individual growth and prosperity, supported by community members. (note 35) Due to this well-knit connection, there is communality in which all members of the community work for the common good and live in solidarity.

There is nothing that expresses these ideals better than the concept of **ubuntu. Ubuntu** is an African philosophy that places emphasis on "being human through other people." It has been succinctly reflected in the phrase, "I am because

---

34. Thorpe, **African Traditional Religions**, 110.
35. Thorpe, 110.

of who we all are." (note 36) This implies that "you cannot live a life of your own; you need other people who will help you to live life to the fullest." (note 37) A community celebrates life together, in bad times as well as in good times. In other words, whatever happens in the community, including disability, affects all – "your pain is my pain." (note 38) As Sinenhlanhla Chisale explains, "Africans defend their communality through the ethic of **ubuntu** by which everyone and everything is seen to be interconnected, interdependent and integrated." (note 39)

African community values and ideals are impacted, both positively and negatively, by the notion of **honour and shame.** This view is perpetuated by the understanding that each society has morals and ideals that are expected to be kept by the individuals, families, clans and tribes that are part of that community. **Honour** is a claim to worth that is publicly acknowledged by the community; therefore to be honoured is to be ascribed value. (note 40) **Shame** is more than the opposite

---

36. Mugumbate and Nyanguru, "Exploring African Philosophy," 83.
37. Masango, "African Spirituality," 76.
38. Masango, 76.
39. Chisale, "Purity Myth," 6.
40. Zulu, **Ancestors, Religion and Worldviews**, 11.

of **honour.** It alludes to unacceptable behaviour that creates or points to an image that should not be present in the society. (note 41)

It is important to note that honour and shame are relative concepts that have been applied differently in various contexts around the world. In his influential book **The New Testament World: Insights from Cultural Anthropology**, Bruce Malina provides extensive insights on these concepts, discussing them predominantly in the context of the New Testament world. In the context of Africa specifically, the notion of honour and shame relates to the pressure on individuals to always strive to leave behind a good legacy, holding onto community values that will not bring individuals and those connected with them into ridicule.

Alignment or categorization of individuals, families, clans or tribes with shame or honour can be passed from one generation to the next. A family that brings honour to the community will always be held in high regard. This echoes Oduyoye, who states, "The concept of individual success or failure is secondary." (note 42) The argument here is that there is a recognition that individual life is lived in a community where one is expected to

---

41. Zulu, 11.
42. Oduyoye, "African Religious Beliefs," 110.

express oneself as a community member. (note 43) A community has support systems to enhance and give space for individual progress.

Therefore, in upholding the above community values and ideals, every person born within the community, in whatever form that person presents him- or herself, is accommodated, embraced and fully supported by the community structures. In view of the above, it is expected that persons with disabilities would be embraced and motivated to live their lives as they please without any hindrance from others.

A Dialogue between the Bible and African Perspectives on Disability

The previous sections have examined four perspectives on disability (disability as curse, disability as inability, disability as a gift from God and disability as being differently abled), looked at the importance of religion in African communities, and outlined an African community perspective. Given the great influence of Christianity on African life whereby some Christian teachings and practices have been adapted to the local cultures (inculturation), it is crucial to understand the interpretation of Christian values in context, since every religion or belief is expressed in the culture

---

43. Oduyoye, 110.

in which it exists, as argued above. This process of inculturation has continued to influence the faith in Africa and cannot be ignored in any process of theologizing on the continent.

In view of the above, disability cannot in any way remove someone from the realm of God and the community. All of God's creation exists by God's design, and therefore humans should not erect barriers that prevent those living with disabilities from belonging and having space in the community. We all belong to God and to community as his creation, made according to his plans. A community is composed of all of God's diverse creation, united by their shared humanity, and the fact that they are created in the image of God irrespective of how they are formed. This is emphasized in both African Traditional Religion and Christianity, both of which influence African community life. Therefore, any segregation and exclusion of human beings, such as persons with disabilities, violates the intentions and fabric of the community. God alone has decided how each person should be made. This variety and diversity strengthens our community. We become one body and we need each other. We are actually one body with all functional parts contributing to the whole. This gives us a number of bases and avenues in which a dialogue between the Bible and disability can be anchored.

Spirituality and Religion

African perspectives need to be situated on the premise of spirituality and religiousness, since everything is religious from birth to death. There is nothing that does not fit into this sphere. This is why even child-bearing is sacred, as alluded to above. Religiousness is what knits the community together and is that from which values are derived. Consequently, spirituality is developed and expressed based on this religiousness.

At personal and communal levels, Africans adhere to a spiritual relationship with a God who influences people's views and perceptions of humans. Humans are held in high esteem due to the fact that they are a creation of God. Human life is sacred and needs to be appreciated as such. Whoever you are, you have come from God.

The Bible, on the other hand, describes a God who is sovereign, reigns and sets values according to which religious communities operate. In the two perspectives, humans are dignified by giving them space to express their humanity without any distraction. The apostle Paul summarizes it emphatically in Romans 2:11, when he points out that "God does not show favouritism." There cannot be segregation of any kind since all human beings, including persons with disabilities, form part of this religiousness and connectedness with the sacred.

Creator and Creation

Belief in the Creator who has brought everything into being and is in control can be another basis for this dialogue. God determines who is born, how one is born and the form one is born in. Mbiti points out that among the Akamba tribe one of the names of God is **Mwatuagi**, the one who determines the shape or design of his creations in detail:

> God is the Giver of details to creation. He makes the hand and cleaves it to give fingers: he cleaves the trees, giving those branches and leaves: he cleaves the land, giving it valleys and hills. God continues his activities of creation and the giving of detailed shapes. That means he is constantly creating in detail and reshaping what he creates or has created. God has set creation in a colossal movement. (note 44)

This is reminiscent of Genesis 1:26–27:

---

44. Mbiti, **Concepts of God**, 92.

> Then God said, "Let us make mankind in our image, in our likeness, so that they may rule over the fish in the sea and the birds in the sky, over the livestock and all the wild animals, and over all the creatures that move along the ground."
>
> So God created mankind in his own image,
> in the image of God he created them;
> male and female he created them.

The image of God in humans is from God, the Creator, and cannot be removed from us. (note 45) In addition, we are created in diversity, and we need to celebrate this reality. This is expressed well in Psalm 139:13–14: "You created my inmost being; you knit me together in my mother's womb. I praise you because I am fearfully and wonderfully made; your works are wonderful, I know that full well."

Therefore, as we view persons with disability in the African context where Christianity is anchored and has impact,

> the Church proposes human dignity as originating from being alive – which is a universal gift, arising not solely out of reason, but out of our belief and from the

---

45. Ssekabira, "Life with Dignity," 86.

Scripture that humans are created in the image of God (Gen. 1:27) and so humans are sacred. The respect due to each other is thus independent of our circumstances. It is intrinsic. (note 46)

We express love and care for everyone because of the dignity and sacredness imparted to all of us by God's own design. Therefore, we agree with the perspective that upholds dignity as a core value of humanity. This is also expressed in the African Charter on Human and Peoples' Rights and the Universal Declaration of Human Rights, to which many African nations have assented. (note 47)

Community and Communality

African community is based on the value of communality. All persons in an African community coexist; one is part of the larger group and this connectedness is complex. There are various concepts that are advocated to emphasize this reality. **Ubuntu**, as alluded to above, points to the fact that no one is alone and lives for him- or herself. Everyone is part of this larger community with all its support structures. This is why the joy or sorrow of the other is mine. As a result, persons

---

46. Ssekabira, 86.
47. Organization of African Unity, "African Charter."

with disabilities are part of this community and they have a stake in all its aspirations.

Similar principles are projected in the Bible. It is clear that we all belong to one family and we need to live as such. (note 48) Even one who is not part of the community is welcome: "God had a particular concern that those in community whose social and economic status was not secure should receive just and proper treatment." (note 49)

Christopher Wright further argues that "the ways of Yahweh in [Deuteronomy 10:14–19] begin with the condescending love for the ancestors of Israel and climax in practical love for the strangers in Israel, the aliens. In between these two all-embracing dimensions of Yahweh's love are sandwiched impartiality, integrity, and commitment to justice." (note 50)

It is unacceptable that persons with disabilities have been subjected to a number of injustices in their communities, such as those noted by Okola: "Employment opportunities for [people with disabilities] in developing countries are most

---

48. Ps 100:3; Isa 43:1.
49. Craigie, **Deuteronomy**, 206. See also Lev 19:14; Deut 27:18–19; Luke 14:12–14.
50. Wright, **Deuteronomy**, 150.

often almost non-existent. Consequently, many [people with disabilities] have to beg for a living whereas, in fact, employment is the only way out of a lifelong exclusion." (note 51) It is common for people with disabilities to be excluded from economic activities.

Compassion and Mercy

African perspectives on community and humanity also teach us about the need to show mercy to others in whatever situations they find themselves. This is not about expressing pity for persons with disabilities, but rather accompanying them so as to lighten their burden as part of the larger community. In other words, we need to give persons living with disabilities a space in which to operate and enjoy their humanity to the full.

The Bible points to a similar position: God's people, Israel, are instructed to show mercy since God has shown mercy to them (Exod 34:6; Isa 63:7; Lam 3:22; Luke 6:36; 1 Pet 3:8; Rom 5:6–9). As Wright rationalizes, "God is love, so to walk in God's way will entail the exercise and practice of love." (note 52)

---

51. Okola, "Education, Employment, and Health," 147.
52. Wright, **Deuteronomy**, 150.

In view of the above, we have a basis on which dialogue with people living with disabilities can be anchored with the purpose of enabling them to have the freedom to enjoy their diversity and have their own space unhindered by bias or discrimination.

Advocacy: Community Values and Ideals in Action

Advocacy in the Bible: A Call to Action

The Bible urges us to stand up for the underprivileged and speak up for the voiceless. There are many examples in the Bible of this stance. One of the best known is 2 Samuel 9:1–13. In this text, we are told how King David showed mercy in an extraordinary manner to Mephibosheth, a person who was lame in both feet (2 Sam 9:3). Given his situation and the position of the society on disability at that time, Mephibosheth was despised (Lev 21:16–23). However, King David did the unexpected by restoring the land that had been confiscated from the family and giving Mephibosheth a place of honour in the king's house. He ensured that Mephibosheth was cared for by making one of his grandfather's servants, Ziba, farm and bring crops to him. This action was unique, restoring Mephibosheth's self-esteem and identity, and ensuring his full reintegration into the community.

We must also discuss one notable matter that needs to be addressed: the issue of stigma and stereotypes in connection with disability. Writing on the book of Job, Claassens highlights that the book demonstrates some stereotypes regarding disability: "one repeatedly finds the notion that disability or disease is the direct consequence of sin." (note 53)

It is imperative for us to completely deconstruct this view and advocate for a hermeneutic of disability. This is an interpretation that recognizes that the narratives on disability were written in different sociocultural and political frameworks. (note 54) For this reason, such texts need to be interpreted for our contemporary times that have a different and positive narrative on disability. Such an interpretation would be devoid of stereotypes and stigma. Actually, all humans are only temporarily able-bodied, and at any moment one could find oneself living with disability, as is evidenced in the book of Job. (note 55)

Further, the Old Testament is full of commands for us to promote justice: "Learn to do right; seek justice. Defend the oppressed. Take up the cause

---

53. Claassens, "Countering Stereotypes," 173.
54. Reynolds, **Vulnerable Communion**, 34–35.
55. Claassens, "Countering Stereotypes," 178.

of the fatherless; plead the case of the widow" (Isa 1:17). Further, Proverbs 31:8–9 says: "Speak up for those who cannot speak for themselves, for the rights of all who are destitute. Speak up and judge fairly; defend the rights of the poor and needy."

The New Testament echoes the need to take action: "If anyone has material possessions and sees a brother or sister in need but has no pity on them, how can the love of God be in that person? Dear children, let us not love with words or speech but with actions and in truth" (1 John 3:17–18).

Despite some Old Testament texts that are more difficult to interpret and that have been used to form views on the origin of disability, God is described as a God of compassion and mercy who desires that all people will receive justice in all aspects of their lives: "This is what the LORD Almighty says: 'Administer true justice; show mercy and compassion to one another. Do not oppress the widow or the fatherless, the foreigner or the poor. Do not plot evil against each other" (Zech 7:9–10).

Advocacy in Church and Community Today

Despite the biblical call for action, the church and wider society are sometimes associated with complacency, and persons with disabilities have often been neglected and unsupported. The concerns of persons with disabilities can end up in policies and guidelines that are forgotten as soon as they are finalized. In addition, while many organizations have been created to deal with matters that relate to disability, these efforts often do not have a genuine impact. It is time that we revisit the issues relating to persons with disabilities in another way. We need to revisit the rich African community values and ideals, and anchor the discourse on disability there for it to make a significant impact on our response to the challenges facing persons with disabilities.

Reflecting on the dialogue between an African community perspective and the Bible, we see it is important to speak out against the stigma and segregation of persons living with disabilities. We should deny any efforts, systems and policies that dehumanize the dignity of persons with disabilities. African communities have always stood for community values that uphold the dignity of all human beings, irrespective of their circumstances. That is why if a person could not uphold the values of a community that had respect for all its members, that person would be punished in some way. For example, if an individual ill-treated a disabled person, the community would reprimand that individual and, in extreme circumstances, would banish the perpetrator from the community.

Consequently, it was the personal responsibility of every member to contribute by helping to uphold the community's values and ideals.

Advocacy also entails that we launch proactive awareness-raising at the community level to bring awareness on various protocols and documentation around the issues of disability. Apart from the Universal Declaration of Human Rights, the African Charter on Human and Peoples' Rights, and the UN Convention on the Rights of Persons with Disabilities, there are a number of helpful organizations that have been formed to bring solidarity to persons with disabilities. The Ecumenical Disability Advocates Network (EDAN), a project of the World Council of Churches (WCC), is one such organization. These can inform and frame our interventions, as people with disabilities will indicate their needs and the space they need in order to enjoy, like others, life in all its fullness.

We also need to point out something that is often overlooked and which has always been advocated by people with disabilities, namely, that in addition to the advocacy promoted by others, people with disabilities themselves need to determine their course by strengthening their own organizations and advocacy strategies. It is imperative that we give them room and space to realize that. This is well summarized by Kabue, who is a thought leader in this area:

Self-advocacy is a major concern of disability rights movements in an attempt to achieve the goal of attaining a dignified life in the community. To achieve this, much work will be needed particularly for persons with disabilities to get themselves out of the low status to which the society has relegated them. It will be necessary to make all the necessary attempts to have persons with disabilities integrated in all aspects of church's and community's spiritual, social and economic development activities. (note 56)

Conclusion

The issue of disability raises diverse views. These views are based on different perspectives on disability prevalent in African communities. In some instances, disability is seen in a negative light as the consequence of sin or a curse, or as inability, whereas in other instances, disability is seen as a gift from God, or as being differently abled. Negative perspectives are often encouraged by particular interpretations of biblical texts that depict disability in a bad light. However, having examined an African community perspective, it is evident that negative perspectives on disability

---

56. Kabue, "Church and Society's Response," 149.

can be re-examined and analysed in a new light, especially when we engage in a meaningful dialogue with the Bible. This dialogue is critical due to the great influence and impact of Christianity and the Bible on African communities' values, and similarities in religious ideals or beliefs that uphold human dignity as a creation of God.

This contribution has highlighted four positions on the matter of disability. First, disability has always been associated with a number of unhelpful perceptions due to a number of myths and inaccurate understandings of disability. This position has been amplified by a traditional reading of some biblical texts and African cultural perspectives. This chapter calls for a deconstruction of these perceptions.

Second, people living with disability are created by God and in his image. This image of God is never erased by any disability. In addition, God created everyone uniquely; therefore we need to celebrate this diversity and create space for everyone in our communities.

Third, there is a need to read the Bible with a liberating mindset to enable people to appreciate the wonderful nature of God's diverse creation. This could enable people to view disability in another light.

Fourth, African perspectives on disability and creation accommodate everyone based on religiousness and community-oriented values supported by the concept of **ubuntu.** This can be a basis for dialogue between the Bible and African perspectives to move towards greater celebration of diversity in God's creation.

Therefore, we have argued in this chapter that re-examining disability from an African perspective informed by community values can assist in some way to deconstruct negative perceptions and prejudices against people living with disabilities. We have emphasized that persons with disability are human beings and have been created in God's own image (see also chapter 6 for more on **imago Dei**). The position that persons with disability find themselves in is dependent on the Creator and has nothing to do with their own or their parents' deeds.

We have urged that a dialogue between the Bible and African perspectives on humanity and community be conducted. This dialogue would assist in changing perceptions regarding persons with disability to move towards greater acceptance and inclusion. This is so because in African communities all persons coexist and are given space to fully exercise their rights and live their own lives with justice. For this reason, stigmatization, segregation and exclusion cannot be part of our communities today. As Christians, we should exercise compassion and mercy as part of our identity, and we need to do so without any distinction. In addition, this needs to form a basis for our advocacy. The general community and the church are called upon to "raise their voices" for justice and the inclusion and participation of people living with disabilities in our communities.

Bibliography

Amenyedzi, Seyram B. "Disability and Healing: Healing Trends in Ghana." 2018. https://www.researchgate.net/publication/322819203_Disability_and_Healing_Healing_trends_in_Ghana.

Chaplin, Kevin. "The Ubuntu Spirit in African Communities." 2015. https://www.readkong.com/page/the-ubuntu-spirit-in-african-communities-7058625.

Chisale, Sinenhlanhla. "The Purity Myth: A Feminist Disability Theology of Women's Sexuality and Implications for Pastoral Care." **Scriptura: Journal for Biblical, Theological and Contextual Hermeneutics** 119, no. 1 (2020): 1–11.

Christaini, Tabita K. "Persons with Disabilities in Indonesia." In **Doing Theology from a Disability Perspective**, edited by Wati Longchar and Gordon Cowans, 1–12. Manila: Association for Theological Education in South East Asia (ATESEA), 2011.

Claassens, L. Juliana M. "Countering Stereotypes: Job, Disability and Human Dignity." **Journal of Religion, Disability & Health** 17, no. 2 (2013): 169–83.

Craigie, Peter C. **The Book of Deuteronomy.** Grand Rapids: Eerdmans, 1996.

Dearman, John Andrew. **Religion and Culture in Ancient Israel.** Peabody: Hendrickson, 1992.

Eiesland, Nancy. **The Disabled God: Toward a Liberation Theology of Disability**. Nashville: Abingdon, 1994.

Galgalo, Joseph D. **African Christianity: The Stranger Within**. Limuru: Zapf Chancery Publishers Africa, 2012.

Hathaway, Bridget, and Flavian Kishekwa. **Included and Valued: A Practical Theology of Disability**. Carlisle: Langham Global Library, 2019.

Idowu, E. Bojaji. **African Traditional Religion: A Definition**. London: SCM, 1973.

Ingstad, Benedicte. "Mpho ya Modimo – A Gift from God: Perspectives on 'Attitudes' Toward Disabled Persons." In **Disability and Culture**, edited by Benedicte Ingstad and Susan R. Whyte, 246–63. Berkeley: University of California Press, 1995.

Kabue, Samuel. "Church and Society's Response to Disability: Historical and Sociological Perspective." In **Doing Theology from a Disability Perspective**, edited by Wati Longchar and

Gordon Cowans, 141–57. Manila: Association for Theological Education in South East Asia (ATESEA), 2011.

Kealotswe, Obed N. "Attitudes towards Disability in Botswana: A Critical Appraisal." In **Disability in Africa: Resource Book of Theology and Religious Studies**, edited by Samuel Kabue, James Amanze and Christina Landman, 42–56. Nairobi: Acton, 2016.

Koopman, Nico. "Men and Women in Church and Society: Equality in Dignity? United Diversity." In **Living with Dignity: African Perspectives on Gender Equality**, edited by Elna Mouton, Gertrude Kapuma, Len Hensen and Thomas Togom, 19–32. Stellenbosch: Sun Media, 2015.

Longchar, Wati. "Culture, Sin, Suffering and Disability in Society." In **Doing Theology from a Disability Perspective**, edited by Wati Longchar and Gordon Cowans, 211–25. Manila: Association for Theological Education in South East Asia (ATESEA), 2011.

Malina, Bruce J. **The New Testament World: Insights from Cultural Anthropology.** Rev. ed. Louisville: Westminster/John Knox, 1993.

Mangany, Jele S., and Johan Buitendag. "A Critical Analysis on African Traditional Religion and the Trinity." **HTS Theological Studies** 69, no. 1 (2013): 1–13.

Masango, Maake J. S. "African Spirituality and Human Dignity." In **African Christian Theology: Focus on Human Dignity**, edited by All Africa Conference of Churches, 62–83. Nairobi: Acton, 2018.

Mbiti, John S. **Concepts of God in Africa.** 2nd ed. Nairobi: Acton, 2012.

———. **Introduction to African Religion.** 2nd ed. Nairobi: East African Educational, 2000.

Mugumbate, J., and A. Nyanguru. "Exploring African Philosophy: The Value of Ubuntu in Social Work." **African Journal of Social Work** 3, no. 1 (2013): 82–100.

Muigai, Salome Wairimu. "Disability and Sexuality." In **Disability, Society, and Theology: Voices from Africa**, edited by Samuel Kabue, Esther Mombo, Joseph Galgalo and C. B. Peter, 199–208. Limuru: Zapf Chancery Publishers Africa, 2011.

Oduyoye, Mercy Amba. "The Value of African Religious Beliefs and Practices for Christian Theology." In **Africa Theology en Route**, edited by Kofi Appiah-Kubi and Sergio Torres, 109–16. Maryknoll: Orbis, 1979.

Okola, Anjeline. "Education, Employment, and Health: A Disability Perspective." In **Disability, Society, and Theology: Voices from Africa**, edited by Samuel Kabue, Esther Mombo, Joseph Galgalo and C. B. Peter, 141–56. Limuru: Zapf Chancery Publishers Africa, 2011.

Organization of African Unity. "African Charter on Human and Peoples' Rights." 1981. https://au.int/sites/default/files/treaties/36390-treaty-0011_-_african_charter_on_human_and_peoples_rights_e.pdf.

Reynolds, Thomas E. **Vulnerable Communion: A Theology of Disability and Hospitality**. Grand Rapids: Brazos, 2008.

Rutachwamagyo, Kaganzi. "A Profile of Tanzanians with Disabilities." In **Disability, Society, and Theology: Voices from Africa**, edited by Samuel Kabue, Esther Mombo, Joseph Galgalo and C. B. Peter, 363–82. Limuru: Zapf Chancery Publishers Africa, 2011.

Shiriko, Joseph. "Disability: Social Challenges and Family Responses." In **Disability, Society, and Theology: Voices from Africa**, edited by Samuel Kabue, Esther Mombo, Joseph Galgalo and C. B. Peter, 170–96. Limuru: Zapf Chancery Publishers Africa, 2011.

Ssekabira, Vincent Kigozi. "Life with Dignity from a Biblical Perspective of Divine Creation." In **African Christian Theology: Focus on Human Dignity**, edited by All Africa Conference of Churches, 84–108. Nairobi: Acton, 2018.

Thorpe, Shirley A. **African Traditional Religions: An Introduction**. Pretoria: University of South Africa, 1991.

United Nations. "Universal Declaration of Human Rights." 1948. https://www.un.org/en/udhrbook/pdf/udhr_booklet_en_web.pdf.

Wright, Christopher J. **Deuteronomy**. Peabody: Hendrickson, 1996.

Zulu, Edwin. **Ancestors, Religion and Worldviews in Genesis 11:28 – 50:1–26.** Beau Bassin: Lap Lambert Academic, 2019.

———. "Interpreting the Exodus among the Ngoni people." **Scriptura** 108 (2011): 365–80.

———. "Possibilities and Constraints of Introducing Disability Discourse in Theological Schools in Southern Africa: A Case for Zambia." In **Christian Identity and Justice in a Globalised World from a Southern African Perspective**, edited by Herman Kroesbergen, 248–56. Wellington: Christian Literature Fund, 2014.

———. "'Watipa Leza': A Critical Re-engagement of Nsenga (African) Religious Values and Disabilities." **Journal of Disability & Religion** 20, no. 1–2 (2016): 84–92.

6

Being Different

Imago Dei in Light of Disability in Africa – Reflections from Kenya

David Tarus

Introduction

This chapter examines the precious doctrine of the image of God as a theological basis for defending, supporting and advocating for people with disabilities, not as projects for our charitable causes or as people we should feel sorry for, but as full human beings who should be treated as such. The chapter begins by recounting a personal experience of disability in my family. My grandmother's story depicts the African church and society's incompetence to serve and treat people with disabilities with the honour due to them. The narrative calls us to rethink how we engage with people with disabilities. It calls us as the body of Christ to live differently; we need to embody a different ethic and practice in how we treat people with disabilities. Further, the chapter examines the doctrine of the image of God by looking at three prominent perspectives and their implications for treatment of people with disabilities. I propose that a relational understanding of the image of God centred on communion with God and on the Christ as God's image and one who enables us to be human as God intended, has better prospects for aiding the church's desire to be with and to minister to people with disabilities. A relational understanding of the image of God coheres with the African ethic of communion, **ubuntu**, the idea that we are all tied up as humanity. When one member of the community suffers, we all suffer. The chapter ends by challenging us to embrace an ethic that actually promotes a more just environment for people with disabilities in Africa. The overall gist of this chapter is that a proper understanding of the image of God liberates people with disabilities to realize their full potential in Africa.

Closer to Home

My grandmother lived with a mental illness. She was free from the disability at birth but contracted cerebral malaria when my father was seventeen years old. The disease permanently damaged my grandmother's brain and left her with adverse effects, such as mood swings and behavioural difficulties, including occasional defiance and violence. Nevertheless, despite the unpleasant reminders of her disease, my grandmother remained, overall, a lovely lady. Yet many, seeing only her erratic behaviour, avoided associating with her. Tragically, it was beyond her capacity to deal with her condition and she longed for conversation and the settling impact of human interaction. She yearned for the normalcy of life, which the disease had robbed her of by irrevocably damaging her neurological faculties and disabling consistent control of her personality.

My grandmother's violent outbursts, as well as misunderstanding of her condition by others, consigned her to live alone, not too far from my childhood home. As the firstborn of her son, I was the only one she accepted into her house. In her home she cooked for me and told me many stories, albeit sometimes incoherently to this then young teenage boy who lacked insight into the workings of mental health. Sometimes she would ask me to pray, and other times she never wanted to hear anything about God. Yet many times, she would simply sing and smile. This was what brought me the most joy and led me to regard her as a uniquely beautiful woman.

My family's effort to treat her condition could not prevent the deterioration of my grandmother's health and she died in 1995. Her death impacted me greatly in many ways. Having grown to accept her and love her, I missed her deeply. Mystifying questions persisted in my mind. For example, why would God allow the undeserved suffering of my family? Why would God allow his servant, my dad, to experience such anguish concerning his mother? Why would God allow my grandmother to suffer such pain?

Furthermore, the church where my father served as a teaching elder was not equipped to care for my grandmother in her condition. In fact, I do not remember ever seeing my grandmother in church. The local community also lacked the necessary understanding to care for her special needs. Instead, she was largely and practically considered a nuisance. Some people attributed some form of wrongdoing to our family. Perhaps a curse needed to be dealt with? Perhaps a sin in our family had led to the misfortune? Distressingly, I realized that many people, even Christians, were not treating my grandmother as a human being made fully in the image of God. I grew up knowing that all human beings were created in God's image. Yet I wondered whether my grandmother was also created in God's image. Did she bear God's image like other human beings? Was she subhuman because she was disabled? It was this reality that pushed me to question what it means to be human in Africa.

My grandmother's story is not unique. There are millions of people living with disabilities in Africa who suffer every day with discrimination, stigmatization and abuse. They feel isolated and rejected. They yearn for recognition. They desire normalcy but they do not get it on a continent that is greatly prejudiced against people with disabilities. They yearn to be fully respected as human beings, and not as problems to be endured or as candidates for social welfare programmes. They desire to be fully embraced by their communities, but they may never experience such an embrace. They long for opportunities to serve God and humanity, but they may never get such opportunities. Considering such realities, it is essential for people to appreciate, apprehend and appropriate a correct understanding of the **imago Dei**.

The Image of God in Historical Context

The affirmation that all human beings are created in the image and likeness of God is an important Christian doctrine. This doctrine, also called the doctrine of the image of God, or **imago**

Dei, has received a lot of attention in Christian theological and biblical scholarship because of its anthropological and ethical significance. For example, many theologians have used it to advance ideas concerning the dignity and sacredness of human life. (note 1) Other topics discussed include the exact meaning of the two words "image" and "likeness," whether there is a distinction between them, and if so, the implications of this; the location of the image of God in humanity; the effects of sin on the image of God; the relationship between the image of God and the image of Christ; the restoration of the image of God in Christians; the significance of the doctrine of the image of God on various issues of life; and the image of God in light of disability. (note 2) The main goal of this chapter is not to delve into the various controversies or views on this important doctrine; rather, I show how it can be used to help build acceptance and honour of people with disabilities in Africa. More specifically, I argue that greater emphasis on a relational understanding of the image of God, especially one centred on Christ as the enabler of an alternative existence,

---

1. Beates, **Disability and the Gospel**, 27, 76–82, 88–124; Cairns, **Image of God**, 16, 248; Gushee, **Sacredness of Human Life**, 39–54; Kilner, **Dignity and Destiny**, 4–17; Middleton, **Liberating Image**, 16.
2. Middleton, **Liberating Image**, 16.

has the potential to positively impact the way in which the church in Africa engages with people with disabilities.

The Image of God in the Bible

The doctrine of the image of God rests upon ample scriptural warrant and accordingly forms the centrepiece of a proper view of all members of humanity. (note 3) The Old Testament includes three explicit references to **imago Dei**, uniting the key terms "image" (**tselem**) and "likeness" (**demut**). Genesis 1:26–27 states the divine intention for humanity:

> Then God said, "Let us make mankind in our image, in our likeness, so that they may rule over the fish in the sea and the birds in the sky, over the livestock and all the wild animals, and over all the creatures that move along the ground."

---

3. As Dyrness notes in the **Global Dictionary of Theology**, although there are few explicit references in the Old Testament, canonical arrangement is significant and the place of Genesis 1:26–27 "as the supreme creational word (with the repetition and the divine deliberation, 'let us make') in the opening chapter determines the way the whole Scripture is to be read" (Dyrness, "Anthropology, Theological," 43).

> So God created mankind in his own image,
> in the image of God he created them;
> male and female he created them.

Genesis 5:1 links with Genesis 1:26–27 and asserts that the divine intention for humanity is propagated to the first human descendants and all subsequent generations. Genesis 9:6 roots the sanctity of human life in the image of God in humanity and implicitly maintains that the image of God extends even to depraved humanity: "Whoever sheds human blood, by humans shall their blood be shed; for in the image of God has God made mankind." In addition to these three references in the Old Testament, Psalm 8:4–6 alludes to the ruling function associated with the image of God and celebrates humanity's most significant place in God's creation.

The New Testament presents numerous direct references to the image of God in various theological contexts. Human beings are created in God's image (1 Cor 11:7; Jas 3:9); Jesus Christ is the image of God (2 Cor 4:4; Col 1:15; Heb 1:3); and believers experience a restoration of the image of God through new life in Christ (Rom 8:29; 1 Cor 15:49; 2 Cor 3:18; Eph 4:22–24; Phil 3:21; Col

3:10). (note 4) In addition, the Apocryphal writings affirm the creation of people in God's image (Wisdom 2:23–24 and Sirach 17:1–12).

The next section explores various approaches to understanding the doctrine of the image of God that have been prominent within theological and biblical studies in the Global North. These approaches are the substantial view, the functional view and the relational view. Considering that African theological anthropology prefers communion over individuality, I see the relational view as having the potential to significantly impact the treatment of people with disabilities in Africa.

Three Perspectives on the Image of God in Light of Disability
The Substantial View

The substantial view finds qualities inherent in human nature as that which constitutes the essence of the image of God. Many proponents specify humanity's intellectual capacity as the main substance of the image of God. (note 5) In addition to intellect, advocates of the substantive view identify additional non-material substances

---

4. Middleton, "Image of God," 516–23.
5. Cairns, **Image of God**, 110; Ramsey, **Basic Christian Ethics**, 250.

such as conscience, aesthetic sense, self-determination, immortality, freedom and moral capacity as constituting the **imago Dei**.

While acknowledging the value of the substantial view, this chapter draws attention to its limitations. Foremost among these is that Scripture does not limit the image of God to cognitive substances. The emphasis on the mind as the centrepiece of the image of God diminishes the significance of the physical body. The human body, even in its brokenness, is beautifully created and reflects the wonder of God's creation. The New Testament affirms the beauty of the human body. Jesus's life and ministry provides hope to the many disenfranchised people on earth. His suffering on the cross and subsequent resurrection in a scarred body affirms the body, even in its brokenness.

Another limitation of the substantial view is that it fosters an individualist notion of life by emphasizing only the endowments of an individual person. Yet Genesis 1:26–27, 5:1–3 and 9:6 unfold not only individual but also corporate dimensions of the image of God. The image of God is construed as "male and female" (Gen 1:26–27), native to all human descendants (5:1–3), and that which is the reason for protecting all human beings from harm (9:6), thus suggesting a corporate orientation rather than an individualistic one. Humanity images God in dynamic relationships.

An overemphasis on the individual image bearer may compromise the dignity of the whole human race because of preferential treatment of certain individuals deemed to bear God's image more than others. If human beings bear the image of God only through substantial attributes, then what implications does this have for someone like my grandmother who suffered from mental illness?

The tendency to view the image of God in terms of innate attributes alone allows room for the justification of mistreatment of people deemed to lack those attributes. John Kilner succinctly summarizes the dangers of such a notion:

> That understanding logically invited the conclusion that some people can be more in God's image than others and so warrant greater respect and protection. What resulted in Nazi Germany were categories of people who were **untermenschen** (subhuman), those in whom the attributes that constituted God's image were most deformed, marred, distorted, etc. They became the targets of Nazi efforts, first to eliminate people with disabilities or other frailties through neglect, forced

sterilization, or killing. Later, the focus turned to exterminating gypsies and Jews. (note 6)

In terms of affirming the place of those with disability, the substantive view falls short of providing a firm rubric that protects people with disabilities.

The Functional View

A second view focuses on the God-given mandate of dominion and responsibility over creation. Its roots can be traced to the Antiochene fathers such as Diodore of Tarsus, John Chrysostom, Theodore of Mopsuestia, Nestorius and Theodoret. (note 7) Richard Middleton, a key proponent of this view, asserts that to act as the image of God is to serve as "God's representatives and agents in the world, granted authorized power to share in God's rule or administration of the earth's resources and creatures." (note 8) To image God is to faithfully exercise the God-given responsibility of nurturing, protecting and tending God's creation.

---

6. Kilner, **Dignity and Destiny**, 21.
7. McLeod, **Image of God**, 236; Middleton, **Liberating Image**, 24–29.
8. Middleton, 27.

The functional view appeals to two lines of support. First, it is rooted in historical-biblical scholarship. Biblical scholars juxtapose "in our image" and "let them rule" in Genesis 1:26 to assert that the phrase "let them rule" should define "in our image." (note 9) Hence to image God is to exercise dominion over God's creation. The divinely ordained function to exercise dominion is commonly termed the "creation mandate." It is a rulership encompassing both the care of creation and culture-making. Under the cultural mandate, human beings are co-creators with God, and God is present in every human cultural activity, even cultural activity tainted by sin.

Second, the functional view looks to ancient Near Eastern backgrounds in its interpretation of the biblical text. Christoph Barth explains the extra-biblical evidence that validates such an understanding of the image of God: "The Ancient Sumerian, Babylonian, and Egyptian texts speak of kings being shaped in the image of their gods. Mesopotamian kings are hailed as the image of Bel or Shamash, Egyptian kings may boast of being the holy image of Re." (note 10) Similarly, Claus Westermann notes, "The background of Gen 1:26

---

9. Middleton, 25–29; Okesson, **Re-Imaging Modernity**, 182–84.

10. Barth, **God with Us**, 27.

is what Egypt and Mesopotamia say about the king as the image of God. A person as the image of God corresponds to the king as the image of God; both are God's viceroy or representative." (note 11) Following this line of thought, image bearers (powerful kings and priests) were significant representatives of a divine being. Their lives and actions were expressions of the gods they represented. They were on earth as ambassadors of the divine. As Middleton notes, "By extension, as imago Dei, embodied humanity is portrayed as responsible for administering the earthly realm as the creator's authorized representatives, with delegated power." (note 12)

Although appreciating the biblio-centric nature of this view, we also recognize one weakness regarding treatment of people with disabilities. An exclusive emphasis on rulership may hinder comprehensive application of the **imago Dei** to every individual. Seemingly not all human beings can exercise rule. People living with profound intellectual disabilities (see Harshaw's chapter in this volume), for example, may be perceived as incapable of exercising rule and consequently may be susceptible to abuse if rule is the locus of God's image.

---

11. Westermann, **Genesis 1–11**, 152.
12. Middleton, "Image of God," 516–23.

To counteract this potential for abuse, proponents have nuanced this view, differentiating rulership as an outcome of being in God's image rather than as the actual image of God itself. (note 13) Stewardship of creation is an outcome of being made in the image of God, not the actual image of God itself. Further, scholars lay emphasis on corporate responsibility rather than individual responsibility, such that people with disabilities join their fellow human beings in a communion of responsible citizens because all human beings are related to one another and to the world they inhabit. (note 14) In this outlook, all human beings, together, become stewards of God's creation. In this regard, no one is excluded from stewardship responsibilities. The next view expounds more on this communal idea of the image of God.

The Relational View

This final view understands humanity's dynamic relationships as constituting God's image. (note 15) Human beings bear God's image in an active sense – through different relationships. Contrary to the substantial view, which construes the image

---

13. McFague, **Models of God**, 68–69.
14. Bonhoeffer, **Creation and Fall**, 79.
15. Barth, **Church Dogmatics**, 195; Berkouwer, **Man**, 68–120; Brunner, **Man in Revolt**, 95–99.

of God exclusively in non-material substances, the relational view sees the image in terms of relationships. Also, in contrast to the substantial view, with its individualistic orientation where an individual in isolation possesses the image of God, the relational view emphasizes holistic relationships where human beings, together, are God's image bearers.

The relational view roots humanity's existence, vocation and responsibility to other human beings in humanity's covenantal communion with God. (note 16) Connecting this view to the functional view, we can say that to be created in the image of God is to subsist in communion with God, which then empowers human beings to exercise stewardship of God's creation. This fortifies the exercise of the God-given mandate of being God's representatives in the world. In other words, without close communion with God (Christ the very image of God), we fail greatly in our God-ordained mandate of creation care. In our fallen condition, we abuse God's creation instead of caring for it.

The relational understanding of the image of God in Africa coheres with the African understanding of humanity as people in communion with each other. The African communal anthropology is summed

---

16. Horton, **Lord and Servant**, 97–98.

up in what is called **ubuntu**. Bishop Desmond Tutu wrote extensively on this understanding. For example, in **No Future without Forgiveness**, he wrote,

> **Ubuntu** is very difficult to render into a Western language. It speaks of the very essence of being human. When we want to give high praise to someone we say, "**Yu, u nobuntu**"; "Hey, so-and-so has **ubuntu**." Then you are generous, you are hospitable, you are friendly and caring and compassionate. You share what you have. It is to say, "My humanity is caught up, is inextricably bound up, in yours." We belong in a bundle of life. We say, "A person is a person through other persons." It is not, "I think therefore I am." It says rather: "I am human because I belong. I participate, I share." (note 17)

Similarly, Mercy Oduyoye takes the idea of **ubuntu** and develops a theology of the church as a family that models ecumenical communion. She writes, "Africans see [the church] as an **Abusua** [association of households] of Christ, the coming together of 'relatives' of Christ to be a new

---

17. Tutu, **No Future**, 31.

community that does the will of God." (note 18) Elsewhere, Oduyoye reminds us that to bear the image of God is to live in communion with other human beings. One cannot be fully human, fully in the image of God, and yet live as if other people do not matter: "No one can claim to be in the image of God who is insensitive to the cry of the afflicted, who invests in structures of domination, or supports them because of vested interests." (note 19)

It is important to note that **ubuntu** is not uniquely African. It is a human attribute. All human beings have **ubuntu** (are relational in nature). In **Imaging God**, Douglas J. Hall succinctly captures this reality:

> Simply in our being there we are being-in-relationship; our sheer existing points beyond itself. We are creatures whose being implies relatedness. The solitary, isolated, self-sufficient human being – the "self-made man" that still exists for us as a rhetorical ideal – is, in fact, a contradiction in terms. To be, to be-in-the-world, is to be with. (note 20)

---

18. Oduyoye, "African Family," 471.
19. Oduyoye, **Hearing and Knowing**, 137.
20. Hall, **Imaging God**, 119.

Affirming the relational nature of being created in the image of God does not exclude the other perspectives. The structural aspects of the image are secondary while the functional and relational aspects are primary. Genesis 1:26–27 does not identify a particular aspect of human nature that can be said to be the image of God. If the text does not identify what the image is, then it is not prudent to overemphasize one aspect at the expense of others. (note 21) Anthony Hoekema provides a good summary of this multifaceted approach to God's image: "The image of God in man must therefore be seen as involving both the structure of man (his gifts, capacities, and endowments) and the functioning of man (his actions, his relationships to God and to others, and the way he uses his gifts)." (note 22) Such a robust understanding of God's image in people, when properly appropriated, yields practical ramifications that would demonstrate love and care for those living with disability. The contemporaries of my grandmother would appreciate her as a true human – one who deserves to enjoy relationships with others, beyond a token acknowledgement that falls short of a comprehensive synthesis and application of the biblical teaching on **imago Dei**.

---

21. Grenz, **Social God**, 200.
22. Hoekema, **Created in God's Image**, 73.

David P. Gushee reasons that creation in the image of God confers a worth to human life, which is intrinsic. (note 23)

Christ the Enabler and the Image of God

An emphasis on the relational view, whereby human beings together image God, aligns with the New Testament's affirmation of Christ as the image of God. As Kilner notes:

> The New Testament . . . reveals that God's purpose all along has not been for humanity to develop into some sort of generic "God's image," but to be conformed specifically to the image of Christ. "For those whom [God] foreknew [God] also predestined to be conformed to the image of [God's] Son, in order that he might be the firstborn within a large family" (Rom 8:29). However, since Christ is God's image (2 Cor 4:4; Col 1:15), conforming to the model of Christ's being and doing is tantamount to conforming to God's image. It is the fulfillment of God's determination at creation that people would be "in" God's image, living and growing in reference to God's standard for humanity. That image/standard is Christ, whose God-

---

23. Gushee, **Sacredness of Human Life**, 33.

given glory – a manifestation of being God's image – was present "before the beginning" (John 17:5; cf. Jude 25). (note 24)

Thus the relational view posits the place of Jesus Christ in restoring the image of God in Christians and enabling them to model an alternative way of life. Jesus, the Christ, shows people how to live differently because he is the "true humanity," (note 25) the "perfect realization of true humanity" (note 26) and "what human nature is intended to be." (note 27) He is the embodiment, the archetype, the definition of what it means to be human. He is the image of God par excellence and the **telos** (goal) of human existence. He exemplifies what humans are called to be and destined to be. He represents a life of complete obedience to God's will on earth. He shows life in its fullness.

Yet Jesus is more than an exemplar. He is the enabler of an alternative existence. Jesus's very presence in the world (incarnation) aided us out of sin that had disabled our relationship with God. He lived among those who are often considered

---

24. Kilner, **Dignity and Destiny**, 52–53.
25. Sherlock, **Doctrine of Humanity**, 18.
26. Cortez, **Theological Anthropology**, 20.
27. Erickson, **Christian Theology**, 532.

broken and disabled. He lifted them up when others passed by. He touched the untouchables. He washed feet and fed the hungry. He broke bread with the rejected, sick and frail members of the society. He went beyond identifying with the disenfranchised members of the society. He was himself disenfranchised and abandoned. He allowed his body to be broken and crushed for our sakes. His broken body is life-giving for it was his broken body that helped us overcome the disability of sin and through the process of sanctification purified us to live as God's image bearers reflecting God's glory on earth. He did all this to save not only individuals but also communities. Consequently, salvation is also corporate. We are saved to live in community with others. Sanctification is renewal in God's image. As a person's image is being renewed, his or her view of others as being fashioned in God's image also goes through a refinery process, resulting in a posture that is less averse to active and intentional participation in the constituency of those living with disability.

We now move to examine implications of the doctrine of the image of God for treatment of people with disabilities in Africa.

Implications of the *Imago Dei* for Treatment of People with Disabilities in Africa

The doctrine of the image of God has serious implications for treatment of people with disabilities in Africa. As shown above, a relational understanding of the image of God, especially one centred on Christ as the enabler of an alternative existence, has the potential to enhance the dignity of people with disabilities in Africa. The following section shows how this is possible within the context of the Christian community, God's church. The church is the centre of formation in the image of God. Though imperfect, the church is an alternative community. It is a community of God's people who have encountered the transformation of God through the Spirit (Rom 8:29; 2 Cor 3:18; Col 1:28–29). The church is the physical body of God on earth. Put differently, the church is the image of God on earth. It is the manifestation of what God has done and continues to do on earth. It is the manifestation of a new humanity being formed in the image of God in Christ by the Spirit (2 Cor 5:18, 20; Eph 4:1). I propose three implications of the doctrine of the image of God regarding treatment of people with disabilities within church and society in Africa.

The Sanctity of Human Life

The doctrine of the image of God affirms the sacredness of all human life. Since all human beings without exception are created in the image of God, the life they have is inherently sacred. The sacredness of a human being does not depend on external conferment. Human beings, not least those living with disability, Christians and non-Christians, are sacred because they are by nature sacred. Consequently, every human life without exception must be revered. One who honours the sacredness of human life lives differently. He or she protects human life and shuns wanton destruction of human life, desecration of human life and compromise of human rights. This is how the dignity of all people is defended unconditionally.

The sacredness of life directly contradicts and confronts abuse of people with disabilities in Africa. There are many cases of denial of their rights in Africa at present. These are expressed in popular beliefs. For example, some communities believe that having sex with someone living with albinism cures HIV and AIDS. (note 28) This exposes these individuals to rape. The practices of forced sterilization and abortion are also very common. A Kenyan newspaper recently reported a

---

28. Rutachwamagyo, "Profile of Tanzanians," 366.

heartbreaking story of a woman who was sterilized when she was twenty-two on account of her disability. (note 29)

For many years, children born with disabilities were killed because they were thought to be burdens to their families and the community, a curse that had to be eliminated. Their presence polluted the community, or, because of various superstitious beliefs, such sacrificing of them would appease the gods. (note 30) This treatment extends even beyond death: people with disabilities are sometimes buried hurriedly, disregarding the cultural and religious rites due to them. If children with disabilities are kept alive, they often lack adequate access to education and health care. (note 31) In contrast to the mistreatment of people with disabilities in Africa, an ethic informed by the **imago Dei** calls for the sanctity of human life. This results in proper treatment of people with disabilities.

---

29. Mwangi, "Disabled Women," 10.
30. Kigame, "Cultural Barriers," 122–26; Rutachwamagyo, 365; Seezi, "Persons with Disabilities," 394.
31. WHO and the World Bank, **World Report on Disability**.

The sacredness of life ethic also contributes to justice for people with disabilities. For many years they have been exposed to great injustice. Justice stems from respecting the image of God that each human being bears. To respect the image of God in people is to respect God (Gen 9:6). To do justice is to right systemic wrongs, such as the destruction of human lives and mistreatment of people with disabilities. But even more significant is the performance of justice through actions of service and compassion, promoting the flourishing of people with disabilities in Africa. What does a more just environment look like for people with disabilities in Africa? We move to this in the next point.

Cultivating an Enabling Environment for People with Disabilities to Flourish

African countries are yet to adequately address the barriers that hinder people with disabilities from flourishing. In the same newspaper article mentioned earlier, another woman living with disabilities recounted her traumatizing experience at a Kenyan hospital:

> When I was pregnant, I was told to climb on the bed. I couldn't. It was too high. A friend who uses crutches gave birth on the hospital corridor, by herself. In public hospitals, you rarely get prompt assistance

even if you're pregnant and in labour. They expect you to walk through those long corridors to the maternity wards using crutches. (note 32)

In the Kenyan context, manufacturers do not consider the needs of people with disabilities when they make their products. For example, "there are no pads that better fit women or girls with deformed or prostheses or no limbs," and "basics such as the expiry date of products are not provided in braille format." (note 33) Most government facilities do not have sign language interpreters, are physically inaccessible to people with mobility impairments, and do not care to fix those barriers. Sadly, churches too have not designed disability-friendly churches and programmes. Many churches, even in cities like Nairobi, do not have sign language interpreters. Most have no programmes to help special needs children. Some parents leave their children with special needs at home when they go to church.

In contrast to this, the church in Africa must cultivate an enabling environment for people with disabilities to flourish and to be able to contribute to the church and society. The

---

32. Mwangi, "Disabled Women," 11.
33. Mwangi, 11.

church must be committed to serving people with disabilities with intentionality and focus. It must overcome "the rigidity, faultiness, deficits, and pathological structures" that hinder people with disabilities from flourishing, (note 34) and instead be a welcoming community. It must open its doors (sometimes literally) to people with disabilities. Opening the doors calls for designing structures, programmes and facilities with people with disabilities in mind. For this to happen, the church must overcome barriers to the inclusion of people with disabilities. Such barriers include "(a) training, (b) physical accessibility, (c) attitudes, (d) programmatic barriers, and (e) behavior management." (note 35) People with disabilities have a right to barrier-free and disability-friendly churches as an expression of the image of God and the consequent dignity which they are due. In addition, the church must confront all the dehumanizing structures and cultures so prevalent in Africa concerning people with disabilities.
It must be a beacon of light for people with disabilities so that they have a place to turn to. The church must advocate for proper treatment of people with disabilities.

---

34. Linton, "Disability Studies," 518.
35. Barnes, "Open Hearts," 88.

Furthermore, the church in Africa must learn to listen to people with disabilities. Therefore, it must go beyond merely implementing programmes for the sake of public image or in compliance with government regulation, for by doing so it treats people with disabilities as projects and not as human beings who are truly created in God's image and so deserve Christian service. A church that truly sees people with disabilities as fully created in God's image will go beyond such motivations. It will truly seek to listen to people with disabilities so that the programmes implemented truly serve the needs of such people. People with disabilities must be in the "kitchen" where the meal (e.g. church programmes) is prepared. They cannot be treated as recipients of church programmes or initiatives, but must be seen also as developers of such programmes and initiatives. They will be key conversation partners, the ones driving the conversation. The church will listen to them and enact robust policies, programmes and structures. Thus people with disabilities must be embraced as genuine members of the body of Christ who participate in the church's witness. They need to receive all the support they need to flourish and to contribute to the enrichment of the church and society.

Empowering People with Disabilities as Equal Partners in the Flourishing of the World

People with disabilities are neither excessive burdens to be carried, threats to be feared, nor projects for charitable causes. On the contrary, they are precious members of society with capacities to enrich the community. What more just way to guard the worth of people with disabilities as bearers of the image of God than to secure equal employment opportunities for them in the church and society? What more just way to uphold the dignity of people with disabilities than to establish that they have a stable source of income to escape poverty? Sadly, the church and society often do not value people with disabilities as employable individuals because they have embraced a capitalist notion of productivity. Such a notion esteems people only if they are competent and capable of creating wealth. Society does not value debility, brokenness and vulnerability. Not only does society not value those characteristics, but society also actively scorns those who have those characteristics. Similarly, the church, under the sway of secularist notions of productivity, may not be mindful of the benefit to the workforce of people with impairments. They would rather employ someone who will work faster, make money more rapidly, think more quickly, talk more swiftly, and present an appealing image of the organization. To avoid undervaluing people with disabilities in the workforce the church must reappraise prevailing notions of productive work and success. The church should welcome less productive contributions of people with disabilities as fruitful contributions and fulfil its calling to encourage, enable and facilitate contributions of disabled church employees.

Let us conclude with a quote from Phitalis Were Masakhwe, who wrote on the church, public policy and disability concerns in Kenya, returning to the dignity of all humans as a starting point:

> Talking about the image and dignity should remind us of the creation stories. The Bible says that all of us were created in the image and likeness of God. The all is a categorical encompassing statement. It means that even those with disability were also made from the same image and likeness of the same God. . . . Any person therefore, whether clergy or otherwise, that demeans persons with any form of impairment is actually defacing and defaming the image and likeness of God. (note 36)

---

36. Masakhwe, "Church," 113.

Conclusion

The doctrine of the image of God is a liberative doctrine and its application to disability in the African context is helpful. A proper understanding of the image of God liberates people with disabilities to realize their full potential in Africa. The thesis of this chapter is that greater emphasis on a relational understanding of the image of God, especially one centred on Christ as the enabler of an alternative existence, has the potential to positively impact the way in which the church in Africa engages with people with disabilities. Christ is the one who recreates people in God's image, shaping them in Christlikeness so that they may reflect God's image, as God intended. Sanctified humanity, or a people formed in the image of God in Christ through the Spirit, embraces a posture that is less averse to active and intentional participation in the constituency of those living with disability. This chapter has also presented three implications of the doctrine of the image of God regarding treatment of people with disabilities. The church that fully accepts the image of God in people with disabilities supports their dignity, justice and service. Such a church cultivates an enabling environment for the flourishing of people with disabilities. It also empowers them as equal partners in the flourishing of the world. A correct understanding and consistent application of the doctrine of the **imago Dei** is essential to this end.

Bibliography

Barnes, Alyssa. "Open Hearts, Open Minds, Open Doors: Including Children with Special Needs in Ministry." **Christian Education Journal** 9, no. 3 (2012): 81–100.

Barth, Cristoph. **God with Us: A Theological Introduction to the Old Testament**. Edited by Geoffrey William Bromiley. Grand Rapids: Eerdmans, 1991.

Barth, Karl. **Church Dogmatics**. Edited by Geoffrey William Bromiley. Edinburgh: T&T Clark, 1958.

Beates, Michael S. **Disability and the Gospel: How God Uses Our Brokenness to Display His Grace**. Wheaton: Crossway, 2012.

Berkouwer, Gerrit C. **Man: The Image of God**. Grand Rapids: Eerdmans, 1962.

Bonhoeffer, Dietrich. **Creation and Fall: A Theological Exposition of Genesis 1–3**. Augsburg: Fortress, 2004.

Brunner, Emil. **Man in Revolt: A Christian Anthropology**. Edited by Olive Wyon. London: Lutterworth, 1939.

Cairns, David. **The Image of God in Man**. London: SCM, 1953.

Cortez, Marc. **Theological Anthropology: A Guide for the Perplexed**. New York: T&T Clark, 2010.

Dyrness, William A. "Anthropology, Theological." In **Global Dictionary of Theology: A Resource for the Worldwide Church**, edited by William A. Dyrness and Veli-Matti Kärkkäinen, 43. Downers Grove: InterVarsity Press, 2009.

Erickson, Millard. **Christian Theology**. Grand Rapids: Baker, 1998.

Grenz, Stanley J. **The Social God and the Relational Self: A Trinitarian Theology of the Imago Dei**. Louisville: Westminster, 2001.

Gushee, David P. **The Sacredness of Human Life: Why an Ancient Biblical Vision Is Key to the World's Future**. Grand Rapids: Eerdmans, 2013.

Hall, Douglas John. **Imaging God: Dominion as Stewardship**. Grand Rapids: Eerdmans, 1986.

Hoekema, Anthony A. **Created in God's Image**. Grand Rapids: Eerdmans, 1986.

Horton, Michael S. **Lord and Servant: A Covenant Christology**. Louisville: Westminster John Knox, 2005.

Kigame, Reuben. "Cultural Barriers to the Disabled People's Participation in Church Life." In **Disability, Society, and Theology: Voices from Africa**, edited by Samuel Kabue, Esther Mombo, Joseph Galgalo and C. B. Peter, 121–37. Limuru: Zapf Chancery, 2011.

Kilner, John F. **Dignity and Destiny: Humanity in the Image of God**. Grand Rapids: Eerdmans, 2015.

Linton, Simi. "What Is Disability Studies?" **PMLA** 120, no. 2 (2005): 518–22.

Masakhwe, Phitalis W. "The Church, Public Policy and Disability Concerns in Kenya." In **Disability, Society, and Theology: Voices from Africa**, edited by Samuel Kabue, Esther Mombo, Joseph Galgalo and C. B. Peter, 111–20. Limuru: Zapf Chancery, 2011.

McFague, Sallie. **Models of God: Theology for an Ecological, Nuclear Age.** Philadelphia: Fortress, 1987.

McLeod, Frederick G. **The Image of God in the Antiochene Tradition.** Washington, DC: Catholic University of America Press, 1999.

Middleton, J. Richard. "Image of God." In **The Oxford Encyclopedia of the Bible and Theology.** Vol. 2, edited by Samuel E. Ballentine, 516–23. Oxford: Oxford University Press, 2015.

———. **The Liberating Image: The Imago Dei in Genesis 1**. Grand Rapids: Brazos, 2005.

Mwangi, Diana. "Disabled Women Face Stigma in Maternity Wards and Sexual Health Clinics." **Business Daily**, July 2021.

Oduyoye, Mercy A. "The African Family as a Symbol of Ecumenism." **Ecumenical Review** 43 (1991): 465–78.

———. **Hearing and Knowing: Theological Reflections on Christianity in Africa.** Maryknoll: Orbis, 1986.

Okesson, Gregg A. **Re-Imaging Modernity: A Contextualized Theological Study of Power and Humanity within Akamba Christianity in Kenya**. American Society of Missiology Monograph Series 16. Eugene: Wipf & Stock, 2012.

Ramsey, Paul. **Basic Christian Ethics**. New York: Charles Scribner's Sons, 1950.

Rutachwamagyo, Kaganzi. "A Profile of Tanzanians with Disabilities." In **Disability, Society, and Theology: Voices from Africa**, edited by Samuel Kabue, Esther Mombo, Joseph Galgalo and C. B. Peter, 363–82. Limuru: Zapf Chancery, 2011.

Seezi, Gidudu Balayo N. "Persons with Disabilities in Uganda." In **Disability, Society, and Theology: Voices from Africa**, edited by Samuel Kabue, Esther Mombo, Joseph Galgalo and C. B. Peter, 383–402. Limuru: Zapf Chancery, 2011.

Sherlock, Charles. **The Doctrine of Humanity**. Downers Grove: InterVarsity Press, 1996.

Tutu, Desmond. **No Future without Forgiveness**. New York: Doubleday, 1999.

Westermann, Claus. **Genesis 1–11: A Commentary**. Translated by John J. Scullion. Minneapolis: Augsburg, 1984.

World Health Organization (WHO) and the World Bank. **World Report on Disability.** Geneva: WHO, 2011. https://www.who.int/teams/noncommunicable-diseases/sensory-functions-disability-and-rehabilitation/world-report-on-disability.

7

From Exclusion to Divine Accommodation of People with Profound Intellectual Disabilities

Jill Harshaw

Introduction

If you type the word "inclusion" into any Internet search engine, it will take you a lifetime to scroll through all the material that greets you – from academic articles, links to disability rights organizations and social policy documents, to images of ethnically diverse gatherings. Among the most prominent depictions are groups of children holding hands in a colourful circle of whom one is seated in a wheelchair. Connections between inclusion and disability seem to be embedded across the global psyche, including Africa.

In Western Christian and Jewish disability theology, the theme of inclusion has been one of the primary catalysts for positive developments in awareness-raising, engagement and practice that acknowledge the reality of embodied experiences of disability and, more recently, intellectual disability – which will be the focus of this chapter – across faith communities. In the Christian context, a campaign for more "inclusive churches" has gathered momentum over a number of decades, driven by the efforts of a number of passionate advocates working in academia, grassroots ministry and what is known in the West as "special education," but most significantly this campaign has been driven by people who have disabilities. Nancy Eiesland's **The Disabled God** (note 1) was the seminal contribution to these early developments. Importantly, however, these developments did not emerge in a vacuum, nor as a result of internal reflection on the part of the Christian church on its long history of prejudice and exclusionary practice that alienated and marginalized people with disabilities. Rather, they were inspired and energized by broader civil rights movements, most notably, though not exclusively, in the United States. The church's work of developing and practising inclusion is, and needs to be, ongoing. While most would accept the principle that

---

1. Eiseland, **Disabled God**, 79–116.

Christian communities ought to be inclusive of people representing every facet of human diversity, it remains clear that practising inclusion is not a priority in Western Christian churches. Effecting the necessary change to make this a reality continues to require an enormous amount of work, determination and courage in order to expose the church's need to confront and repent of historical and contemporary injustices. This too affects the global and African church. At the same time my writer positionality remains that of a Northern Irish based disability theologian.

Of course, inclusion is not the only theme that has captured the attention of disability theology in recent years. One key focus of interest is the issue of human personhood or theological anthropology. This is an important subject, not least because of the social and cultural values that prevail in Western, self-proclaimed "liberal," "tolerant" societies which, as Yong explains, produce notions of normalcy which have not only been socially, politically and economically oppressive to disabled people, but also theologically. (note 2) He rightly insists that "whatever else disability is, it is also the experience of discrimination, marginalization, and exclusion from the social, cultural, political

---

2. In Eiseland, 79–116.

and economic domains of human life." (note 3) This is evident in the under-representation of people with disabilities in decision-making bodies as well as in mainstream media. A persistent undercurrent that elevates values of independence and productivity inevitably dehumanizes and marginalizes those whose capacity to contribute economically to society is inherently curtailed by the way in which they inhabit the world.

In theological discussions the anthropological theme now extends beyond a defence of the personhood of people with intellectual disabilities, and profound intellectual disabilities in particular, to a quest for what they can teach about what it means to be human. Indeed, in recent years there has been an increasing emphasis on this role or vocation of "teacher." We are encouraged to think about people with profound intellectual disabilities as "prophetic signs" (note 4) pointing more intellectually able Christians to the supposed virtue of vulnerability, although it is vital that we acknowledge the differences between an intellectually able person's experience of vulnerability and that of those who are dependent on the care of others and have no means of expressing any maltreatment they may

---

3. In Eiseland, 99.
4. Cf. Young, **Arthur's Call**.

suffer. These individuals are further described as educators in relation to our need of and place within communities, thus illuminating an authentic Christian ecclesiology. This perception of the prophetic or teaching role of people with profound intellectual disabilities may well reveal significant insights, but there is a danger of imposing our explanation of the purpose of their lives. We must guard against inadvertently aligning ourselves with what David Pailin terms "a contributory theory of human worth" (note 5) in which someone is valued for what he or she can teach or contribute to others, rather than simply for who he or she is, without regard to anything he or she can offer.

Returning to the theme of inclusion, while increasing theological reflection has taken place on the subject, there is space for deeper investigation, particularly into what it is to be inclusive and whose responsibility it is to make it happen. As we challenge others to take inclusion seriously, those of us who advocate for, research, write, speak and teach about inclusive ecclesiologies in the context of intellectual disability need to ask searching questions of ourselves in relation to how far we have allowed the implications of inclusion to impact the trajectory and depth of our reflection. Indeed, I wonder whether inclusion

---

5. Pailin, **A Gentle Touch**, 116.

is any longer a useful word in this context, and whether we need to critique our well-established perspectives on the subject, challenging any lazy theologies that depend on useful but less-than-comprehensive explorations of the biblical text, the historical tradition and the experiences of people with intellectual disabilities within or beyond the church.

Do not misunderstand me: I do not suggest that inclusion is not a core theological principle. On the contrary, it has a fundamental role in the Christian tradition, epitomized in the life and teaching of Jesus who intractably oriented his ministry and his lifestyle towards those who were socially and religiously excluded. The Jewish and Christian understanding of an inclusive God whose first encounter with Abram was to promise that through him, and his obedient response to God's call, all nations would be divinely blessed (note 6) has enormous importance in our understanding of how to live faithfully and missionally, both individually and corporately, as citizens of the counter-cultural kingdom of God. My purpose here is to encourage a conversation about how to engage in deeper theological reflection that builds on the considerable progress that has been achieved to date in promoting conversations about

---

6. Cf. Gen 18:18.

inclusion alongside those that have their origins in disability rights, by exploring the place of people with intellectual disabilities within our theological frameworks of relationships, with God and others, as well as the spiritual life and church. When we develop more critical questions about the ways in which we understand inclusion and the church's role in effecting it, we create space for important issues to come to the surface.

There is a critical difficulty lying at the heart of what we mean by inclusion and building inclusive communities, and how we use the Bible, and particularly Paul's ecclesiology, to advocate for them. This difficulty lies in the unspoken and potentially unrecognized power dynamic inherent in the debate. Building inclusive communities is deemed to mean to create, or at least to draw attention to, an obligation to include and to carry it out in a contextually relevant way. Yet to promote the need for and carry out the practice of inclusion requires someone, or more aptly, "someones," to assume responsibility for that obligation: members of a church community, apart from those who are deemed to need to be included, must assume the role of the "includer." We are on the inside, and our reading of Scripture encourages us to act compassionately towards those whom we believe to be on the outside. This in itself is an incomplete view of the foundational impetus for what we term "inclusion." In the Bible, inclusion is as much a matter of justice as it is compassion. "This is what the LORD Almighty said: 'Administer true justice; show mercy and compassion to one another.'" (note 7) It is our failure to practise justice, as much as our failure to show compassion, that leads to unfaithful expressions of Christian community.

This does not negate the fact that, in many ways, people with intellectual disabilities do find themselves on the outside or margins of our faith communities, but this is not because they do not belong; it is because in our distorted practices and mindsets, we have perpetuated the discrimination to which they have long been subject in society as a whole, perceiving them as essentially "the others" who do not intrinsically or automatically belong with "us." Not only does this assume an unfounded superiority on the part of the self-designated includers in relation to those waiting to be included, but it distorts and usurps the dynamic between the includers and the One who is the origin of the inclusion of any of us – God himself.

Apart from the ingrained contemporary and historical influences of our social and political environments, where does this sense of

---

7. Zech 7:9.

entitlement in relation to our right/obligation to include people who have intellectual disabilities in our churches originate? I want to suggest that, ironically, it emerges from the same source as that which inspires our desire to "include" in our theological understanding of what it means to be a Christian – what qualifies us to be a "member" of the church and what it looks like to have a life-giving relationship with God. Sadly, even those of us who are working to implement practical inclusion often still cling, perhaps subconsciously, to a pernicious theological exclusion. This is most evident in how we understand, engage with and speak about the spiritual lives of people who have profound intellectual disabilities.

Tensions Inherent in Discussions about Intellectual Disability

Before we proceed, I want to briefly clarify who I'm referring to when I talk about people with profound intellectual disabilities and, in so doing, to acknowledge some significant tensions. First, the most widely recognized core criteria for diagnosing an intellectual disability are threefold: a significant impairment of intelligence (the extent of which is determined by use of the Intelligent

Quotient); (note 8) a significant impairment of social functioning; and an age of onset prior to adulthood. So, while I use the widely accepted IQ spectrum as a mode of identification of the level of disability to which I am referring – the score in question is below 35 – I am conscious that this is only one indicator of this category. Second, in categorizing at all, I am in danger of perpetuating the "us" and "them" culture that is so disavowed in disability theology and in disability rights movements as a whole. I, and others in this field, experience intense discomfort in categorizing people according to the degree of their capacity or incapacity. I do not imply any lack of respect for the uniqueness and inestimable value of any human being, all of whom are loved into being by God and invested with a dignity that cannot be limited by the way in which they inhabit and experience their own personas and the world at large. If, however, I do not indicate the people whose relationship with God I am exploring, nothing I am about to say would have any value at all. I believe that it is genuinely important that we discuss these issues, fundamentally because the kind of theological exclusion I am challenging takes shape in either denial of or indifference to the spiritual capacity of those with limited

---

8. World Health Organization, International Classification of Diseases.

intellectual prowess. It is worth noting also that the situation in which people with profound intellectual disabilities find themselves in relation to ambivalent attitudes towards their spirituality is evidenced by the fact that were I to discuss the potential spiritual experience of those whose IQ exceeded 140, and who are considered "gifted," it is unlikely that criticism would be levelled to the same extent.

The Shape of Theological Exclusion

I should say that my interest in the world of intellectual disability did not come out of the blue. My daughter, Rebecca, has profound intellectual disabilities. Rebecca has opened my eyes to what is truly important in life and faith but, as is typically the case in an experience of profound intellectual disabilities, she does not use words to express herself, nor does spoken or written language form any part of how she engages with or conceptualizes her own life, those around her and the world in general. In this sense it seems obvious that in light of the Christian faith's inherent attachment to words, primarily in its sacred text, a profound intellectual disability can appear highly problematic.

There is no denial here of the absolute necessity of and infinite riches embedded and inherent in the verbal revelation of God. Nor should we deny the centrality of the spoken word at, or around, the introductory point to the Christian faith, as well as in obedient Christian living, clearly presented within the text itself. The apostle Paul, for example, states that "faith comes from hearing the message, and the message is heard through the word about Christ." (note 9) Christ continually emphasizes to his followers the imperative of acting in accordance with his Father's verbally expressed commands, just as he, the self-identified Son of God, does, in fulfilling the mission for which he came to earth. (note 10) Perhaps it's not surprising then that discussions of the spiritual experience of people with profound and complex intellectual disabilities often have to contend with those who are committed to the absolute necessity of personal engagement with the text. Swinton highlights the difficulty of "offering the Word to those who have no words." (note 11)

Morris articulates the challenge clearly: "The role and significance [of the Bible] is increasingly perceived by many ordinary Christians as the benchmark for how to live and what to

---

9. Rom 10:17.
10. See John 15:10: "If you keep my commands, you will remain in my love, just as I have kept my Father's commands and remain in his love."
11. Swinton, "Restoring the Image," 22.

believe," (note 12) and this, to some extent, contributes to the assumptions that those with little or no access to the text might be perceived as "less Christian." (note 13) Consequently, conversations persist in which doubts as to the capacity of Rebecca, and other individuals who have profound intellectual disabilities, to encounter God at all hang in the air because not only can Rebecca not access the text, she cannot access the traditional, intentional steps in the Christian perspective on the establishment and development of a human person's relationship with God. The cognitive responses of confession, repentance and expression of belief in Christ as the way to God are inaccessible to Rebecca, as they are to others who have profound intellectual disabilities. Peter Jensen, for example, unequivocally states that the "achievement of the gospel is that people come to know God through informative and hortatory words about him. Whatever else the gospel is, it is verbal, an announcement by way of speech." (note 14) Scott Swain agrees, writing that while "'communication,' theologically understood, involves more than the simple exchange of words . . . communication,

---

12. Morris, "Does the Church Need the Bible?," 166.
13. Morris, 167.
14. Jensen, **Revelation of God**, 36.

theologically understood, is **never less** than an exchange of words." (note 15) Again, Morris describes the impact of these assertions:

> What is assumed . . . in practice, however much we might wish to redefine what faith is, [is that] in order to be saved, a person will normally have language and the intellectual capacities to learn a set of beliefs and make choices and decisions about them; what is assumed is able-bodied normativity. (note 16)

Any suggestion that, without apprehension of the words, no fruitful revelation or communication by God is possible is a matter of enormous importance for those who are working to establish inclusive communities of faith. If intellectual reflection on language-based sources were to be an indispensable part of how a human being might meaningfully encounter God, then for people with profound intellectual disabilities there would be little hope for such encounters. As Creamer suggests, "within a discourse dominated

---

15. Swain, **Trinity, Revelation and Reading**, 8 (emphasis mine).

16. Morris, "Transforming Able-Bodied Normativity," 236–37.

by intellectual and academic rigour, it is difficult to know where an entry point for the cognitively disabled might appear." (note 17)

Perhaps this is why reflection on the spiritual experience of people whose intellectual disabilities are profound has, despite progress in other areas, been so deficient. This cannot continue if there is a desire to understand and practise authentic inclusion in our Christian communities, because its absence entrenches the ethos that conceptualizes individuals who have profound intellectual disabilities as of lesser value and objects of pity to whom good must be done, rather than people from whom good might be received. Genuine inclusion means recognizing and valuing their relationships, not only with other members of the community, but with God. This vacuum perpetuates prejudicial, ableist assumptions, in which the potential for a relationship with God is assumed to be predicated solely on human intellectual capacity, of which the disturbing statement below is just one example:

> Severely mentally handicapped people are denied the very substance of a rational productive existence. . . . Such an existence gives no real opportunity for inner spiritual growth, or the nourishment of the human spirit, both of which are important when

---

17. Creamer, **Christian Theology**, 108.

> coming to terms with the meaning of Christianity. It gives no real opportunity to experience the joy of seeking a lifetime relationship with the Almighty, because concepts involved are complicated and require a level of awareness which the profoundly mentally handicapped do not have. (note 18)

While the tone of this comment by eminent UK professor of nursing Peter Birchenall seems particularly offensive, and one might imagine that the time that has elapsed since it was made would make it irrelevant to our current discussion, the underlying perspective he is describing remains a very real one, even within academic and church circles, where views on the spiritual experience of people whose intellectual disabilities are profound remain hazy and ambiguous.

With the lack of a first-person articulation of spiritual life on the part of those who have profound intellectual disabilities, disability theology scholars, uncomfortable to leave the issues unaddressed, have sought to look elsewhere for evidence of a relationship with God. This search has primarily taken shape in theological reflection on anecdotal behaviours and events,

---

18. Birchenall and Birchenall, "Caring for Mentally Handicapped People," 150.

especially in the context of qualitative research projects. In the absence of first-hand accounts from the individuals who are the objects of this reflection, researchers have sought evidence of their spiritual lives by asking questions of those who are closest to them.[19] While such attempts reveal an important desire to reverse the neglect of the spiritual experience of people who have profound intellectual disabilities, it must be acknowledged that all narratives are subjective and interpretative and that it might be particularly difficult to describe the inner life of someone else, no matter how well known to us, on the basis of what we ourselves experience as we spend time with that person, rather than on what he or she communicates directly. Drawing robust theological conclusions on the basis of this work research seems difficult.

If we are determined to uncover such evidence, the ambiguity of second-hand accounts begs the question of where we might find a reliable source – a question that is perhaps not so problematic as has been presented. If one party to a relationship is unable to articulate his or her experience of that relationship, it seems obvious that we should invite the party who can communicate it to tell

---

19. Swinton, Mowat and Baines, "Whose Story," 5–19.

us. Should we not address our enquiries to the One who knows the answers? I suggest that questions about whether, or more appropriately, how people with profound intellectual disabilities might enjoy a relationship with God should, in fact, be addressed to the rich theological sources of the Christian tradition. In doing so, we might discover that the cognitive deficits of persons with profound intellectual disabilities do not prejudice their capacities or opportunities for being either recipients or conduits of a revelation of God – or perhaps more appropriately expressed: God is not incapacitated by reason of their cognitive deficits from communicating and disclosing himself to and through them.

Divine Revelation and Accommodation

The identification and comprehension of God's self-revelation has been the task and objective of believers and theologians across two thousand years of church history. As Headlam states, "the primary question in theology must be what the source of our knowledge of God is." (note 20) While Scripture is second only to the incarnation in its significance as one of these sources, it is important to acknowledge that Scripture in itself cannot comprise all there is to communicate, nor

---

20. Headlam, **Christian Theology**, 7.

is the communication its own end. Temple explains that "what is offered to man's apprehension in any specific Revelation is not truth concerning God but God Himself." (note 21) The foundational theological truth here is not that Scripture is God's revelation but that God reveals himself. Thus the quest for a valid apprehension of the nature of God's revelation must be pervaded by the understanding that a revelation of God can only ever come from God. Demarest agrees that any understanding or belief in relation to God "can . . . only consist in what is revealed by God of Himself. . . . Only God can make known God." (note 22) Crucially, this divine self-disclosure, in its nature as well as its content, takes the form of a God-designed bridge which spans the otherwise unbridgeable gap between the infinite God and a finite humanity, without which humanity remains helpless to construct such a bridge and, moreover, to conceive of the need for one.

As God's desire for communication with human beings is played out, the core challenge of finite humanity's incapacity to apprehend God in the fullness of who he is assumes enormous significance. Sparks explains that "there is simply no way to transfer God's infinite perception

---

21. Temple, **Nature, Man and God**, 322.
22. Demarest, **General Revelation**, 13.

of reality into a finite human mind." (note 23) Accepting this, there must be an accessible bridge – a means (or a range of means) by which such communication can take place. The important question, in the context of a discussion of the theological inclusion of people who have profound intellectual disabilities, relates to how God discloses himself to offer the possibility of a relationship of intimacy with all human beings in a way that is accessible and appropriate to the variously embodied limitations of their finitude.

A Theological Response: Divine Accommodation

A significant contribution to Christian (and Jewish) (note 24) theology's answer to this question has been formulated in terms of the theory of accommodation. (note 25) Van Bemmelin

---

23. Sparks, **God's Word**, 243.

24. Theories of accommodation proliferate in historical Jewish theology. One of their most prominent exponents, writing in the twelfth century AD, was Maimonides (Mosheh ben Maimon) (1135–1204). See Maimonides, **Guide of the Perplexed**; Benin, "'Cunning of God,'" 179–91.

25. Accommodation is variously referred to in theological scholarship as a "theory," "idea," "concept" and "doctrine."

provides a helpful definition of the theory: "God, in His self-revelation to humanity, accommodates Himself to the mental and spiritual capacity of human beings so that they can come to know Him, learn to trust Him and ultimately love Him." (note 26) The theory has been adopted throughout history by a remarkably diverse cross-section of theological scholarship. As Benin further comments, "the breeze of accommodation . . . blows . . . through the nooks and crannies of almost countless works, and an examination of each work would fill volumes." (note 27)

The theory has most commonly emerged as a general response to the challenges of biblical interpretation and the historical and ongoing difficulties inherent in appropriating the ancient text within a contemporary context. Benin, for example, refers to accommodation as "an exegetical device" (note 28) although there is considerable debate about its origins. Some locate them in a Jewish and a legal, rather than a Christian and an exegetical, context. (note 29)

---

26. Van Bemmelin, "Divine Accommodation," 221.
27. Benin, **Footprints of God**, 93.
28. Benin, 1.
29. Cf. Funkenstein, **Scientific Imagination**, 213. He points out that its mediaeval manifestation in the form of the Latin phrase **Scriptura humane**

Van Bemmelin, though, identifies the origins of the term within the rhetorical tradition of the ancient Romans who "used the word [accommodation] . . . in rhetoric to express the idea that an orator would adapt himself to his audience in his choice of words, gestures and emotions so that he could move their hearts and persuade their minds in whatever direction he wanted." (note 30)

Accommodation in Hermeneutics

In biblical interpretation, there are a number of significant questions or issues to which a theology of accommodation is purported to supply a justifiable response. These include the fact and degree of diversity of perspectives within Scripture, the dissonance between Scripture's worldview and that of the contemporary reader, the balance between divine inspiration and the human authors' limitations and capacity for error, and, to a lesser extent, differences between what Scripture seems to convey and objective scientific fact. (note 31)

---

loquitor is a translation of the Jewish phrase **dibra tora kileshon bne 'adam**, literally, "Torah spoke like the language of [the sons of] man."

30. Van Bemmelin, "Divine Accommodation," 221.

31. Recent modes of interpretation have attempted to present a way of reading the text and understanding the origins of the text which

In outlining a brief, selective overview of the forms in which these specific issues have been addressed by use of the theory of accommodation, the aim is to provide a foundational case on which conclusions about the spiritual relationship open to people with profound intellectual disabilities can be drawn.

When Sparks poses the important question of how we know that accommodation has occurred, he evidences those points where Scripture is perceived to be self-contradictory, presenting "diverse viewpoints on the self-same matter, respecting . . . matters of history, linguistics, ethics, theology and religious practice." (note 32) Although encompassing aspects of New Testament teaching, for example with regard to some contradictions in chronology and narrative between John's Gospel and the Synoptics, the most commonly perceived manifestation of the challenge of diversity or inconsistency relates to the differences between the obligations imposed by God in the Old and New Testaments – Peter's conversion to the eating of

---

mean that the divergence between scientific explanations in Scripture and in science are not so problematic as would prima facie appear to be the case. See Wolterstorff, **Philosophical Reflections**, 228–29.

32. Sparks, **God's Word**, 230.

animals deemed unclean under the Old Testament law provides a vivid example. (note 33) While some contemporary scholars do not characterize the issue of biblical interpretation in which the theory of accommodation arises as a dilemma and are content to allow for a discrepancy between the Old and New Testament obligations God places on his people as an instance of progressive revelation, (note 34) its use has a lengthy provenance in Christian theology, going right back to the church fathers and mothers who, Young explains, "recognized that God accommodated the divine word to the human level not only in the incarnation, but also in the human language of the Scriptures, which necessarily used types and symbols to speak of what transcends everything in the created order." (note 35) What is generally agreed is that God's accommodative, self-revelatory action is ongoing and often changes in both form and content to meet the requirements of specific people living in specific contexts, within the framework of his cosmological and eschatological plan to bring all things to perfection. (note 36)

---

33. Acts 10–11.
34. Cf. Swain, **Trinity, Revelation and Reading**, 23–24.
35. Young, **Art of Performance**, 34.
36. Rom 8:19–21.

In relation to divergences in culture and worldview between the world of Scripture and the myriad different social, historical and geographical contexts that have followed, Sparks explains that "ancient authors used literary genres quite different from our own to audiences living in contexts and facing concerns that were sometimes considerably different from ours." (note 37) In an early contribution, Young cautions against overemphasizing the importance of cultural diversity, insisting that within the text "there are realities which it takes to be realities: God, covenant, atonement, worship" (note 38) Later, however, she agrees that the tool of accommodation is necessary in light of "the limited realm of human understanding, with its risks, potential for distortion in transmission, [and] inevitable particularity within a particular culture and time." (note 39)

Discrepancies are found between biblical explanations of aspects of scientific and historical realities and those offered by objectively established knowledge in relation to, for example, the creation narrative and the statement that the sun stood still for a day in Joshua 10:13.

---

37. Sparks, **God's Word**, 230.
38. Young, **Art of Performance**, 19.
39. Young, **God's Presence**, 27.

Copernicus's heliocentric theory (note 40) provides further evidence for the significance of a theology of accommodation. Both Catholics and Reformers (note 41) denounced Copernicus's perspective because of their literal interpretation of the text. Copernicus's supporters used the theory to contend for an allegorical interpretation of the recorded event.

Accommodation in the Text?

Calvin's perspective on this subject is particularly interesting. He understands accommodative action in which explanations are tailored to fit the intellectual or educational background of their audience.

> Nor did Moses wish to withdraw us from this pursuit by omitting such things as are peculiar to the art; but because he was ordained a teacher of the unlearned and ignorant as well as the learned, he could

---

40. The debate is commonly referred to as the "Copernicus Revolution" – a sign of the magnitude and rarity of the challenge it presented to the geocentric beliefs of ancient Israel.
41. Cf. Luther, **Tischreden**, 232.

not fulfil his office unless he descended to this more elementary method of instruction. (note 42)

He makes the point that the absence of specific information in the text does not preclude the existence of such information; the human author of the text in which this scientific "information" was recorded was relaying only what was needed and could be apprehended by its hearers.

One of the difficulties maintained by those who express scepticism about the spiritual capacity of people with profound intellectual disabilities is predicated on the absence of direct biblical material on the subject. In the face of this absence, the weight of other material in the text which stresses the centrality of intentional engagement with the propositions, ideas and instructions conveyed in its words seems to support their case. On the other hand, there is much in the biblical content on which to sustain an alternative position. Arguably, then, the linguistic revelation which cannot be apprehended by some provides knowledge which others have sufficient capacity to process, so that an understanding of the position of the former in relation to the God who is the source of the revelation can be discerned.

---

42. Calvin, **Commentaries**, 86–87.

Significant discussions and theories of accommodation emerge with regard to the limitations of the human authors of the text. Augustine's (354–430) comment on John's teaching on the incarnation serves as a key example.

> John spoke of the matter not as it is but even he, only as he was able . . . it was a man that spoke of God. Inspired indeed by God, but still a man. Because he was a man he said something; if he had not been inspired he would have said nothing. But because he was a man inspired, he spoke not the whole, but what a man could, he spoke. (note 43)

Modern theologians (and philosophers) would describe this perspective as practical realism – an understanding that "'perfect' human knowledge is an illusion which mistakenly confuses good and useful knowledge with perfect, God-like knowledge." (note 44)

On the wider issue of divine accommodation to the limitations of the human authors and readers of the text, and the infallibility of God, Sparks insists that "the voices of accommodationists

---

43. Augustine, **Homilies on the Gospel of John**, 1.1 (**NPNF** 1 7:7); cited in Sparks, **God's Word**, 246.
44. Sparks, **God's Word**, 43.

from the first century to the present are on this point unanimous. . . . Accommodation does not introduce errors into Scripture; it is instead a theological explanation for the presence of human errors in Scripture." (note 45) Many different views persist on the existence of error and the extent to which and how account should be taken of human fallibility in the text. (note 46) In the context of profound intellectual disability, however, the vital principle is that because human beings (even divinely inspired human beings) cannot know God as he is, he condescends (a vital element of accommodation) to reveal to them what he wants them to know of himself.

Modes of Accommodation

Beyond arguments for the existence of accommodation in God's self-revelation, it is particularly insightful to explore the ways in which God accomplishes it and what this tells us about his nature and disposition towards human beings. The first element that becomes visible as we trace

---

45. Sparks, 256.

46. For an interesting synopsis of the issues involved in the modes of interpretation of errantists and inerrantists, see Wolterstorff, **Philosophical Reflections**, 227–29; also Young, **Art of Performance.**

God's accommodative disclosure throughout the biblical canon is its flexibility. In what is arguably one of the most striking prophetic texts, Ezekiel 20, the prophet relates God's condemnation of the unfaithfulness of his people following their escape from Egypt and how they disobeyed his specific instructions for how to live well. These instructions were not portrayed by God as burdensome, but as life-giving and relationship-nurturing, notwithstanding their misconduct: "I gave them my decrees and made known to them my laws, by which the person who obeys them will live. Also I gave them my Sabbaths as a sign between us, so they would know that I the LORD made them holy" (vv. 11–12). The fact that this text emphasizes the "goodness" of God's laws renders it remarkable that, a little later in the same declaration, God speaks the extraordinary words, "I gave them other statutes that were not good and laws through which they could not live; I defiled them through their gifts – the sacrifice of every firstborn – that I might fill them with horror so that they would know that I am the LORD" (vv. 25–26). In a dramatic instance of his accommodated revelation, God's response to his people's disobedience involves giving them commands and obligations which would be life-draining. Bowen describes these as God's "shock therapy to move Israel out of their persistent rebelliousness." (note 47) By drastically disturbing and even horrifying his people, God demonstrates the importance he attaches to a life-changing revelation of God's self to human beings. As Bowen goes on to comment, in contrast to the thrust of its earlier part, the fact "that God gave 'not good' laws suggests that God's reputation is not . . . the overriding concern of this chapter." (note 48) On the contrary, it is the re-establishment of a broken relationship brought about by a fresh revelation of himself.

In our context, this stunning portrayal of the diversity and particularity of God's modes of accommodation challenges any belief that an inability to engage cognitively with the words of the gospel, which some hold to be indispensable, stands as an insurmountable obstacle. In fact, the idea that a relationship between God and any human being would depend on finite human ability, rather than infinite divine ability, seems untenable and in contradiction of the purpose of divine accommodation – to bridge the gap between the infinite and the finite. It is only the infinite that can create the bridge.

---

47. Bowen, **Ezekiel**, 117.
48. Bowen, 117.

The flexibility demonstrated so vividly in Ezekiel 20 is not an isolated case. The general understanding of accommodation as a device for continual adaptation of the divine revelation to meet the demands of a particular time, circumstance and culture to facilitate a divine–human relationship was also used to legitimize the considerable degree of diversity within the practices of the church. (note 49) These variances further demonstrate the flexibility within the spectrum of God's approach to his communication with humanity, for which Strabo (paraphrased by Funkenstein) argues, "God Himself has set an example." (note 50) Reflecting on this continuous flexibility, when held alongside the aspects of the revelation which stress God's love for and desire for relationship with all of humanity, a vision for God's intervention in the lives of those for whom engagement with a word-based revelation is not accessible begins to emerge.

Accommodation as Condescension

The second element of the insight provided by a theology of accommodation is its illumination

---

49. Funkenstein, **Scientific Imagination**, 225 (the author cites the work of Walahfrid Strabo to substantiate this position).
50. Funkenstein, 225.

of divine condescension. Calvin's work offers a significant contribution to the debate. Battles explains that "for Calvin, the understanding of God's accommodation to the limits and needs of the human condition was a central feature of the interpretation of Scripture and of the entire range of his theological work." (note 51) He sets his perspective on accommodation within the tradition of classical rhetoric in which "the verb **accommodare** . . . [denotes] fitting, adapting, adjusting language, of building a speech-bridge between the matter of discourse and the intended audience." (note 52) His argument is helpfully summarized in a statement in which he draws particular attention to God's response to the limitation of human comprehension:

> For who is so devoid of intellect as not to understand that God, in . . . speaking [in human language], lisps with us as nurses are wont to do with little children? Such modes of expression do not so much express what kind of a being God is as accommodate the knowledge of him to our feebleness. In so doing He must, of course, stoop far below His proper height. (note 53)

---

51. Battles, "God Was Accommodating," 22.
52. Battles, 22.
53. Calvin, **Institutes**, 263–64.

This is perhaps the central metaphor of the theory of accommodation. It describes the way in which God stoops to the level of human beings in the same way that an adult stoops to the level of a child. The underlying principle here is pivotal. Divine revelation is always attuned to the level of understanding of its particular recipients. In the case of Moses' hearers of scientifically unsustainable explanations, (note 54) these are people whom Calvin would describe as having limited intellectual understanding; in the context of this discussion, they are people with profound intellectual disabilities.

Calvin's perspective is predated by much earlier theological voices. Chrysostom, for example, as well as highlighting the anthropomorphic language of the Bible as God's accommodation to human limitations, explains God's condescension to weaker natures by illustrating how he does so in relation to all created beings, whether angelic or human. (note 55) Benin agrees, describing this kind

---

54. Calvin, 131–32.

55. With regard to Isaiah's extraordinary vision of God on his throne, described in Isa 6:1–2, in which the seraphim must cover their faces in God's otherwise unendurable presence, Chrysostom comments that "C'est, pour Dieu, le fait d'apparaître et de se montrer non pas tel qu'il est,

of imagery as "proportional revelation. . . . If one hears a prophet claim to have seen God, this does not mean the divine essence but a manifestation achieved through divine condescension." (note 56) This, Sparks argues, is the "true nature of accommodation: accommodation provides greater access to the divine truth by depicting some things as other than they are." (note 57) And thus human beings are, on the whole, permitted by the linguistically based accommodation of Scripture to see more of God than they naturally could, by seeing less of him than there actually is to see, as the full revelation would render him entirely inapprehensible by or blindingly incapacitating to not only the human eye but the entirety of the human person. In Isaiah's record of his vision in chapter 6, for example, it is the language that paints the picture, but even the picture is far removed from the reality. Clearly, words are not the only means of divine revelation, and those for whom words are not relevant should not be

---

mais tel qu'il peut être vu par celui qui est capable de cette vision, en proportionnant l'aspect qu'il se présente de lui-même à la faiblesse de ceux qui le regardent." Chrysostome, **Sur l'incompréhensibilité de Dieu**, III.3 722/200 (my translation).

56. Benin, **Footprints of God**, 68.

57. Sparks, **God's Word**, 239.

deemed incapable of accessing an experience of God that might perhaps be even more immediately present than that which words can depict.

Divine Motivation

The third interpretative lens through which we can understand divine accommodation is in its divine motivation: the expression of God's goodness and desire. Origen sets the use of accommodative biblical language firmly within the positive parameters of the desire and benevolence of God in disclosing himself to human beings, despite their inability to apprehend him as he is.

> Just as when we are talking to very small children we do not assume as the object of our instruction any strong understanding in them, but say what we have to say accommodating (**harmosamenas**) to the small understanding of those whom we have before us . . . so the Word of God seems to have disposed the things that were written, adapting the suitable parts of his message to the capacity of its hearers and their ultimate profit. (note 58)

---

58. Origen, **Against Celsus** 5.16, cited in Benin, **Footprints of God**, 12.

Gregory of Nyssa describes the "ultimate profit" to which Origen alludes in terms of an apprehension of the love of God:

> We account for God's willingness to admit men to communion with Himself by His love towards mankind. But since that which is by nature finite cannot rise above its prescribed limits or lay hold upon the Superior Nature of the Most High, on this account, He [brought] His power, so full of love for humanity, down to the level of human weakness. (note 59)

Here, accommodation is revealed to be a depiction of the extent of God's loving desire for self-disclosure and relationship. We might ask whether this self-disclosure must be confined within the text, or is it possible that out of the reservoirs of the same love that motivated God's accommodated communication found within the biblical text, it continues to take place in ways that are appropriate to the capacity of other potential recipients of his revelation? It seems at best incongruent, at worst unsustainable, to conclude that, at some point on this continuum or spectrum of human capacity, the divine accommodation process must come to an end.

---

59. Gregory of Nyssa, **Answer to Eunomuius' Second Book**, in Schaff, **Gregory of Nyssa**, 292.

Gregory of Nyssa's perspective goes even further. He presents the view that the metaphor for understanding God's accommodative action should not only encompass the use of simpler language than might be the case, but be extended to include the idea of God not using comprehensible language at all:

> so the Divine power . . . though exalted far above our nature and inaccessible to all approach, like a tender mother who joins in the inarticulate utterances of her babe, gives to our human nature what it is capable of receiving; and thus in the various manifestations of God to man He both adapts Himself to man and speaks in human language, and assumes wrath, and pity, and such-like emotions, so that through feelings corresponding to our own our infantile life might be led as by hand, and lay hold of the Divine nature by means of the words which His foresight has given. (note 60)

His metaphor depicts God communicating by non-linguistic means, like the mother of a newborn infant, stooping below or beyond the level of verbal expression. She communicates her deepest emotion to her baby in a way in

---

60. Gregory of Nyssa, 292.

which the infant will be capable of grasping the essence of that emotion – her love for her child. Not only does this mother set aside her natural way of speaking; she adopts the baby's own mode of expression: she adopts the precise "non-verbal" sounds and gestures which are the infant's sole options for expressing him- or herself. Imagining the encounter, we would discover no ambiguity in our perception of what is occurring; what is passing between mother and baby is non-linguistic, but a no-less-comprehensible, immediate, intimate communication of love. While Gregory's explanation might be criticized as an overly dramatic description of accommodation, we should take into account evidence in the biblical text of the parenthood of God both as reality and metaphor, and the expressions of love and intimacy that accompany it.

Fundamentally, the significance of such a depiction of God's accommodative self-disclosure lies in what might be described as God's chosen accommodative range. God does not simply water down the more complex aspects of his being in order to disclose himself to those he has created for loving and faithful relationship. Rather, he does what needs to be done in order to reveal himself and his love. Gregory's explanation of God's range of accommodation suggests that God will use whatever form of communication is necessary to bridge the gap between himself and any human being's ability to apprehend him.

There are many more examples of accommodation to be found within the biblical text that cannot be discussed here. What is most important is its fundamental aim – divine–human communication. Benin comments that for Augustine, "communication is the key." (note 61) The latter's focus is particularly interesting in this context: in his perspective on accommodation, communication, both in its means and content, is not confined to words. God has "played with our infantile character by providing parables and similes – such as fire and smoke and the cloudy pillar, as by visible words." (note 62) Undoubtedly words are, for him, both the greatest communicative tools and the greatest signs by which revelation was accomplished, yet they remain only tools and signs. Particular words in themselves are not the beginning and end of any communicated revelation; they are to be understood as more than their immediate meaning

---

61. Benin, **Footprints of God**, 94.
62. Benin, 99, referring to Augustine, **De vera religione**.

might convey; they are signs to realities beyond themselves and they stimulate or emerge in response to a quest for such realities. (note 63)

Accommodation in the Incarnation

It is, of course, impossible to explore any concept of biblical revelation without acknowledgement of the foundational premise of Christian theology that God's ultimate revelation was not accomplished in human words but in the divine Word or **logos** (λογοσ), (note 64) God's incarnate presence among human beings. (note 65) In its fullest expression, the Word of God as revealed to human beings is not a "word" in its common sense at all, but a human being, flesh and blood, tangible and vulnerable (albeit one whose divinity was not diminished by the humanity in which he participated). (note 66) Benin summarizes the prominent perspective on the incarnation among theologians who emphasize the theory of accommodation as "the extreme example of

---

63. Benin, 94.
64. John 1:1.
65. John 1:14.
66. So Barth argues that "genuine deity includes in itself genuine humanity." Barth, **Humanity of God**, 50.

accommodation and condescension." (note 67) As Young explains, "Christian theology affirmed that God had accommodated the divine self to the limitations of human language and our creaturely existence, both in Scripture and in the incarnation," (note 68) further arguing that "the complete incarnation of one who was totally transcendent was the crown of accommodation." (note 69) The foundational principle of christological thought is that Christ is not simply an additional revelation but the ultimate revelation of God; the revelation who supersedes all that has come before. (note 70) For Karl Rahner, as Carr comments, "the single mystery of divine self-communication is given in the doctrine of Christ." (note 71)

As a statement of Christ's divinity and revelatory essence, John 1:1 is one of the most significant: "In the beginning was the Word, and the Word was with God, and the Word was God." While the most common translation of **logos** is "word," it is much more complex and multidimensional than a basic usage of this term conveys, with inherent

---

67. Benin, **Footprints of God**, 65.
68. Young, **God's Presence**, 71.
69. Young, 395.
70. Heb 1:1–3.
71. Carr, "Theology and Experience," 367.

connotations of "mind," "idea," "thought" and "rational plan." It was not an exclusively Hebraic idea but was commonly found in other religious traditions and, significantly, given the New Testament context, in Greek philosophy, where it "denoted something like the world-soul . . . the rational principle of the universe." (note 72) As such, the term would have been widely recognized by its first hearers and understood as signifying something very important. There are contrasting views on the cultural and religious contexts from which John's thinking here emerged, and there is no definitive explanation, but William Temple's concise articulation of the Hebraic and Greek understandings and roots of **logos** is helpful: "[The **logos**] alike for Jew and Gentile represents the ruling fact of the universe, and represents that fact as the Self-expression of God." (note 73) Leon Morris's conclusion on the issue is that "for [John], the Word was not a principle, but a living Being and the source of life; not a personification, but a Person and that Person divine." (note 74) Brunner argues that "the fact that He Himself takes the place of the spoken word is precisely the category which distinguishes the Old Testament revelation – the revelation through speech – from

---

72. Morris, **Gospel According to John**, 115.
73. Temple, **Readings in St. John's Gospel**, 4.
74. Morris, **Gospel According to John**, 123.

the New Testament revelation, the revelation in Christ." (note 75) Thus it is clear that the "Word" in the Old as well as the New Testament is both a word and much more than a word, and that the **logos** of the New Testament is a person, the person of Christ, the Second Person of the Godhead.

Nonetheless, the use of the incarnation to support ideas of revelation without verbal communication based on the **logos** passage in John 1 is strongly contested by some scholars, of whom Jensen's is a representative voice: "The revelation is not the proper nouns 'Jesus Christ,' but the proposition, 'Jesus is Christ, the Lord.' The divine word comes to us in, and not apart from, the words of this gospel." (note 76) It might be asked whether Jensen is confusing the content of revelation – that Jesus Christ is Lord, albeit that this is perhaps a somewhat limited account of its content – with the revelation itself, which or who is Christ. If what God "said" through human authors is an accommodation of who he is, then, in the coming of Christ, we actually have who he is. The concept of the revelation of God as a proposition rather than a person is far from convincing.

---

75. Brunner, **Doctrine of God**, 27.
76. Jensen, **Revelation of God**, 49.

What is clear is that this revelation in Christ challenges "all abstract presuppositions about God's nature, both ancient and modern. To know God, we begin not with general definitions of the 'divine,' but with the particular Person, Jesus of Nazareth." (note 77) Yet Jesus Christ, the **logos** of God, not only respected but continued to utter the words of God, (note 78) thus precluding any possibility that God's self-disclosure in Christ negates or undermines either the spoken words of the Old Testament or the spoken words of the New. On the contrary, Jesus declared his purpose to be that of fulfilling the law, not abolishing it, (note 79) and yet it was in his personal engagement with humanity in its own place and within its own limitations that this fulfilment of the law was achieved. God's engagement with humanity is not distant or propositional but present and relational. The **logos** of God and all that the person of Christ does to bridge the gap between God and human beings both reveals the depth of God's desire to engage in relationship with them and demonstrates that, in the enacting of this desire, he is not only far from constricted by linguistic methods, but that such methods alone are entirely inadequate to the task. On

---

77. Campbell, "Between Text and Sermon," 396.
78. John 14:10.
79. Matt 5:17.

the contrary, the language which communicates so much of what is known of God is merely a communicative tool used to point to the reality which is God himself.

The Importance of Mystery

There is some irony in the fact that an argument for the spiritual experience of people who do not use words is predicated on the interpretation of words, but it is important to stress that its validity does not rest on a need to dispense with words in order to experience God. This is an additional and not a contradictory perspective which pertains specifically to people with profound intellectual disabilities as people whom we must conclude God loves and with whom he desires relationship, but who cannot learn of this truth in one of the primary ways that others can. Acknowledging the complexities of the **logos** concept – the reality that the greatest act of accommodation is not verbal but relational, not a proposition but a person – indicates that access to words cannot be the defining aspect of any person's potential to be reached by and experience God.

What, then, might be the appropriate theological "vocabulary" for persons who do not apprehend verbal communication to encounter or be encountered by God? Whatever it is, it cannot be beyond the capacity of God. Those who argue for the indispensability of words, and the intelligence to understand and respond to them, are in danger of underestimating the depths of all humanity's incapacity when it comes to understanding God. As Battles states, "[we] try to measure God's immeasurableness by our small measure. But it is God who knows the incalculable difference in measure between His infinity and our finiteness, and accordingly accommodates the one to the other in the way in which He reveals Himself to us." (note 80) To ask whether Rebecca's and others' limited intellectual capacity precludes them enjoying a life-giving relationship with God is an irrelevant exercise. The only thing that matters is God's infinite capacity to generate and energize that relationship in light of his indisputable revelation of his desire to do so.

At its core, the Christian revelation of God is a mystery, crafted and implemented by the supernatural power and activity of its divine author; its content cannot be fully accommodated to human understanding. Norris emphasizes this point: "Intellectual activities may lead us part of the way; they may even point to God's existence, but God's essence is beyond our powers of expression. Enfleshed human beings do not have the capacity to grasp God's nature except in

---

80. Battles, **God Was Accommodating**, 35.

faithful acceptance of the mystery." (note 81) On what authority would we attempt to restrict the depth of this mystery, as Birchenall seeks to do, and view that the revelation might be inaccessible to some of those created human beings, simply as a consequence of their lack of linguistic ability? As Sparks warns, "We are wise to hesitate before we say what God can and cannot do." (note 82) When assessed via the IQ scale, the gap between my knowledge of the world and Rebecca's seems enormous. Yet the gap between my knowledge of God and what there is to know of God makes the gap between us no more than a hair's breadth. If God accommodates himself to human beings in order to draw them into loving relationship, it is no more credible to assume that this accommodation would arbitrarily stop at some point based on limited intellectual capacity than that it would stop at the other end of the scale.

Returning to Swain's comment that "communication, theologically understood, is never less than an exchange of words," (note 83) the counter-question that might be posed is whether a non-verbal encounter with God should inevitably be perceived as less than words. Does

---

81. Norris, **Faith Gives Fullness**, 112.
82. Sparks, **God's Word**, 253.
83. Swain, **Trinity, Revelation and Reading**, 8.

the absence of words inherently mean a lesser degree of revelation than that which might be achieved by linguistic means? Cannot God be encountered personally, either before or apart from their utterance? The substantial theological scholarship which perceives verbal expression and cognitive appropriation of truth to be essential for apprehending God creates tensions in relation to the view that, for some, words or the lack of them do not have the last word.

Concluding Remarks

How then can we find a way to hear about the spiritual experience of those who, as a consequence of their profound intellectual disabilities, cannot speak? We cannot. The question is, does this really matter? Rather than asking them for information – the questions which we might or might not believe require to be asked concerning the spiritual lives of people with profound and complex intellectual disabilities – the rich vein of God's self-disclosure in the sources of the faith tradition provides an appropriate focus for our attention. Accommodation as a model of divine self-disclosure lies at the heart of the history of the Jewish and Christian tradition of revelation. God stoops to the level of finite humanity in order to welcome them into his infinite reality. As such, God's methodology for communication is multifaceted and inevitably entirely appropriate to meeting the needs of people with profound intellectual disabilities and their incapacity to receive and apprehend information by cognitive and linguistic means. Ultimately, it is not human incapacity in any form that matters, but God's infinite capacity to accommodate his revelation to it. It would, then, be inappropriate to attempt to restrict the depth of this mystery in a way that supports a view that the revelation might be inaccessible to some of those created human beings, simply as a consequence of their lack of intellectual and linguistic ability. As quoted above, Sparks warns that "we are wise to hesitate before we say what God can and cannot do." (note 84) As Baillie emphatically argues, "we must not limit the competence of God by saying that He cannot reveal His will to stocks and stones." (note 85)

The content of the accommodation expressed in Scripture and the wider sources of the faith tradition reveal crucial insights from which a theological understanding of whether and how the spiritual experience of people with profound intellectual disabilities might take shape. This theory does not provide a comprehensive

---

84. Sparks, **God's Word**, 253.
85. Baillie, **Our Knowledge**, 21.

picture – there are many other sources from the faith tradition that could be explored. Biblical material on the unpredictable activity of the Spirit, perspectives emerging in wider systematic theologies, and a philosophical analysis of the reasonableness of accepting evidence of a mystical, non-cognitive and non-sensory encounter with God (note 86) have potential to further illuminate this discussion. It is not possible to explore these here, but it is important to ground our previous discussion in our church communities and remind ourselves why it is vital in the contemporary life of the church and its attempts to develop communities of inclusion.

This chapter began with highlighting shortcomings in contemporary understandings of inclusive Christian communities and the continuing theological exclusion of those who, despite their equal and God-imbued value, are often perceived as essentially different by reason of their limited intellectual capacity. The effects of these perceptions are all too real and damaging to their experience of Christian community, or lack thereof, and that of those who know and love them most. At the time of writing, I have been invited by one of the largest Reformed denominations in the United

---

86. An excellent discussion of the subject can be found in Alston, **Perceiving God.**

Kingdom to join a designated group of church leaders tasked with creating a church policy to address the "dilemma" of whether people who have intellectual disabilities should be allowed to receive the sacrament of communion and be admitted to full membership of their churches. Here is theological exclusion at work in an era of the purported development of inclusivity in Western churches.

This oppression and exclusion are undoubtedly detrimental in the extreme to people who have intellectual disabilities and to their families who once again experience and witness the pain of discrimination, ostracization and rejection in the one place where they might most expect to be safe, respected and loved. But they are also detrimental to the church, which should mourn the absence of some of its indispensable members and the loss of the gifts they have to bring to the life of the community. (note 87) And for its members' understanding, experience and practice of what it means to be a Christian and the nature of the church, such exclusion denies them theological and spiritual insight that could be genuinely transformative. It distracts us from our missional task and the blessings of mutuality and interdependence inherent in authentic

---

87. See 1 Cor 12, for example.

relationships within the body of Christ. (note 88) It erodes the virtue of humility that will keep us from thinking of ourselves more highly than we ought (note 89) and our ability to follow the Christ who set aside his ego for the sake of others. (note 90) It represents a misunderstanding of the counter-cultural kingdom of God, of which simplicity is a hallmark and where the last will, in the end, be first. It fosters the arrogant over-intellectualism that seeks to process spiritual things solely through our cognitive processes and inhibits our ability to be content to rest in the mystery at the heart of the Godhead, rather than joining the psalmist who submits and responds to his own finitude in light of the infinite God.

> My heart is not proud, LORD,
>> my eyes are not haughty;
> I do not concern myself with great matters
>> or things too wonderful for me.
> But I have calmed and quietened myself,
>> I am like a weaned child with its mother;
>> like a weaned child I am content.
>
> Israel, put your hope in the LORD
>> both now and for evermore.
>
> (Ps 131)

---

88. 1 Cor 12.
89. Rom 12:3.
90. Phil 2:4–6.

Bibliography

Alston, William. **Perceiving God: The Epistemology of Religious Experience**. New York: Cornell University Press, 1991.

Baillie, John. **Our Knowledge of God**. Oxford: Oxford University Press, 1946.

Barth, Karl. **The Humanity of God.** London: Fontana, 1967.

Battles, Ford Lewis. "God Was Accommodating Himself to Human Incapacity." In **Readings in Calvin's Theology**, edited by Donald McKim, 21–42. Eugene: Wipf & Stock, 1998.

Benin, Stephen. "The 'Cunning of God' and Divine Accommodation." **Journal of the History of Ideas** 45, no. 2 (1984): 179–91.

———. **The Footprints of God: Divine Accommodation in Jewish and Christian Thought**. New York: State University of New York Press, 1993.

Birchenall, Peter, and Mary Birchenall. "Caring for Mentally Handicapped People: The Community and the Church." **The Professional Nurse** 1, no. 6 (1986): 148–50.

Bowen, Nancy. **Ezekiel**. Nashville: Abingdon, 2010.

Brunner, Emil. **The Christian Doctrine of God.** Vol. 1 of **Dogmatics.** Translated by Olive Wyon. Philadelphia: Westminster, 1950.

Calvin, John. **Commentaries of the First Book of Moses Called Genesis.** Vol. 1. Translated by John King. Grand Rapids: Eerdmans, 1948.

———. **Institutes of the Christian Religion.** Vol. 1. Translated by Henry Beveridge. 2 vols. Edinburgh: Calvin Translation Society, 1844.

Campbell, Charles. "Between Text and Sermon: John 1:1–14." **Interpretation: A Journal of Bible and Theology** 49, no. 4 (1995): 394–98.

Carr, Anne. "Theology and Experience in the Thought of Karl Rahner." **Journal of Religion** 53, no. 3 (1973): 359–76.

Chrysostome, St Jean. **Sur l'incompréhensibilité de Dieu (Homélies I–V)**. SC 28 bis. 2nd ed. Edited by Jean Daniélou, Anne-Marie Malingrey and Robert Flacelière. Paris: Editions du Cerf, 1970.

Creamer, Deborah Beth. **Disability and Christian Theology: Embodied Limits and Constructive Possibilities**. Oxford: Oxford University Press, 2009.

Demarest, Bruce. **General Revelation: Historical Views and Contemporary Issues**. Nashville: Zondervan, 1992.

Eiesland, Nancy. **The Disabled God: Towards a Liberatory Theology of Disability**. Nashville: Abingdon, 1994.

Funkenstein, Amos. **Theology and the Scientific Imagination from the Middle Ages to the Seventeenth Century**. Princeton: Princeton University Press, 1986.

Headlam, Arthur. **Christian Theology.** Oxford: Cheltenham, 1934.

Jensen, Peter. **The Revelation of God**. Leicester: IVP, 2002.

Luther, Martin. **Luther's Works, Vol 4: Letters.** Translated and edited by G. Krodel. Philadelphia: Fortress Press, 1963.

Maimonides, Moses. **The Guide of the Perplexed.** Vol. 1. Translated by Shlomo Pines. Chicago: University of Chicago Press, 1963.

Markus, Robert Austin. "St. Augustine on Signs." **Phronesis** 2, no. 1 (1957): 60–83.

Morris, Leon. **The Gospel According to John**. London: Marshall, Morgan and Scott, 1972.

Morris, Wayne. "Does the Church Need the Bible? Reflections on the Experiences of Disabled People." In **Education, Religion and Society: Essays in Honour of John M. Hull**, edited by Dennis Bates, Gloria Durka and Friedrich Schweitzer, 162–72. Abingdon: Routledge, 2006.

———. "Transforming Able-Bodied Normativity: The Wounded Christ and Human Vulnerability." **Irish Theological Quarterly** 78, no. 3 (2013): 231–43.

Norris, Frederick W., ed. **Faith Gives Fullness to Reasoning: The Five Theological Orations of Gregory Nazianzen**. Leiden: Brill, 1991.

Pailin, David. **A Gentle Touch: From a theology of handicap to a theology of human being.** London: SPCK, 1992.

Schaff, Philip. **Gregory of Nyssa.** Vol. 5 of **Nicene and Post-Nicene Fathers**, Second Series. New York: Cosimo Classics, 2007.

Sparks, Kenton. **God's Word in Human Words: An Evangelical Appropriation of Critical Biblical Scholarship**. Grand Rapids: Baker Academic, 2008.

Swain, Scott. **Trinity, Revelation and Reading**. London: T&T Clark, 2011.

Swinton, John. "Restoring the Image: Spirituality, Faith and Intellectual Disability." **Journal of Religion and Health** 36, no. 1 (1997): 21–27.

Swinton, John, Harriet Mowat and Susannah Baines. "Whose Story Am I? Redescribing Profound Disability in the Kingdom of God." **Journal of Religion, Health and Disability** 15, no. 1 (2011): 5–19.

Temple, William. **Nature, Man and God: The Gifford Lectures, 1932–34.** Whitefish: Kessinger, 2003.

———. **Readings in St. John's Gospel**. London: Macmillan, 1947.

Van Bemmelin, Peter. "Divine Accommodation in Revelation and Scripture." **Journal of Adventist Theological Society** 9, no. 1–2 (1998): 221–29.

White, Andrew D. **A History of the Warfare of Science with Theology in Christendom.** Vol. 1. New York: Appleton, 1920.

Wolterstorff, Nicholas. **Philosophical Reflections on the Claim That God Speaks**. Cambridge: Cambridge University Press, 1995.

World Health Organization. International Classification of Diseases. 11th Revision. 1 January 2022.

Young, Frances. **Arthur's Call: A Journey of Faith in the Face of Severe Learning Disability.** London: SPCK, 2014.

———. **The Art of Performance: Towards a Theology of Holy Scripture.** London: Darton, Longman and Todd, 1990.

———. **God's Presence: A Contemporary Recapitulation of Early Christianity**. Cambridge: Cambridge University Press, 2014.

8

Attitudes and Accessibility

The Church's Response to People with Disabilities in Ghana

Dan Nyampong Asihene

Introduction

Negative attitudes and lack of accessibility are barriers that people with disabilities face. They are inextricably linked when it comes to the area of disability. According to James Charlton, barriers to the inclusion of people with disabilities within the church can be grouped into three distinct categories: "attitudinal," "architectural" and "communicative." (note 1) Some churches in Ghana claim to work against these three barriers: first, people with disabilities are not prevented from meeting and talking to persons without disabilities in the church; and second, people with disabilities can enter the buildings with ease to worship God. (note 2)

The apostle Paul explained that Christ "has destroyed the barrier, the dividing wall of hostility." (note 3) These walls or barriers – attitudinal, architectural and communicative – are human-made and they contradict Christ's ministry of reconciliation. A ministry of inclusive community will tear down the walls that are prevalent in the church and in the wider culture and society.

Peter Coleridge states that it is negative **attitudes** that disable: "if other people did not react with horror, fear, anxiety, hostility or patronizing behaviour towards People With Disabilities (PWDs), (note 4) then there would not be a problem." (note 5) Coleridge emphasizes that many

---

1. Charlton, **Nothing About Us**, 54.
2. Adjasah, "How Are We Faring?"
3. Eph 2:14.
4. Whenever the term "PWDs" is used in quotations it stands for "people with disabilities."
5. Coleridge, **Disability**, 6.

people with disabilities claim that their disability is caused by the environment and society, because if society provided support and understanding for them, they would not be disabled. (note 6) According to James Charlton, beliefs and attitudes about disability are experienced individually but socially constituted, reiterating that it is an individual's beliefs that produce his or her attitudes towards people with disabilities. (note 7) C. B. Peter avers that some persons with disabilities are denied accessibility to employment, including ordination into church leadership, as well as the opportunity to inherit from their family members. (note 8)

In contrast, certain inherent religious beliefs and teachings of the church have influenced congregants' attitudes towards people with disabilities in positive ways. For instance, the sociocultural and Christian beliefs attached to humanity as individuals and communities are helpful. African culture has a high regard for the individual as well as for the community in which the individual lives. This conception supports the

---

6. Coleridge, 6.
7. Charlton, **Nothing About Us**, 57.
8. Peter, "One in Christ," 59–79.

belief in individual Christians coming together to form the "body of Christ," where they share their lives. (note 9)

In general, then, sociocultural and religious beliefs appear to influence attitudes towards people with disabilities. As Amenyedzi explains, the old adage "there is no smoke without fire" also becomes relevant in this discussion. For the African, there are always spiritual reasons behind any occurrence, be it fortune or misfortune. Disability has been socioculturally constructed in most African societies as a curse meted out by the gods due to some kind of abomination committed by the person with the disability, a relative or an ancestor. (note 10) The Ghanaian sociocultural understanding of communalism is found to have contributed to positive attitudes towards people with disabilities within the church and society when it comes to issues of welfare and charity, but there are some gaps to be filled, and these will be discussed below.

The study that forms the basis of this chapter was limited to the Akan-speaking group within the selected communities or geographical areas. It was observed that what was found about the Akan

---

9. 1 Cor 12:26.
10. Amenyedzi, "Equity and Access," 46–47.

people, the largest ethnic group in Ghana, could in many ways be applied to other ethnic groups in Ghana as well. This chapter is structured as follows: first, we will examine how certain inherent cultural and religious beliefs tend to influence actions taken towards people with disabilities. For the most part, people acquire these beliefs in their formative years through storytelling by family members. Second, we will explore disability models in the African/Ghanaian understanding. Third, we will argue that the sociocultural beliefs of the church and society at large have influenced people's attitudes towards people with disabilities. We will then conclude with recommendations for the church's response to different types of disabilities.

Language Terms, and Inherent Cultural and Religious Beliefs

African theologians writing on the theology of disability, such as Reuben Kigame, (note 11) Esther Mombo (note 12) and Phitalis Masakhwe, (note 13) do not exclude the possibility that myths and "unhealthy beliefs" associated with disability have led to negative attitudes towards people

---

11. Kigame, "Cultural Barriers," 121–38.
12. Mombo, "Society and Leadership," 157–68.
13. Masakhwe, "Church," 111–20.

with disability in the wider African context. Here, disability is believed to be caused by evil spirits, and it is important to engage with such beliefs, rather than ignore them.

In some parts of Ghana, as in most African societies, there is a strong belief that nothing just happens for no causal reason. As Shiriko states, "everything is caused by a variable; it could be real, imagined or figurative." (note 14) Disability is also considered a punishment or curse for sin committed either by the parents of the person or one of the ancestors. (note 15) Belief in the reincarnation of people with disabilities in some Ghanaian communities, as noted by Agbenyega, "has somehow affected people's attitudes towards PWDs believed to be reincarnated." (note 16) Others believe that those with disabilities are superhuman and wield supernatural mystical powers that can either benefit or harm the community. (note 17) Therefore, attitudes towards people with disabilities and how they are treated depend on the perception of the community. Masakhwe notes that the beliefs, attitudes and practices

---

14. Shiriko, "Disability," 169–96.
15. Shiriko, 169–74.
16. Agbenyega, "Power of Labeling."
17. Rutachwamagyo, "Profile of Tanzanians," 363–82.

of a society contribute to the limitations of the normal lives of people with disabilities. (note 18) It is believed that people with disabilities will always need physical assistance from others to be able to manage their daily activities. They are sometimes prevented from using their talents either in the church or in society due to challenges related to mobility.

However, contrary to such attitudes, there is a lot that people with disabilities are able to do. For instance, they can distribute tracts, bulletins and flyers to visitors. They can play musical instruments and be part of the church choir, and also be ushers to direct visitors to their seats. Yet their perceived vulnerability has often become a source of oppression, causing people to exercise authority over them against their wishes. The writer experienced something of this when attending a conference organized for people with disabilities. When the main speaker at the conference, a person living with a disability, was introduced to present his lecture, the writer attempted to assist him to the podium. The speaker, however, politely resisted, saying, "Thanks, I can walk to the podium." The assumption that

---

18. Masakhwe, "Church," 111–20.

people with disabilities are intrinsically weak and unable to take responsibility for their own lives needs to be revisited.

Words are used as barriers for people with disabilities but have evolved, with different terms being thought appropriate at different times, and then being challenged over time (see appendix 1). Terminology "ranges from derogatory to sympathetic." (note 19) To quote Michael Masutha, a South African politician and human rights lawyer, "we must take language very seriously. The feeling I have is that language is always a reflection of attitude." (note 20)

Akan Language Terms Related to Disability

Ghanaians have various descriptions for people with disabilities which appear to be similar in meaning. It is worth paying attention to the terminology and words in use, as these tend to be derogatory and discriminate against people with disabilities. Paying close attention to the use of language terms can reveal underlying attitudes and beliefs. "Language terms" in this context

---

19. World Health Organization, "International Classification," 28.

20. Quoted in Charlton, **Nothing About Us**, 58.

means words that are used by persons without disabilities to describe the disability associated with someone else.

Beliefs concerning inappropriate terms used for persons with disabilities within the Akan community in Ghana – the largest community in Ghana – appear to be similar to the belief systems of the wider community, though there are a few dissimilarities in the use of language. (note 21)

One of the terms used within the Akan community to describe persons with disabilities is **wafi Nipa mu**, which literally means "one cannot take part in community activities." **Nipa** means a human being

---

21. The Akan people of Ghana are the largest ethnic group, constituting 49 percent of the Ghanaian population, according to the 2020 Worldometer report. According to Kuada and Chachah, they migrated from the Chad–Benue regions of Africa and settled first at the confluence of the Pra and the Offin rivers in the forest regions of Ghana around the eleventh century (Kuada and Chachah, **Ghana**, 12). They speak dialects of the Akan language, the major ones being Twi and Fanti. The use of their language has been one of the major factors in unifying the Akan people (Omenyo, **Pentecost outside Pentecostalism**). The language of the Akans can in many ways be applied to other ethnic groups in Ghana as well.

created by God. Persons with disabilities expect society to treat them with dignity as human beings and as equals. In this regard, the Akan concept of a human being will be useful in this analysis.

According to Peter Sarpong, "a human being is both a social being and an individual species." Human beings are called **Homo sapiens** (literally, thinking beings). (note 22) The term **Homo sapiens** (Latin) can be broken down into **homo** (human being) and **sapiens** (wise). In contrast, the Akan idea of human beings is based on their beliefs and practices. According to Sarpong, for the Akan, a human being must consist of the following main components: **mogya** or **bogya** (blood), **sunsum** (spirit), **ɔkra** (soul), **honhom** (breath of life), and **sasa**, **saman**, **ntoro** or **bosom** (different forms of spirit). (note 23)

Sarpong maintains that the "Akan conception of [the] human being is dualistic: the visible side and the invisible side, the spiritual and material side." (note 24) Cephas Omenyo echoes that in Akan religious thought, the "human person is a complex of both physical and spiritual elements received from God, father and mother that are

---

22. Sarpong, **Peoples Differ**, 89–90.
23. Sarpong, 90–91.
24. Sarpong, 92–93.

bonded together." (note 25) He adds that apart from the body, the person is believed to have **sunsum**, **ɔkra** and **mogya**.

Another Akan term used for persons with disabilities is **wadidɛm**, and this goes beyond restriction and impairment. This word represents anything that is "damaged or disfigured physically and irreversibly beyond repair." This could be as a result of a personal tragedy, for example through a traffic accident. **Wadidɛm** is seen as a deformity that cannot be improved or repaired back to its former state. Another Akan description for persons with disabilities is **watɔsin**, which could literally be defined as a defective or incomplete human being. **Watɔ** means "to acquire." In the Akan sense, **sin** means "deficient or not up to the full measure," or abnormal.

The Akans describe persons with learning disabilities as **Nea wayin agya n'adwene ho** or **Nea n'adwene mu ye hare**, which means "feeble-minded" and is dehumanizing. On the basis of these terms, we can see that disability is assumed to mean either not being included in the category of human beings, or not measuring up to their required standard. In this instance, if the beauty of the human body becomes defective,

---

25. Omenyo, **Pentecost outside Pentecostalism**, 28.

it is mistaken for ugliness. Similarly, when one's strength and intelligence are defective, weakness and intellectual disability are assumed. The word **sin** is believed to establish a hierarchical system in which certain kinds of people have higher worth than others. Some Akan traditions assume such distinctions, but the biblical Scriptures suggest otherwise: "in humility count others more significant than yourself." (note 26)

Models of Disability in the African/Ghanaian Context

The challenge of defining disability persists since disability is relative to sociocultural context; however, there are several models that seek to define disability within various settings. (note 27)

The term "disability" can be understood from different perspectives, such as social, medical or cultural (see introduction to this volume). According to Michael Oliver, there are many models of disability, but the global definition of the term "disability" falls into two main categories: the medical model and the social model. The medical model sees disability as a problem (caused by disease or another health condition) on the part

---

26. Phil 2:3, ESV.
27. Cf. Amenyedzi, "3D Disability."

of the person with the disability and not any other individual. The social model of disability, in contrast, sees the issue of disability as caused by the community and the social environment that requires equal access and inclusion within the society. (note 28) Under the social model, there is differentiation between impairment and disability, promoting the view that persons with disabilities need to be treated equally as their non-disabled counterparts. Furthermore, the social model depicts disability as a process which can be overcome and managed, while the medical model seeks to provide a cure or medical care to treat the medical aspects of the disability.

Amenyedzi states that in the social model, disability is the external factors that prevent people with disability from accessing their rights, privileges, roles and the environment. She adds that the moral model associates disability with sin and affliction, particularly within religious settings. The expectation here is that the able-bodied must serve and care for people with disability by means of charity. In the moral model, the attitude towards people with disability is one of extreme exclusion, seen in the way that disability is culturally constructed as a curse/punishment in

---

28. Oliver, **Understanding Disability**, 17–20.

the Ghanaian traditional belief culture. (note 29) The moral model therefore overlaps with the cultural model.

According to Rod Michalco, interdisciplinary research has proposed new insights and other related models of disability, including the cultural model. The cultural model of disability sees societal beliefs, attitudes and practices that have become the norm as contributing to the limitations of the normal lives of people with disabilities. (note 30)

Whereas the medical model locates the cause of disability as disease in the body, the cultural model places the cause directly in spiritual matters. The social and human rights models view disability as a socially constructed issue where people with disabilities are not fully integrated into society. In this context, disability is assumed to be a complex construct mostly caused by the social environment and not by the attitude of an individual. To resolve this challenge requires social action and it is the corporate responsibility of the church and society at large to modify the environment to enable the full participation of people with disabilities in all areas of life in the society.

---

29. Amenyedzi, "Equity and Access," 15.
30. Michalko, **Difference**.

For many Africans, as stated by Francis Appiah-Kubi, an understanding of the causes and effects of any variable is often attributed to the world of spirits. It is important to note that myths, superstitions and beliefs can affect people's attitudes towards disability. (note 31) This is the case when people consider afflictions that result from accidents and disability and death to be the consequences of bad actions by the persons affected. This suggests that the positive or negative side of an in-built sociocultural belief system tends to work on our psychology to affect our attitudes towards people with disabilities. For this reason, to achieve a comprehensive understanding, it is important to consider cultural models of disability in African contexts.

Sociocultural Attitudes and Disabilities

As we have established, in the Ghanaian context, disability is often considered a curse or punishment for sins committed either by an ancestor, a parent or the person living with the disability. (note 32) The following study explores sociocultural attitudes towards disability in greater depth.

---

31. Appiah-Kubi, "African Traditional Religion," 27–39.
32. Amenyedzi, "3D Disability," 292–325.

Overview of Methods

The sociocultural and religious attitudes of people towards different categories of disabilities were the focus of empirical research conducted in 2019 among 273 persons. (note 33) Interviews were used as tools to explore the type of Akan language that expresses the different attitudes towards different kinds of disabilities. The scope of the interviews was locations in Akan-dominated areas in Ghana, specifically the Ashanti and eastern regions. Empirical methods were used to collect both quantitative and qualitative data for the research.

The writer participated in the collection of the data. Questionnaires were used to assess the various sociocultural belief systems concerning disability within churches, public institutions and communities in Ghana. Available ethnographic research based on Akan cosmology on the subject was used, especially regarding beliefs, myths, rituals and symbols.

For the administration of the interviews, research volunteers sometimes helped with the qualitative selection of respondents and, when necessary, with translation of the languages. For the survey, volunteers were used to help with

---

33. Academic thesis submitted to the South African Theological Seminary, South Africa.

the administration of the questionnaires. In this research, observation was used to study behaviour towards persons with disabilities; for example, how people behave and what their body language is when meeting a person with disability on the street. These observations gave insights into attitudes towards people with disabilities.

The writer joined fifty local churches in Ghana, including four deaf ministry churches, and participated in their activities to investigate attitudes towards people with disabilities using dialogue and observation. The writer also took notice of how people with disabilities were referred to in public and whether they were welcomed or discriminated against. The research data was critically analysed to demonstrate the genuine attitudes and language terms expressed towards people with disabilities.

The quantitative survey helped to collect relevant data from a large number of respondents. The research population was spread over five out of ten regions in Ghana. Due to the scope of the research, it was not possible to visit all of the districts in each region. Ten districts were selected from each region, to get results from both rural and urban settings. To ensure a spread in the selection of respondents, the research volunteers were instructed to interview only four persons per community in each town or village. Research assistants considered an equal division between the number of male and female respondents and a range of respondents from towns and villages. It should be clear, though, that the sample is not representative for the total population in Ghana, and the results of this research should therefore not be over-generalized.

The final measurement of attitude and language terms was done by adding together the different items that measured the same disability language terms. Some of the statements reflected positive attitudes towards persons with disabilities and others, negative attitudes. The data collected was processed using Excel and SPSS. (note 34) Since the research was based on language terms and attitudes towards persons with disabilities, these

---

34. The information gathered in the survey was processed into three different SPSS (Statistical Package for the Social Sciences) and Excel files. In the analysis of the results for the total sample of language terms, the group of persons with disabilities registered a lower weighting factor and the group of persons without disabilities a higher weighting factor. Because of the large sample of certain types of disabilities, it was possible to make a comparison between attitudes of people towards different types of disabilities. A large portion of the data collected consisted of two

unratified proposals were tested by means of the attitude scale. (note 35) Table 1 provides an overview of the interviews conducted and the data analysis results.

The following findings from the church and general public were noted (see Table 1): different language terms and attitudes were observed for different kinds of disabilities. The identified results of different attitudes towards people with disabilities can be expressed as follows: fear of unpredictable actions of persons with mental health disabilities led to an attitude of rejection; sympathy towards persons with hearing and speech disabilities resulted in an attitude of inclusion; persons with visual disabilities were welcomed and tended

---

attitude scales: the scale for disability language terms and the scale for attitudes towards different categories of disability.

35. (1) Persons who identify themselves as having a disability have more positive attitudes towards persons with disabilities than people who do not identify themselves as having a disability. (2) People with certain inherent cultural and religious beliefs have particular language terms and attitudes towards persons with certain disabilities. After the test analysis using data from the respondents which included persons with and without disabilities, the second scale of attitude was ratified.

to experience an attitude of inclusion into the community, while people with physical disabilities tended to be ridiculed and discriminated against. This suggests that attitudes towards people with disabilities differ for different types of disabilities.

Table 1

Categories of disabilities under investigation	Number of non-PWDs (note 36) who were interviewed as respondents	Language terms used to describe PWDs by non-PWDs
Persons with physical disabilities	145	1. **Wadidem** 2. **Ayarefo**
Persons with visual disabilities	149	**Watɔsin**
Persons with hearing disabilities	156	1. **Ayarefo** 2. **Asotifo**
Person with mental / intellectual disabilities	138	1. **Wafi nipa mu** 2. **Adwenmu yare**

---

36. "Non-PWDS" refers to people without disabilities.

Respondents who used same language terms	Meanings from non-PWD respondents' language terms	Attitudes as expressed by non-PWDs towards PWDs
84%	The person's disabilities are beyond recovery	They are ridiculed and stigmatized
86%	The person is disabled in some parts of the body	They are admired and welcomed
90%	The person is considered a weak person	They are empathized with and included
80%	The person has lost his or her identity as a human being	They are feared and isolated from the community

According to some respondents, stigmatization and language terms took the form of words; others noted labelling descriptions that highlighted their disabilities rather than abilities. These language expressions, consisting of words and descriptions to label persons with disabilities, pushes them to the periphery to conform to the characteristics of the language terms and stigmatization.

Accessibility and the Church's Response

Accessibility differs according to disability. Amenyedzi states that the matters of access and disability cannot be lumped together as one issue. There is therefore a need to categorize "what works better for whom." So accessibility requirements for people with physical disability will not be the same as those for people with visual/hearing disability. Accessibility requirements for people with disability differ according to the disability. (note 37)

In this next section we move from attitudes to accessibility. The issue of accessibility concerns our neglect of people with disabilities in our prevention of them from entering church auditoriums and public halls by building walls of separation that cannot be overcome by the use of mobility aids. Here, I draw from the example of

---

37. Amenyedzi, "Equity and Access," 152–54.

making churches accessible for those with mobility impairments (i.e. physical disabilities), which is an important category to consider.

In Ghana, the Ministry of Works and Housing has not prioritized the accessibility of people with disabilities in recent housing projects, even though the Disability Act 715 of 2006 in Ghana states, "The owner of a place to which the public has access shall provide appropriate facilities that make the place accessible to and available for use by PWDs." (note 38) Section 60 of the Act adds, "The owner or occupier of an existing building to which the public has access within 10 years of the Act must make that building accessible and available for use by PWD." (note 39) Despite the provisions in the Disability Act, many public and religious buildings have no lifts and their escalators are so narrow and cumbersome that PWDs cannot use their mobility aids to move around freely. In addition, not many stairs in church buildings are professionally made in consultation with people with mobility impairments. Some stairs and facilities give only partial access to important areas: washrooms, the pulpit, the pastor's office and church halls. In June 2015, as I was entering a beautiful church building, I saw a group of

---

38. Ghana Persons with Disability Act, 5–6.
39. Ghana Persons with Disability Act, 5–6.

congregants in front of the building holding a physically challenged person who had fallen from the stairs of the building together with his crutches. I encouraged the person to rejoin the congregation. Initially, he declined my advice, preferring to wait until the church service was over, but later he joined the service. He had fallen because the stairs were too steep and slippery.

In activities of daily life, an accessibly built environment that can be used by people with disabilities involves the design of buildings/spaces, stairs, management of the environment, tactile sidewalks/crossings, transport and auditory traffic signs, ramps, escalators, wide doors and corridors, and sign language interpreters. Specific barriers in the built environment include the following: steep stairs, steep ramps, smooth tiles, narrow toilets and bathrooms, no sign language interpreters, inaccessible over- or underpasses, lack of aids at street crossings (for the visually impaired) and lack of Braille (in public meetings). Each of these can be improved. Unnecessary isolation and exclusion from full participation in society has marginalized people with disabilities.

Recommendations for the Ghanaian and Wider African Church

The findings from this chapter have informed the following recommendations to Christian communities and the wider society to better facilitate full participation of all categories of people with disabilities in the church and society.

Cultural and Religious Beliefs

The church should utilize every opportunity to raise awareness and help change inherited cultural and religious beliefs about the causes of disabilities. Preferably, this should be done through seminars and open fora. They should address topics such as the causes and prevention of disability, discrimination, isolation, violence and negative attitudes experienced by persons with disabilities. Unhelpful attitudes and beliefs can also be addressed through the preaching in church services.

Chiefs, queen mothers (note 40) and other traditional leaders should be invited to engage with church members on how certain unhealthy beliefs and superstitions surrounding disability can be handled for the benefit and well-being of people with disabilities. They look forward to being empowered by the church through advocacy. Advocacy in Ghana means reaching out, not only to people with disabilities, but to and with everyone. In this way, the church, society and people with

---

40. Queen mothers are traditional female leaders in Ghana.

disabilities will understand their sociocultural beliefs and work together to promote everybody's well-being. Advocacy is carried out by sharing one another's burdens and ideals such that each person in the community, including those living with disabilities, becomes empowered.

Models of Disability

Models of disability prevalent in the Ghanaian understanding tend to shroud both the society and members of the church such that they are unable to see the hidden talents of people with disabilities. Persons with disabilities are usually treated gently and given all the privileges associated with weakness of the body; they are denied opportunities to participate in social or church activities for fear that they will not be able to do them well or navigate the physical environment. But on the contrary, and as we have established, people with disabilities can be engaged in church life. The church needs to engage with the religious and cultural models of disability that implicitly influence member attitudes.

Akan Language Terms and Disabilities

Akan language terms range from the derogatory to the sympathetic. They include **Wadidem** (impaired), **Ayarefo** (diseased), **Watɔsin** (handicapped), **Wafi**

nipa mu (retarded) and **Adwenmu yare** (mental health disability).

The following words are offensive and must be discouraged because they tend to discriminate against people with disabilities: **Ayarefo** (diseased), **wafi nipa mu** (retarded) and **watɔsin** (handicapped). **Wadidem** (impaired) and **adwenmu yare** (mental health disability) connote some sympathy with people with disabilities, but could be prefixed with more polite words.

Churches must be careful in their use of certain language to describe people. For example, metaphors of deafness and blindness can be applied in subtle ways to build linguistic barriers to exclude persons with disabilities and contribute to disabling attitudes among disabled people. To make full participation possible, inclusive language is extremely important in church contexts.

Sociocultural Attitudes and Accessibility

The church is sensitive regarding the recognition and acceptance of the provision of physical access such as stairs in church buildings, but such provisions should be made to meet international standards. For effective communication, the use of projectors during church services and other activities of the church could facilitate accessibility to information by those with physical or speech impairments. Churches must be disability friendly by ensuring the provision of ramps, special toilet facilities and special parking spaces. The church ought to train sign language interpreters and deploy their services to their communities.

Conclusion

The outcome from the plethora of attitudes and accessibility issues has confirmed some positive and negative attitudes towards people with disabilities within church and society.

It has been observed that many people in society and the church use diverse language terms and have varying attitudes towards different categories of people with disabilities. It was noted that some causes of disabilities are biological, medical, genetic, nutritional and biochemical. Accidents can also result in disability. According to the traditional Ghanaian perspective, another cause of disability is the work of evil spirits, including witchcraft. This chapter took into consideration the sociocultural and religious beliefs of people in dealing with different categories of disabilities. The sources of different attitudes were noted for different kinds of disabilities. Identifiable results from the interviews conducted on these attitudes towards people with disabilities were in some instances explained. It is important for churches to be aware of these different attitudes in Ghanaian society and to constructively engage with them, so that people with disabilities can meaningfully participate in churches. As we have established, the cultural beliefs, language terms and bodily expressions of the society are important to note. The results of the study demonstrated that attitudes towards people with disabilities differ for different types of disabilities, with the most positive attitudes being towards persons with visual, hearing and mental health disabilities. These are important insights for church leaders.

This chapter highlights that most Christians' attitudes towards people with disabilities reflect certain cultural and religious beliefs of the broader society in Ghana. In conclusion, until people's attitudes are changed to show empathy and understanding, people with disabilities are unlikely to experience inclusion, accessibility and integration into the church and the wider society.

Bibliography

Adjasah, Ann. "How Are We Faring in Making Buildings Accessible to the Disabled?" **Accra Daily Graphic**, 10 September 2015.

Agbenyega, Joseph. "The Power of Labeling Discourse in the Construction of Disability in Ghana." 2003. https://www.semanticscholar.

org/paper/The-Power-of-labeling-discourse-in-the-construction-Agbenyega/dbf7cbaed55503793265f51e6a5c642ca383ec7b.

Amenyedzi, Seyram Bridgitte. "Equity and Access for Persons with Disability in Theological Education, Ghana." Doctoral diss., Stellenbosch University, 2016. http://scholar.sun.ac.za/handle/10019.1/100118.

———. "3D Disability: Tapping into a Womanist Theology of Disability." In **The Changing Scenes of Disability in Church and Society: A Resource Book for Theological and Religious Studies**, edited by Samuel Kabue et al., 292–325. Nairobi: Ecumenical Disability Advocates Network, 2021.

Appiah-Kubi, Francis Kwame. "African Traditional Religion and Disabilities: A Critical Theological Reflection." In **Perspectives on Disability: A Resource for Theological and Religious Studies in Africa**, edited by Samuel Kabue, Helen Ishola-Esan and Deji Ayegboyin, 27–39. Nairobi: Ecumenical Disability Advocates Network, 2016.

Asihene, Dan Nyampong. "The Edumfa Prayer Camp: A City of Refuge." Unpublished master's thesis, University of Ghana, 2008.

Charlton, James I. **Nothing About Us Without Us: Disability Oppression and Empowerment**. Berkeley: University of California Press, 2000.

Coleridge, Peter. **Disability, Liberation and Development**. Oxford: Oxfam, 1993.

Ghana Persons with Disability Act, 2006; Act 715. https://sapghana.com/data/documents/DISABILITY-ACT-715.pdf.

Kigame, Reuben. "Cultural Barriers to the Disabled Person's Participation in Church Life." In **Disability, Society, and Theology: Voices from Africa**, edited by Samuel Kabue, Esther Mombo, Joseph Galgalo and C. B. Peter, 121–38. Limuru: Zapf Chancery, 2011.

Kuada, John, and Yao Chachah. **Ghana: Understanding the People and Their Culture**. Accra: Woeli, 1999.

Masakhwe, Phitalis Were. "The Church, Public Policy and Disability Concerns in Kenya." In **Disability, Society, and Theology: Voices from Africa**, edited by Samuel Kabue, Esther Mombo, Joseph Galgalo and C. B. Peter, 111–20. Limuru: Zapf Chancery, 2011.

Michalko, Rod. **The Difference That Disability Makes**. Philadelphia: Temple University Press, 2002.

Mombo, Esther. "Society and Leadership: Challenges and Opportunities for People with Disabilities." In **Disability, Society, and Theology: Voices from Africa**, edited by Samuel Kabue, Esther Mombo, Joseph Galgalo and C. B. Peter, 157–68. Limuru: Zapf Chancery, 2011.

Oliver, Michael. **Understanding Disability: From Theory to Practice.** Basingstoke: Palgrave Macmillan, 1996.

Omenyo, Cephas N. **Pentecost outside Pentecostalism: A Study of the Development of Charismatic Renewal in the Mainline Churches in Ghana**. Uitgeverij: Boekencentrum, 2006.

Peter, C. B. "One in Christ: Priesthood of the Disabled and the Exercising of Gifts." In **Disability, Society, and Theology: Voices from Africa**, edited by Samuel Kabue, Esther Mombo, Joseph Galgalo and C. B. Peter, 59–79. Limuru: Zapf Chancery, 2011.

Rutachwamagyo, Kaganzi. "A Profile of Tanzanians with Disabilities." In **Disability, Society, and Theology: Voices from Africa**, edited by Samuel Kabue, Esther Mombo, Joseph Galgalo and C. B. Peter, 363–82. Limuru: Zapf Chancery, 2011.

Sarpong, Peter K. **Peoples Differ: An Approach to Inculturation in Evangelisation**. Accra: Sub-Saharan, 2002.

Shiriko, Joseph. "Disability: Social Challenges and Family Responses." In **Disability, Society, and Theology: Voices from Africa**, edited by Samuel Kabue, Esther Mombo, Joseph Galgalo and C. B. Peter, 169–96. Limuru: Zapf Chancery, 2011.

World Health Organization. "International Classification of Impairments, Disabilities and Handicaps." Geneva, 1980. Repr. 1993.

9

Worshippers with Disabilities in the Nigerian Church Community

The Role of Inclusive Theological Education

Tongriang Daspan and Noah Daspan

Introduction

This chapter highlights the global prevalence of disability, focusing on Africa, particularly Nigeria. It examines the causes of disability in Nigeria and the experiences of individuals with disabilities in Nigerian society, church settings and theological education. The literature review explores disability concepts, theoretical models and perceptions of disability in Nigeria and other African countries. Tarayyar Ekklesiyoyin Kristi a Nigeria (note 1) (TEKAN) was the study population. In English, this means the Fellowship of the Churches of Christ in Nigeria. TEKAN was founded in 1955 and comprises fifteen church denominations and two associate members. The TEKAN churches are All Nations Christian Assembly (ANCA), the Christian Reformed Church of Nigeria (CRCN), the Church of Christ in Nations (COCIN), Ekklisiyar Yanuwa a Nijeriya (note 2) (EYN), the Evangelical Church of Christ in Nigeria (ECCN), the Evangelical Reformed Church of Christ (ERCC), Haddadiyar Ekklisiyar Kristi a Nigeria (note 3) (HEKAN), the Lutheran Church of Christ in Nigeria (LCCN), Mambila Baptist Convention (MBC), Nigeria Reformed Church (NRC), Nongo Kristu ui Ser u sha Tar (note 4) (NKST), the United Methodist Church of Nigeria (UMCN), the Universal Reformed Christian Church (URCC), the United Missionary Church of Africa (UMCA), the Christian Evangelical Fellowship of Nigeria (CEFN),

---

1. Hausa language.
2. Hausa language. EYN is also known as the Church of the Brethren.
3. Hausa Language. HEKAN is also known as the United Church of Christ in Nigeria.
4. Tiv language. NKST is also known as the Universal Reformed Christian Church.

and the two associate members: the Church of Nigeria, Anglican communion (CNAC), and the Presbyterian Church of Nigeria (PCN). The TEKAN fellowship has over 30 million worshippers from these church denominations in Nigeria. (note 5) Various TEKAN denominations have founded individual seminaries (TEKAN denominational seminaries). (note 6) However, TEKAN jointly owns the Theological College of Northern Nigeria as the primary and central institution servicing the ministerial formation needs of all TEKAN church denominations. An interview with worshippers with disabilities in some TEKAN church denominations, and with theological educators/administrators during a content analysis of the theological education curricula and practices of some TEKAN denominational seminaries, revealed persistent barriers that continue to limit the participation of worshippers with disabilities in church life and theological education. The study concludes by suggesting ways forward for the church and theological education, and future research.

---

5. Ebuga, "General Secretary's Report."
6. "TEKAN denominational seminaries" refers to seminaries or theological colleges owned by TEKAN member churches.

Methods

A qualitative approach was used to explore the experiences of worshippers with disabilities in some TEKAN member churches including the Theological College of Northern Nigeria (TCNN) Chapel, and to explore theological education curricula and practices of TEKAN denominational seminaries. There are no official statistics on the number of worshippers with disabilities in TEKAN churches (no sampling frame). Therefore, to explore the experiences of worshippers with disabilities, we used a non-probability sampling method – snowball sampling – to select participants. (note 7) The snowball technique helped us to use one participant who met the study criteria to locate the next participant in the same TEKAN denomination and region or in a different TEKAN church denomination in another region of the country. All participants identified as worshippers with visual, hearing or mobility impairments, who either underwent part or all of their educational journey in a TEKAN denomination

---

7. This is a technique in which the researcher finds someone who meets the criteria for the research and then that person helps in referring the researcher to the next person who also meets the criteria. This approach assumes that people with or in similar situations are more likely to know each other.

school or experienced the worship life of a TEKAN member church. A sample of twenty-six worshippers with disabilities (nineteen males and seven females) consented to be a part of the study. By type of impairment, seventeen participants (65.4 percent) had a visual impairment; seven participants (26.9 percent) had a hearing impairment; and two participants (7.7 percent) had a mobility impairment. Fourteen participants were between the ages of thirty and forty; four participants were between the ages of twenty and thirty; and eight participants were over the age of forty. Twelve worshippers with disabilities were from different COCIN churches, three participants were from the ERCC denomination, one participant was from the TCNN Chapel, four participants were from ANCA, two were from HEKAN, one was from CRCN and three were from the Anglican Church. Participants were mainly from north-central and north-western Nigeria.

To explore theological education curricula and practices, eight curricula from eight of the eleven seminaries owned by TEKAN member denominations were purposively selected. Additionally, at least one theological educator or administrator involved in curriculum planning or implementation was purposively selected from each seminary for interaction about curriculum content and evaluation of college practices. In total, eleven theological educators, including academic deans and administrators, participated in the content analysis of the curricula.

Two data collection tools were used to collect information on the same questions. The first was a Computer-Assisted Self Interview (CASI). This was used to obtain information from theological educators and from worshippers with disabilities whose impairment did not affect their sight. The same interview questions were administered through telephone interviews for worshippers with disabilities whose impairment affected their sight but not their hearing, and face-to-face interviews (with sign language interpretation) were conducted for some participants with a hearing impairment. Each interview lasted between thirty and forty-five minutes. The semi-structured interview protocol used was based on deductive codes focused on common practices and traditions of many TEKAN churches. The following deductive codes were used to collect and analyse the interview data: giving offerings, praise worship sessions, hymn singing, hearing and proclaiming God's word, communion, unpleasant experiences, ratings of the church's awareness of and attitudes towards disability, and availability of specialized services/facilities. We analysed variations and similarities across participants using the deductive codes and interpreted our findings through the lens of the social model of disability. Descriptive analysis was done with a computer-based Statistical Package for Social Sciences (SPSS).

Literature Review
The Prevalence of Disability and Problems of Inaccessibility

According to a 2011 report from the World Health Organisation, more than one billion people in the world live with some form of disability. Eighty-four million are estimated to be in Africa and 29 percent of that population live in Nigeria. (note 8) In other words, around twenty-five million people in Nigeria live with a disability. (note 9) According to the World Health Organization, "Almost everyone will temporarily or permanently experience disability at some point in life, and those who survive to old age will experience increasing difficulty in functioning." (note 10) The increase in the number of people with disabilities (note 11)

---

8. WHO and the World Bank, **World Report on Disability**, xi.
9. Oduu, "Over 25 Million."
10. WHO and the World Bank, **World Report on Disability**, 7.
11. We choose "identity-first language" in this chapter. In line with Brown, we find that "people-first identity vs. disability-first identity/approach

has been linked to chronic health conditions and ageing populations. In Nigeria, the major causes of disability include poor maternal and neonatal care, poor trauma care, injuries, and resultant poor management of infections leading to cataracts, amputations, poverty, malnutrition, reduced access to education and poor access to quality medical care. (note 12)

The evidence indicates that most people with disabilities in Nigeria are unable to access services due to a litany of barriers. (note 13) Blessing Ocheida, the executive director of Platinum Interventions Care Initiatives, reports a lack of access to and inclusivity of public structures and transport systems in Nigeria. She explains that she has had to install ramps in places where she "schooled, lived and worked," and laments

---

is more respectful." So, instead of saying "disabled persons" or "disabled worshipper," we choose the term "people with disabilities" or "worshippers with disabilities." This puts the person first before the disability, while not denying that there is a disability (Brown, "Identity-First Language").

12. Abang, "Disablement, Disability," 71–77.
13. Smith, "Face of Disability," 35.

the "systemic barriers and institutionalized discrimination that have continued to hold back" people with disabilities in Nigeria. (note 14)

Perceptions of Disability in Africa

Negative cultural and religious beliefs about the causes of disability in Africa include perceiving disability as **an ancestral curse** (Cameroon, Ethiopia, Senegal, Uganda, Zambia and Ghana), perceiving disability as **ancestral violations of societal norms** (Nigeria) or perceiving disability as **the consequence of bad actions of parents**, mainly the promiscuity of mothers (in Kenya, this may include broken taboos by the mother, such as eating eggs during her pregnancy or lying down on her stomach. More specifically, the Nandi people believe killing an animal without provocation during a woman's pregnancy can cause disability to her child, while the Ambagusil believe cleft palates result from parents making fun of someone with a disability). (note 15) In some parts of Africa, such as northern Ghana, persons with disabilities experience not only social death but actual death by being killed. (note 16) Other cultural and religious beliefs include

---

14. PICI, "Stakeholders' Dialogue."
15. Rohwerder, "Disability Stigma," 5–6.
16. Amenyedzi, "Equity and Access," 46.

perceiving disability as **demonic possession** (the belief that people with disabilities are not really human or that they are cursed and afflicted by bad spirits), perceiving disability as **witchcraft** (in Nigeria, false beliefs about disability include the perception that it is caused by witches and wizards or "juju") (note 17) and perceiving disability **as fate or punishment from God.** (note 18) Misconceptions about disabilities include the idea that people with disabilities cannot contribute to anything, cannot have normal relationships/ are sexually inactive, will not be able to report sexual abuse, bring bad luck, and have "magical" properties in their bodies. (note 19) In Nigerian culture, disability is synonymous with being less capable. (note 20) Omigbodun et al. describe some negative attitudes and misconceptions towards people with congenital or mental disabilities in Ibadan, western Nigeria. Their study shows that

---

17. Cbanga, "Juju." Juju is an object that has been deliberately infused with magical power, or the magical power itself. Juju is practised in West African countries such as Nigeria, Benin, Togo and Ghana, and its assumptions are shared by most African people.

18. Rohwerder, "Disability Stigma," 5–6.

19. Rohwerder, 8–10.

20. Omigbodun, Odejide and Morakinyo, "Highlights from the CAR Study," 191.

the general populace believes gaining employment, getting married and having a family will be severely affected by a disability. (note 21) Such beliefs and misconceptions about the causes and nature of disability have led to negative attitudes towards people with disabilities such as maltreatment and restricted their participation in social activities. For instance, some families stigmatize their relatives with disabilities by hiding them away or forbidding them from public participation because of shame or to protect them from stigma. (note 22) Nyangweso recounts an incident in southern Nigeria, where a woman with severe kyphosis (colloquially known as "hunchback") was killed for ritual purposes. The woman was kidnapped and her body mutilated because her community believed that the hump contained a mercury-like magical substance that could make people rich. (note 23) In contrast, some African communities, cultures, and families treat people with disabilities positively by taking good care of them. Among the Chagga in East Africa, persons with physical disabilities are seen as pacifiers of evil spirits; they are also selected as law enforcement personnel in Benin. The Turkana people of Kenya perceive children with disabilities

---

21. Omigbodun, Odejide and Morakinyo, 192.
22. Rohwerder, "Disability Stigma," 7.
23. Nyangweso, "Disability in Africa," 117.

as a gift from God who must be taken care of to avoid punishment from the deity. (note 24) The Ga people from Accra, Ghana, treat individuals with intellectual disabilities with awe as reincarnations of a deity, and the Igbos of Nigeria treat people with disabilities from the two extremes of pampering or rejection. (note 25)

Nigeria passed a bill prohibiting discrimination against people with disabilities in January 2018. (note 26) However, the journey towards achieving an inclusive Nigerian society seems to still be far away. Negative attitudes continue to undermine people with disabilities in Nigerian society even when African worldviews about disability seemed to have gradually faded. (note 27)

The Concept of Disability and Popular Theoretical Models

"Disability" is an umbrella term that includes impairments, limitations on activity and restrictions to participation. It can be viewed through different models, such as charity, medical,

---

24. Rohwerder, "Disability Stigma," 8.
25. Nyangweso, "Disability in Africa," 119.
26. Ewang, "Nigeria Passes."
27. Ishola-Esan, "Remnant of African Worldviews," 103–18.

individual and social models. (note 28) The charity model of disability treats people with disabilities as objects of charity who always need help. People with disabilities are pitied and considered liabilities requiring charitable resources or support. The medical model treats people with disabilities as sick, needing to be cured, fixed and cared for through medical intervention and therapy. Most services focus on healing people with disabilities or making them appear non-disabled (an example is providing wheelchairs) instead of making the environment (such as restrooms) more accessible. (note 29) The individual model of disability treats disability as a personal tragedy. (note 30) However, the social model views disability as caused by how society is structured and locates disability within societal barriers rather than in individuals. (note 31) For example, a person using a wheelchair is considered "disabled" because the roads and buildings in society are not usually structured for wheelchair users. Finkelstein beautifully argues that so-called "abled" people would be disabled if the environment were not

---

28. WHO and the World Bank, **World Report on Disability**, 7.
29. Mobility International USA, "Models of Disability."
30. Barnes and Mercer, **Social Model**, 18–31.
31. Barnes and Mercer, 18–31.

structured with them in mind. In an imaginary upside-down world where "disabled" people live in a different village and design buildings or roads according to their needs, the "abled" will notice that they are "disabled" and, for example, hit their heads against 5 feet-high door lintels when they come to settle in this village. (note 32) In that sense, environments **en**able or **dis**able people.

To identify barriers that limit worshippers with disabilities within the theological education system and consequently the church, the social model of disability was employed as a lens of analysis and interpretation in this chapter. Critics of the model argue that the model tends to deny or dismiss the pain of impairment. (note 33) Others propose that the focus should be on building a sense of affirmation within people with disabilities to overcome societal obstacles and to think differently about being different. (note 34) Nevertheless, this study adopted the social model as part of the desire to first draw the attention of theological education towards identifying barriers and rethinking its practices and curricula through the eyes of the experiences of worshippers with

---

32. Finkelstein, "To Deny or Not to Deny."
33. Emens, **Disability and Equality Law**, 47.
34. Swain and French, **Disability on Equal Terms**, 185.

disabilities. In this way, theological education can better enable the church to carry out its mandate of preaching the gospel to all creation (Matt 28:18–20) and equipping God's people "for works of service, so that the body of Christ may be built up until we all reach unity in the faith and in the knowledge of the Son of God and become mature, attaining to the whole measure of the fullness of Christ" (Eph 4:12–13). The model's focus on the disabling (environmental, cultural and other) barriers rather than on the impairment itself also helps in transforming consciousness by identifying and addressing issues that can be changed through collective action beyond individual tragedy. (note 35) In a social model perspective, equipping all of God's people would mean ministering to and with worshippers with disabilities as co-workers and co-benefactors of the ministries of all God's people within the church community, as opposed to the charity or medical models of only ministering to worshippers with disabilities.

Experiences of Worshippers with Disabilities in Church and Theological Education

The African church has often neglected worshippers with disabilities. The case in Nigeria is

---

35. Emens, **Disability and Equality Law**, 48, 51.

no different. Nigeria, the largest African nation with an estimated population in 2019 of over 190 million people, (note 36) is one of the most religious countries in the world. (note 37) In 2011 it had "the largest Christian population of any other country in Africa, with more than 80 million people in Nigeria belonging to various denominations." (note 38) It also has the highest rate of church attendance globally. (note 39) However, Osukwu observes that persons with disability in Nigeria are still grappling with unpleasant experiences that make them feel excluded from the church community. (note 40) Moreover, people with disabilities need more pastoral care than persons without disability (8.1 percent versus 4 percent) (note 41) due to potential trauma, depression and feelings of hopelessness that result from societal exclusion. Yet they are the same people who are "less likely to attend worship services, Bible studies, and other church activities than those without disabilities (47

---

36. IndexMundi, "Nigeria."
37. Pew Research Center, "Age Gap."
38. Wikipedia, "Christianity in Nigeria."
39. **The Economist**, "World's Most Popular Religion."
40. Osukwu, "Disability," 52–64.
41. Evanson, Ustanko and Tyree, "Promoting the Inclusion," 97.

percent versus 65 percent), largely due to barriers that limit accessibility to church." (note 42)

Kabue categorized three forms of excluding people with disabilities in church as paternalistic and patronizing attitudes, exclusion from participation, and unjustified emphasis on physical healing. (note 43) Osukwu affirms this as being true to her own experiences in Nigeria. (note 44) Judging by the statistics, the Nigerian church alone has great potential for influence in championing any course in Nigeria and Africa as a whole. However, the more significant determinant of the church's potential to make the right impact is theological education, because it is the system that equips men and women for church ministry and leadership.

There are not many examples of experiences of worshippers with disabilities in churches or theological education. As Jacobs observes, not much research has been done on the experiences of those living with disabilities in churches globally. (note 45) However, a few researchers have reported the experiences of worshippers

---

42. Evanson, Ustanko and Tyree, 99.
43. Kabue, "Persons with Disabilities," 18.
44. Osukwu, "Disability," 52–64.
45. Jacobs, "Upside-Down Kingdom," 249.

with disabilities especially in Europe (note 46) and North America. (note 47) One of the few African examples of the experiences of worshippers with disabilities in the church community was reported by Samuel Kabue. Kabue's church in Kenya did not ordain him even though he met all the criteria to be ordained except that he was blind. Although the Presbyterian Church of East Africa had softened its stance and had been very supportive of Kabue's efforts, including making him an elder, he was not ordained. Kabue observed that discrimination robs the church of the benefit that people with disabilities bring to the table of Christ and denies worshippers with disabilities the opportunity to contribute their immense skills and gifts to the church. (note 48) Another African example from Amenyedzi is the story of a presiding church elder in Ghana who attended a two-year Bible school and completed a diploma but faced discrimination when the institution proposed to award him a one-year certificate due to his disability. After a heated debate, the individual insisted on receiving the deserved diploma and refused to participate in the graduation unless it was rightfully granted. (note 49) Outside Africa,

---

46. Jacobs, 1–305.
47. White, "People with Disabilities," 11–35.
48. WCC, "Workshop on Disability Discourse."
49. Amenyedzi, "Equity and Access," 173.

George White reported the experiences of some worshippers with disabilities in North America. One of the worshippers said, "A communion rail was removed without asking me. Now, I can no longer go up to the rail for communion, and I feel excluded from the central practice of my church." (note 50) Another man reported, "My daughter, who couldn't speak, was enjoying the music, and one of the elders got offended when she was making what he called noises. The elder said she should not be brought into the service anymore." (note 51) Another worshipper with disabilities was asked to leave the church because his behaviour was "unmanageable." A group of worshippers with disabilities were also approached by a pastor and told they were inappropriate for his church. The pastor advised them to find somewhere with special classes to go to. (note 52) These experiences illustrate a discouraging church community for worshippers with disabilities. Although some of these examples are from the Global North, not Nigeria, they offer some insight into what church communities and theological education may need to do differently.

---

50. White, "People with Disabilities," 29.
51. White, 26.
52. White, 30.

Services and Facilities for People with Disabilities in TEKAN Member Churches

Nigerian churches, particularly some notable examples within the TEKAN circle, have contributed significantly to providing special services to people with disabilities within educational and medical contexts. Church facilities and services for people with disabilities in Nigeria include church-run special schools and hospitals. Of note in the TEKAN circle is the Church of Christ in Nations (note 53) (COCIN hereafter). The Sudan United Missions (SUM) established a hospital/rehabilitation centre for individuals with leprosy, polio and other physical disabilities in 1949 and handed it over to COCIN in 1976. (note 54) COCIN also established a school for blind children in Gindiri in 1953 (note 55) and Gindiri Materials Centre for the Handicapped in 1989. (note 56) However, most of these services are educational and medical. In contrast, little inclusiveness seems to have been expressed in the immediate practice and life of the church community in terms of the

---

53. Formerly, Church of Christ in Nigeria.
54. International Leprosy Association, "COCIN Hospital and Rehabilitation Centre."
55. Adebiyi, "Visually Impaired Education," 2.
56. Thompson D. Damwesh, personal interview with the coordinator, GMCH in Gindiri, Plateau State, Nigeria, 1 February 2020.

worship culture generally. This example is typical of the church's perception of and response to disability through charity and medical models. There is a need to sensitize the church on the social model response to disability, especially through theological education.

Theological Education Curriculum

Like any other curriculum, a theological education curriculum involves both instruction and the experiences of learners. Albert Oliver defines "curriculum" as the school's program and divides it into four essential elements: a program of studies, a program of experiences, a program of service and a hidden curriculum. (note 57) A curriculum goes beyond the instructional content of a course of study alone to include the entire program and practice of a school. The sum of the experiences of learner programs and practices of a school will encompass courses studied, admission processes, the diversity of the staff and student population, appointments in leadership and other special roles, and so on. The curriculum is built with goals and objectives, and one of the goals of theological education curricula is to train men and women for the service of the church. As Ishola-Esan puts it,

---

57. Oliver, "Curriculum Improvement," 111.

> Theological education is part of the life and mission of churches in their respective situations. It equips people to participate in their church's evangelical drive, witness, and service to the different contexts in the world. From a narrow sense, theological education is concerned with preparing and continuing professional leadership training for churches. (note 58)

This connection between theological education and the church is fundamental because until we establish what link or obligation theological education has to the church and vice versa, we will be wrong to advocate for or demand certain outcomes in the church from it. What is the church responsible to theological education for? And what is theological education responsible to the church for? If it is unclear what purpose each serves to the other, we will one day awake to a theological education separated from the church and a scholarship that will not impact Christian living and ministry. It is for this reason that the International Council for Evangelical Theological Education notes that theological education must be in the service (aligned to the expectations) of

---

58. Ishola-Esan, "Relevance of Theological Institutions," 5.

the Christian community. (note 59) The former president of Gordon-Conwell Theological Seminary Dennis Hollinger is reported to have quoted the famous saying, "As goes the seminary, so goes the church." (note 60) Therefore, theological education has an impact on the church and it is crucial for theological educators to always bear in mind its correct purpose: "The content and task of theological education is inseparable from its purpose. The purpose decides the content, and the content serves the purpose." (note 61) It is therefore important to explore what the purpose of theological education is. Until this is defined, the content cannot serve that purpose and desired outcomes may not be achieved. Ervin Budiselić puts it across beautifully in pointing to the direction for the future of theological education: "The future of theological education is in the use of the Bible as the foundation for theology, in the importance of **practice** as the final goal of theological education, and in serving and helping the church to reach maturity and unity of faith." (note 62)

---

59. ICETE, "The ICETE Manifesto II."
60. Chao, "Spiritual Formation."
61. Chao.
62. Budiselić, "Apology of Theological Education," 131–54.

Little attention has been paid to disability discourse in the curricula of theological colleges of Africa towards building inclusive churches. (note 63) In the Nigerian context, Ishola-Esan writes, "A cursory look at the curriculum of theological institutions reveals a drought of courses on disability studies or courses that relate to people with disabilities." (note 64) Jacobs also reports that "there is a lack of critical examination of disability in theology, and little ethnographic research exploring the experiences of disabled people in churches." (note 65) Ishola-Esan further notes that even though a few courses related to disability are occasionally taught to interested students in some theological institutions, there is a critical need for a more intentional approach to including disability discourse in the curricula of theological colleges to ensure it includes ministering with and among people with disabilities, whose needs and concerns are included in the task of the Great Commission. (note 66) The work and mission of the

---

63. Ishola-Esan, "Relevance of Theological Institutions," 1; Amenyedzi, "Equity and Access," 170.

64. Ishola-Esan, 5.

65. Jacobs, "Upside-Down Kingdom," 249.

66. Ishola-Esan, "Relevance of Theological Institutions," 5.

Ecumenical Disability Advocates Network (EDAN) has been focused on bridging this gap through networking with theological associations and institutions to influence curriculum development – especially one that includes disability concerns towards the formation of ministers who will promote an inclusive church community of all and for all. (note 67) EDAN has gone beyond rhetoric to model this by appointing people with disabilities to key leadership positions. Theological education should also model inclusive practices and participation in the entirety of its approach to ministerial formation beyond including disability courses in the curriculum.

Until theological education develops a strategy for educating prospective pastors in setting the tone for inclusive church communities, it is by its silence or faint voice (at least in the curriculum) and college practice excluding worshippers with disabilities. Could the Nigerian theological education system and consequently the church community be unconsciously contributing to excluding worshippers with disabilities? To answer this question, the rest of this chapter aims to do the following:

---

67. WCC, "Ecumenical Disability Advocates Network (EDAN)."

1. Examine the experiences of worshippers with disabilities within the Nigerian church, specifically TEKAN member churches.

2. Identify available services and facilities for worshippers with disabilities in some Nigerian church communities within TEKAN.

3. Examine how theological education addresses the issue of disability and inclusiveness in the curriculum and practices of some TEKAN denominational seminaries.

Results and Discussion
Church Experiences of Worshippers with Disabilities

We will first discuss the findings related to the church experiences of worshippers with disabilities, before discussing the findings regarding the theological education curricula.

Giving Offerings

Almost half of the participants cited "giving offerings" as a critical aspect of difficulty during church services. Worshippers with mobility and visual impairments explained that moving out of their seats to drop offerings in a container is challenging. A worshipper with a visual impairment said she once missed her seat after returning from dropping her offering, and sometimes she feared she might drop her offering on the floor instead of in the offering box. Another participant said she once handed her offering to someone sitting next to her to help her drop it in the offering box. However, the person didn't go out during the offering collection time. When she asked why the person was still seated during the collection, there was no reply.

Praise Worship Sessions

Worshippers with hearing impairments explained that many of the local songs sung during the service were unfamiliar and not printed out or projected for them to "sing" or sign along. A worshipper with a visual impairment said that although she can participate in praise worship sessions which are usually accompanied by dancing, she is cautious because she is not sure about the dance style or special actions that may go with a song. So, "to avoid embarrassment," it was safer to stand still and sing. The respondent added that some pastors tell the congregation to sit down only with a wave of the hand. She once found that she was the only one still standing alone while other worshippers were already seated after the praise worship session.

Hymn Singing

Most participants mentioned difficulties related to hymn singing. Although many hymns are printed out, unlike local songs/choruses, those with hearing impairments explained that they struggle to keep pace while signing with the congregation. They suggested being taught rhythm and "reading music notes." Worshippers with visual impairments lamented that there were no Braille hymns; they wished churches could produce a Braille sheet with the hymn(s) for each Sunday. Eventually, the complete hymnal would be in Braille. In addition, church-based devotionals and Bible study materials could be in Braille or made available to them in soft copies so that text-to-speech software programs can read to them.

Hearing and Proclaiming God's Word

A worshipper with a hearing impairment explained that he did not access sign language services in his church for the first twenty years of his life, so he did not have any meaningful input or explanation of the word of God, especially as a child. Two other respondents, independently of each other, reported that they tried numerous church denominations searching for sign language services, including organizations that held incorrect beliefs and practices. They shared that they almost lost their faith through exposure to harmful teachings, all in search of sign language services. Another participant said that, for over thirty years, there was no sign language interpreter in his church or any other church in his locality, so he stopped attending church services. He only began attending church again when he moved to another state for higher education. Another participant also lamented that the pastor in his church speaks so fast that the interpreter is unable to keep pace when interpreting the message in sign language. Moreover, the interpreter sometimes gets distracted. When there is humour in the sermon, the interpreter stops signing to join the congregation in enjoying the moment, before resuming to sign again. "We see people laugh, but we are not a part of it." One of the respondents with a visual impairment who had an enabling church community said that he is occasionally given preaching opportunities in his church and other churches around, especially during special services for worshippers with disabilities. However, he finds the glass pulpit in many of the TEKAN churches too narrow for him to be able to spread his large Braille Bible comfortably.

Holy Communion

A worshipper with visual impairment explained, "The element is fragile, I cannot see it or know where to pick it from. I am careful not to break it into pieces, and I am also careful not to contaminate other pieces in the tray before I can pick the piece I need." Another respondent with a visual impairment who plays the keyboard said, "The communion element and wine were once placed for me on top of the keyboard. I moved my hands very carefully to locate the wine cup but never found the element or asked for a replacement." Yet another respondent with a visual impairment explained that the person sitting next to him refused to help him by picking up and placing the element in his hands because, in that person's traditional belief, communion was sacred and private and became violated if one picked it up on another's behalf.

Bible Reading

For more than half of the participants, Bible reading during church services was difficult. Worshippers with visual impairments explained that the Braille Bible is so large and voluminous it cannot easily be taken to church. One respondent said, "It would be easier if the church announced which book and chapter of the Bible would be read the Sunday ahead, or better still, it would be easier if the church gave everyone a copy of the preaching roster." Failing that, "we will need a pickup van or truck to convey the complete Braille Bible to church."

Unpleasant Experiences

A worshipper with a visual impairment said he was surprised that other worshippers drove past his way without offering him a lift. "Someone saw me getting lost and came to tell me, 'This is the wrong way,' without putting me on the right one. Another time, someone just walked past without saying a word to help me find my path. It is shameful," he lamented. Another participant recalled, "Someone once pulled my mobility cane to lead me in the right way. Although I appreciate the good intention to help, I do not appreciate that there was no clue or communication before my cane was suddenly grabbed. People need to be taught to say, 'Excuse me, please' because I can't see them; they need to hold my hand, not my cane, because that is dangerous for me." The participant also said that one time, he tried teaching an eight-year-old girl to hold his hand instead of his mobility cane, but the girl got angry and left him stranded. Another respondent explained that she once went to church alone. After the service, people walked past and asked, "Where is your guide? Who will take you home?" She wondered, "Why don't you take me home? My guide is not the only person with the responsibility of taking me home!" She was quick to mention that one of her colleagues no longer goes to church because he gets dirty from the waterlogged clayey paths that are untarred while trying to find his way to and from church. Recalling a particularly unpleasant experience, the same respondent said, "I once made an outstanding Bible memorization presentation during a church service. As people came by to commend my effort after the service, a fellow said, 'She stays home all day doing nothing, what do you expect? She has all the time to learn Bible verses.'" Another participant explained that a lady in his church was supposedly helping him go upstairs, but all she did was stand from a distance and shout, "Go up! Just go up, hold the rail, and go up!" "I thought she would hold my hand!" he said. He was also shocked at the attitude of another Christian lady whom he visited. "She just stood by the door to say goodbye, not minding the complex road network and unkept gutters around her house." Another participant said a Christian man stopped his daughter from playing around her because he believed her blindness was contagious.

Another respondent recounted the experience of his friend who no longer attends church services. After presenting a song with the choir, the friend was left standing on the stage alone while the other choir members left. He stood on stage until the end of the sermon when someone noticed him and went up for him. He was so hurt that he left the church completely. Another respondent reported that security officers by the pastorium refused him entrance to see the pastor, because, according to them, "The reverend does not attend to people like him." In a similar vein, another respondent visited a new cleric in his region. On seeing him the cleric said, "The person who used to help you [referring to his predecessor] is not around." Although worshippers with disabilities commended a few churches for giving them financial support or other welfare packages, they were unhappy about some people's misconception of them as automatic beggars who come to church in search of money, miracles, healing or deliverance, instead of seeing them as people who have come to worship God. This kind of response to disability follows a charity and medical instead of a social model.

Worshippers with Disabilities' Ratings of Church Awareness and Attitudes about Disability

Table 1

SN	Treatment of worshippers with disabilities by the church (as perceived by worshippers with disabilities)	No. and % (n=26)
1	With ignorance	(12) 46.2%
2	With pity	(8) 30.8%
3	With care	(5) 19.2%
4	As a friend	(6) 23.1%
5	As a co-labourer	(4) 15.4%

Table 2

SN	Frequency of being assigned to play special roles in the church	No. and % (n=25) One participant did not respond to this question.
1	Weekly	(3) 12%
2	Monthly	(3) 12%
3	Quarterly	(5) 20%
4	Yearly	(2) 8%
5	Rarely	(9) 36%
6	Never	(3) 12%

The responses of worshippers with disabilities are based on Elim Christian Services and Dan Vander Plaats's "5 Stages" of disability attitudes. (note 68) The results in table 1 show that nearly half of the worshippers with disabilities (46.2 percent) perceived that their church was ignorant about disability and worshippers with disabilities. In comparison, 30.8 percent felt that the church treated them well but out of pity for their condition, reflected in questions like, "So how do you manage to run your life in this condition?" Some participants (19.2 percent) felt cared for by their church, but this mostly meant that their needs were to some extent met through

---

68. See Anabaptist Disabilities Network, "Changing Attitudes."

assistance (cash and kind). Only a few worshippers with disabilities said that care meant someone was checking to find out how they were doing. Some participants (23.1 percent) felt their church treated them on a friendship level because they felt noticed and appreciated in many ways. However, only 15.4 percent said they were not only appreciated and loved, but given an opportunity and trusted to the level of being considered co-workers or given responsibility. Of the worshippers with disabilities, 80.8 percent belonged to one church fellowship group or another, but 36 percent of them rarely played any role, and 12 percent had never played a role in over ten years of church or fellowship attendance (see table 2). Among the roles played, some worshippers with disabilities led Bible studies, midweek prayers or church services, preached and taught Sunday school. Virtually all participants who played special roles had visual or mobility impairments; worshippers with hearing impairments did not report playing any special roles, except in a deaf service.

When asked about the skills they could contribute to the church, worshippers with disabilities mentioned skills such as teaching church members sign language, decorating the altar, acting/drama, ushering and preaching (with the help of a translator). Some worshippers with visual or mobility impairments mentioned skills such as editing, evangelism, maintenance of electronic equipment, a talk show about inclusion, and social networking. More than half of worshippers with disabilities (53.3 percent) said no special service or week in the church's calendar was set aside for them. They reported that while there was a special service/week for widows, orphans and other target groups of worshippers in the church, there was no special programme or week for them. The remaining 46.7 percent said their churches observed special services (a day or week set apart for worshippers with disabilities to feature special activities). Churches that observed special services for worshippers with disabilities were mostly located near a department of special education where special services were readily available or had a different section dedicated to worshippers with disabilities, which some participants considered a form of exclusion from the general church. Coincidentally, participants who had a deaf church section/service were from a denomination in north-western Nigeria that does not have a denominational seminary. Therefore, the Theological College of Northern Nigeria (TCNN) is the primary seminary servicing this church denomination. As a mother seminary, TCNN has people with disabilities among its staff. Although disability discourse is not emphasized in its curriculum, it models an aspect of an inclusive curriculum in its practice, which is a good starting point that could influence the practice of other TEKAN member denominational seminaries.

Services and Facilities for Worshippers with Disabilities

Table 3

SN	Facility or service	Percentage availability in churches of respondents (n=25) One participant did not respond to this question.
1	Projector	(15) 60%
2	Sign language interpreter	(6) 24%
3	Bulletin	(7) 28%
4	Braille hymnals	0%
5	Ramp	(3) 12%
6	Accessible restrooms	(1) 4%
7	Assistive listening devices	(0) 0%

Table 3 provides an overview of services and facilities available in the churches. When the worshipper who uses a wheelchair was asked how he copes without accessible restrooms in his church, he said he can generally manage the long hours (four or more) between leaving home and attending Sunday school, the main service and returning home without using the restroom. However, he leaves before the end of the service on those days when he is unable to handle it.

Regarding services generally, some worshippers with disabilities noted that they had joined COCIN from other denominations and had their spiritual foundations in COCIN schools where they had enrolled to benefit from the special educational services that COCIN provided. However, they left the COCIN church as a denomination in later life because they did not find the services and facilities to support worship within the church community that they had found within the school structure. For instance, students with visual impairments at the School for Blind Children or any of the three COCIN secondary schools located within the Gindiri Mission Compound had had their various textbooks translated into Braille at the Gindiri Material Centre for the Handicapped. Some participants, however, lamented that after completing their education, COCIN, one of the few churches providing special services in the country, did not provide special services for continuing spiritual growth for them outside the school setting. Such services could include Brailling or providing soft copies (for text-to-speech translations) of the COCIN daily devotional and Bible study manual for them to access from churches or bookstores. Some of the participants applauded COCIN for its programs, such as Theological Education by Extension (TEE). Although they completed the program, they wished the learning materials had been more accessible.

Theological Education Curriculum and College Practices

While evaluating the curricula of the eight seminaries, eleven theological educators or administrators who played a role in curriculum planning or execution were interviewed. The tables show information about the theological education curriculum (table 4) and practices (tables 5 and 6) of the eight seminaries.

Table 4

Courses on disability, inclusive theological education or accessible worship in the curriculum	No. and % of seminaries (n=8)
Yes	0
Yes (related courses)	3 (37.5%)
No	5 (62.5%)

Table 5

Field work posting destinations	No. and % of seminaries (n=8)
Churches	8 (100%)
Church schools	6 (75%)
Chaplaincies	4 (50%)
Special needs/rehabilitation centres	1 (12.5%)
Counselling centres	2 (25%)

Table 6

School evangelism groups	No. and % of seminaries (n=8)
Children	8 (100%)
Prisons	5 (62.5%)
Youth	8 (100%)
Hospitals	5 (62.5%)
Special needs/people with disabilities	0

The tables show that no seminary had inclusive theological education or accessible worship courses. Three seminaries had related courses such as elective modules on "special education." The eight seminaries had field trip destinations that included churches, church schools and chaplaincies, but only one had a field trip posting destination to a rehabilitation centre. No seminary had an evangelism group that reached out to people with disabilities in the community.

A brief assessment of the seminaries also showed that, for the award of a bachelor's degree in theology/divinity, a total of 122–140 credit units were offered by most schools. One of the colleges offered only a diploma programme and offered thirty-nine credit units in total. Of the eight theological colleges, no theological college had a course in disability. **Only one** college offered a credit unit course in special education (elective). The same college's curriculum also had a course called "specialized ministry." Two colleges provided courses related to disability studies, such as trauma healing, Christian/pastoral counselling, cross-cultural missions and new community recovery missions (elective). Five colleges did not have even one course "related" to disability in the curriculum. Note that the course's rating with regard to disability studies was based only on how theological educators or administrators in each theological college perceived it. While one theological educator/administrator considered a course to be related to disability studies, another theological educator/administrator did not consider the same course as related to disability studies.

A close look at the courses that were listed as related to disability discourse in the theological education curriculum also revealed a response to disability that likely draws from the charity and medical models, in which worshippers with disabilities may need healing, recovery, counselling or comfort. This reflects the view of worshippers with disabilities as recipients of ministry rather than as co-workers or potential contributors to the body of Christ.

Considerable inclusivity was practised by some of the theological education institutions studied. One of the colleges admitted a person with low vision. Three students had partial mobility impairments in two other colleges at the time of this research. According to two theological administrators, their seminaries have trained a student with visual impairment. Another administrator said their college trained a student with partial hearing loss. While this is commendable, the statistics on the number of students with disabilities who were served by the seminaries may have been over- or underestimated because they were based only on the memory and knowledge of the individuals interviewed. None of the theological institutions in the study had any structure or office/officer dedicated to disability services or kept good records about students with disabilities in their colleges.

Overall, the formal course of study (i.e. the curriculum of many theological colleges in the TEKAN circle and outside TEKAN) presumably does not include worshippers with disabilities or at least does not emphasize disability sufficiently. The only theological education institution that offered a course in special education provides a 140-credit unit load to award a bachelor's degree in divinity. However, special education is only a credit unit **elective** course. To say this is the best example of the eight is worrisome. Similarly, none of the seminaries included a statement on their admission forms explicitly indicating that individuals with disabilities could apply and would receive specialized services and accommodation for any special needs.

Without planning to include worshippers with disabilities, the current silence or weak emphasis in theological education translates into excluding worshippers with disabilities. As noted by Wolfe, "excluding people affected by disability typically is not an intentional act. However, having no form of disability ministry outreach [or plan], lack of awareness, and accessibility issues routinely keep" worshippers with disabilities from church communities and theological education. (note 69) Theological education must not only give disability

---

69. Wolfe, "What Does It Mean."

a voice in its curriculum, but it must further model what an enabling, inclusive and accessible church community could look like using every opportunity in its practices.

Ways Forward

Theological education should be deliberate about including and emphasizing disability discourse in its curriculum. Beyond course inclusion, theological education should model inclusive practices within theological education training, such as in worship culture in chapels, policy statements, admission statements, and staff and student recruitment, which explicitly show that persons with disabilities can enrol in theological education and will receive maximum support or accommodation to thrive. Theological education must raise adequate consciousness about disability to give prospective pastors the experience of ministering with and among worshippers with disabilities, especially from a social model perspective. There is a need for structured offices and staff who will provide disability services, networks, support, advice, statistics, and so on, in theological institutions.

Special services such as sign language interpretation/translation and facilities such as ramps, assistive listening devices, Braille hymnals, projection of information during services and accessible restrooms should be found in every theological college chapel. Fieldwork destinations should include special/rehabilitation centres or rehabilitation chaplaincies and there should be an evangelism group that targets people with disabilities and especially invites people with disabilities into its membership. It is important that theological education graduates not only hear about disability but also see it and imbibe some hands-on skills that will contribute to setting the tone for a welcoming church community. This is key considering the very few worship centres that are inclusive of worshippers with disabilities in Nigeria. Theological colleges should take proactive steps to provide specialized services and not wait until worshippers with disabilities show up before making accommodation for them. It is not always possible to know when worshippers with disabilities come to worship because some disabilities, such as hearing impairment, are hidden. Worshippers with disabilities are only likely to come when they know that special services and facilities are available, and theological college chapels should undoubtedly be such places where worshippers with disabilities are sure to belong anywhere, any time. Theological education institutions may also consider opening centres to train people to provide special services, not like any other special education service, but with ministry in mind. Such centres could organize workshops, seminars and symposiums to prepare pastors and other Christians for ministry with and among people with disabilities. Churches should also serve theological education by sponsoring people, including people with disabilities, for such trainings and workshops.

Limitations and Areas for Further Research

For further research, investigating ministers' approaches to ministry with and among worshippers with disabilities in the colleges that offered a course in special education may show what impact that exposure had on pastors' practice in ministry. Ishola-Esan and Nihinlola have reported on disability and theology in south-western Nigeria. However, as Nihinlola recommends in his study covering ten theological seminaries in south-western Nigeria, there is a need for further research that covers other parts of the country, as well as departments of religious studies in universities or colleges of education. (note 70) While this research covered some of the regions recommended (north-central and north-western), it was limited to only TEKAN and to eight out of the eleven theological education institutions within the TEKAN circle. The small sample size, the limited scope of

---

70. Nihinlola, "Disability Discourse," 43.

disabilities covered, and the non-probability sampling used limit the generalizability of the findings of this research to all worshippers with disabilities in Nigeria. However, the findings reveal that worshippers with disabilities are still grappling with very basic accessibility problems including access to worship. While some parts of the world are working at improving assistive devices for people with disabilities and other "higher-order issues," the experiences of many Nigerian people with disabilities still revolve around basic access problems. (note 71) Outside of the few churches where worshippers with disabilities are localized, due to the availability of special services, the small numbers or invisibility of worshippers with disabilities may be indicative of their exclusion or inadequate participation in the life of many churches.

More research needs to be done involving larger sample sizes of theological education institutions, worshippers with disabilities within and outside TEKAN, and other regions of the country. Of particular interest may be north-eastern Nigeria, which has the highest incidences of disability, illiteracy, unemployment and

---

71. Eleweke and Ebenso, "Barriers to Accessing Services," 116.

conflict. (note 72) A wider range of disabilities (e.g. albinism, intellectual disabilities, mental illness, multiple disabilities) also needs to be explored. Outside the TEKAN circle, denominations worth investigating include the Catholic Church, which some participants reported as enabling. (note 73) More research on developing disability theology courses in theological education also needs to be considered. The sample curriculum recommended during the EDAN workshop by the World Council of Churches in 2004 is a rich resource for interested theological institutions. (note 74) Such course development projects can be done in clusters such as TEKAN and other coalitions of theological education institutions.

Most of the worshippers with disabilities in this research were educated, could understand English or sign language even when they could not understand some of the facilities being referred to (an indication of the lack of basic resources), could speak Hausa or English, and could afford mobile phones to receive calls or pay the cost of data to fill out the CASI. However, the experiences of worshippers with disabilities at the grassroots and the inclusivity of churches in some of the remotest

---

72. Yohanna, Carter, Malgwi et al., "'They Called Us.'"
73. Fox, "Pope Francis."
74. WCC, "Workshop on Disability Discourse."

regions of the country are worth examining. This may open up new insights for theological education and for pastors serving in these areas.

TEKAN should take advantage of its prominent presence in northern Nigeria to play a leading role in modelling inclusive worship practices for worshippers with disabilities. This is especially important because of the prevalence of disability in northern Nigeria due to conflict-related causes and insurgency. (note 75) TCNN can also play a leading role in inclusive theological education by maximizing its influence and tapping into the advantage of having a solid network and collaboration of many church denominations, to model inclusive worship practices to other seminaries.

Conclusion

The challenges faced by worshippers with disabilities in this study highlight the significant barriers and lack of access within the church community, some of which are worse than for people with disabilities outside the church. When society provides an interpreter for a social programme or news broadcast and the church does not, something is wrong. The Nigerian church, with its vast population of over eighty million

---

75. Yohanna, Carter, Malgwi et al., "'They Called Us.'"

attendees, will undermine its potential to influence societal change if it does not pay serious attention to worshippers with disabilities. We should demand reasons for the exclusion of worshippers with disabilities from the education system that prepares people for the service of the church, and theological education in Nigeria owes this obligation to the Nigerian church by emphasizing and modelling disability discourse in its curriculum and practices.

Bibliography

Abang, Theresa B. "Disablement, Disability and the Nigerian Society." **Disability, Handicap & Society** 3, no. 1 (1988): 71–77.

Adebiyi, B. A. "Visually Impaired Education: Yesterday, Today, and Tomorrow." **Essays in Education** 22 (Fall 2007), 3 pages. https://openriver.winona.edu/cgi/viewcontent.cgi?article=1019&context=eie.

Amenyedzi, S. B. "Equity and Access for Persons with Disability in Theological Education, Ghana." PhD diss., Stellenbosch University, 2016.

Anabaptist Disabilities Network. "Changing Attitudes: The Journey of Disability Attitudes." Accessed 24 February 2022. https://www.anabaptistdisabilitiesnetwork.org/Resources/AccessibilityAwareness/Attitudes/Pages/default.aspx.

Barnes, Colin, and Geoffrey Mercer. **Implementing the Social Model of Disability: Theory and Research**. Leeds: Disability Press, 2004.

Brown, Lydia. "Identity-First Language." ASAN: Autistic Self Advocacy Network. Accessed 25 February 2022. https://autisticadvocacy.org/about-asan/identity-first-language/.

Budiselić, Ervin. "An Apology of Theological Education: The Nature, the Role, the Purpose, the Past and the Future of Theological Education." **Evangelical Journal of Theology** 7, no. 2 (2013): 131–54.

Cbanga, Ibo. "Juju." Britannica online. Last modified 28 March 2017. https://www.britannica.com/topic/juju-magic.

Chao, Hannah. "Spiritual Formation and the Purpose of Theological Education." China Partnership. 3 December 2014. https://www.chinapartnership.org/blog/2014/12/spiritual-formation-and-the-purpose-of-theological-education.

Ebuga, Moses. "TEKAN General Secretary's Report." Presented at TEKAN 65th General Assembly, TEKAN Headquarters, Kaduna, Nigeria, 17 January 2020.

The Economist. "The Future of the World's Most Popular Religion Is African." 25 December 2015. https://www.economist.com/international/2015/12/25/the-future-of-the-worlds-most-popular-religion-is-african.

Eleweke, C. Jonah, and Jannine Ebenso. "Barriers to Accessing Services by People with Disabilities in Nigeria: Insights from a Qualitative Study." **Journal of Educational and Social Research** 6, no. 2 (2016): 113–24.

Emens, Elizabeth F. **Disability and Equality Law**. London: Routledge, 2017.

Evanson, Tracy A., Lois Ustanko and Elizabeth Tyree. "Promoting the Inclusion of Persons with Disabilities in Faith Communities: The Faith Inclusion Forum." **Community Development** 37, no. 3 (2006): 97–105.

Ewang, Anietie. "Nigeria Passes Disability Rights Law: Offers Hope of Inclusion, Improved Access." Human Rights Watch. 25 January 2019. https://www.hrw.org/news/2019/01/25/nigeria-passes-disability-rights-law.

Finkelstein, Vic. "To Deny or Not to Deny Disability – What Is Disability?" Independent Living Institute. 1975. https://www.independentliving.org/docs1/finkelstein.html.

Fox, Thomas C. "Pope Francis Envisions an Inclusive Church." National Catholic Reporter. 12 June 2013. https://www.ncronline.org/blogs/ncr-today/pope-francis-envisions-inclusive-church.

IndexMundi. "Nigeria – Population." 28 December 2019. https://www.indexmundi.com/facts/nigeria/population.

International Council for Evangelical Theological Education (ICETE). "ICETE Manifesto II 2022: Call and Commitment to the Renewal of Evangelical Theological Education." https://icete.info/resources/manifesto/.

International Leprosy Association. "COCIN Hospital and Rehabilitation Centre." https://leprosyhistory.org/database/archive302.

Ishola-Esan, Helen. "Impact of the Remnants of African Worldviews on Perception of Pastors towards Ministering to Persons with Disabilities in Nigeria." **Journal of Disability & Religion** 20, no. 1–2 (2016): 103–18.

———. "Relevance of Theological Institutions in Disability Discourse and Advocacy in Nigeria." **European Journal of Special Education** 2, no. 3 (2017): 1–5.

Jacobs, Naomi L. "The Upside-Down Kingdom of God: A Disability Studies Perspective on Disabled People's Experiences in Churches and Theologies of Disability." PhD diss., SOAS University of London, 2019.

Kabue, Samuel. "Persons with Disabilities in Church and Society: A Historical and Sociological Perspective." In **Disability, Society, and Theology: Voices from Africa**, edited by Samuel Kabue, Esther Mombo, Joseph Galgalo and C. B. Peter, 3–25. Limuru: Zapf Chancery Publishers Africa, 2011.

Mobility International USA. "Models of Disability: An Overview." 3 October 2018. https://www.miusa.org/resource/tipsheet/disabilitymodels.

Nihinlola, Emiola. "Disability Discourse in the Curriculum of Nigerian Theological Institutions: Constraints, Possibilities and Recommendations." **Journal of Disability & Religion** 20, no. 1–2 (2016): 40–48.

Nyangweso, Mary. "Disability in Africa: A Cultural/Religious Perspective." In **Disability in Africa: Inclusion, Care, and the Ethics of Humanity**, edited by Toyin Falola and Nic Hamel, 115–36. Woodbridge: Boydell & Brewer, 2021.

Oduu, Ode. "Over 25 Million Nigerians Excluded Due to Disability." Dataphyte. Last modified 20 January 2020. https://www.dataphyte.com/latest-reports/governance/over-25-million-nigerians-excluded-due-to-disability/.

Oliver, Albert I. "Curriculum Improvement: A Guide to Problems, Principles and Processes." **NASSP Bulletin** 62, no. 417 (1978): 111–12.

Omigbodun, Olayinka, Adebayo Odejide and Jide Morakinyo. "Highlights from the CAR Study in Ibadan, Nigeria." In **Disability and Culture: Universalism and Diversity**, edited by T. B. Üstün, Somnath Chatterji, Jürgen Rehm, Shekhar Saxena, Jerome E. Bickenbach, Robert T Trotter II and Robin Room, 185–94. Seattle: Hogrefe & Huber, 2001.

Osukwu, Celine. "Disability, Performance, and Discrimination in the Service to Humanity." **International Review of Mission** 108, no. 1 (2019): 52–64.

Pew Research Center. "The Age Gap in Religion around the World." 13 June 2018. https://www.pewresearch.org/religion/2018/06/13/the-age-gap-in-religion-around-the-world/.

Platinum Interventions' Care Initiative (PICI). "Stakeholders' Dialogue on the Need to Build an Inclusive and Accessible Society for Persons with Disabilities in Nigeria." Platinum Intervention Care Initiative. 15 November 2019. https://m.facebook.com/platinumintervention/posts/802179846899186/.

Rohwerder, Brigitte. "Disability Stigma in Developing Countries." K4D Helpdesk Report. 9 May 2018. https://assets.publishing.service.gov.uk/media/5b18fe3240f0b634aec30791/Disability_stigma_in_developing_countries.pdf.

Smith, Natalie. "The Face of Disability in Nigeria: A Disability Survey in Kogi and Niger States." **Disability, CBR & Inclusive Development** 22, no. 1 (2011): 35.

Swain, John, and Sally French. **Disability on Equal Terms.** Thousand Oaks: SAGE, 2008.

Thompson, Stephen. "Nigeria Situational Analysis. Version II – June 2020." Disability Inclusive Development. https://opendocs.ids.ac.uk/opendocs/handle/20.500.12413/15561.

White, George F. "People with Disabilities in Christian Community." **Journal of the Christian Institute on Disability (JCID)** 3, no. 1 (2014): 11–35.

Wikipedia. "Christianity in Nigeria." https://en.wikipedia.org/wiki/Christianity_in_Nigeria.

Wolfe, Ryan. "What Does It Mean to Be Inclusive?" Ability Ministry. 15 April 2018. https://abilityministry.com/what-does-it-mean-to-be-inclusive/.

World Council of Churches (WCC). "Ecumenical Disability Advocates Network (EDAN)." Accessed 24 February 2022. https://www.oikoumene.org/what-we-do/edan.

———. "Workshop on Disability Discourse for Theological Colleges, Kenya." 21 August 2004. https://www.oikoumene.org/resources/documents/workshop-on-disability-discourse-for-theological-colleges-kenya.

World Health Organization (WHO). "Disability." Last modified 7 March 2023. https://www.who.int/news-room/fact-sheets/detail/disability-and-health.

World Health Organization (WHO) and the World Bank. **World Report on Disability.** Geneva: WHO, 2011. https://www.who.int/teams/noncommunicable-diseases/sensory-functions-disability-and-rehabilitation/world-report-on-disability.

Yohanna, Timothy Ali, Holly Cartner, Prof. Anna Mohammed Malgwi et al. "'They Called Us Senseless Beggars': Challenges of Persons with Disabilities in North-Eastern Nigeria, Grassroots Researchers Associations." 2018. Wathi, 10 October 2019. https://www.wathi.org/they-called-us-senseless-beggars-challenges-of-persons-with-disabilities-in-north-eastern-nigeria/.

Epilogue

Towards an Inclusive Theology of Disability for Africa

Emmanuel Murangira and Sas Conradie

Introduction

Bringing together the diversity of contributions in this volume is no easy task. The authors and editors have taken the reader on a journey inside the African church, its faith, beliefs and the foundations of its practice in relation to those living with various forms of disabilities. In this concluding chapter, we want to reflect on some of the principles mentioned by the contributors and how these could be applied further in the African church.

Reading through the preceding chapters, one cannot help but draw on personal experiences to illustrate the challenge of disability in the African church. I (Sas) come from a family living with disabilities. My brothers in South Africa are both paralysed and when I visited them recently, I was struck by the magnitude of the challenges that they face. (note 1) When one of them looked for a place to live in Cape Town, he could find only one flat out of two hundred that was accessible for people living with disabilities. But how often are people living with disabilities in Africa left in tin shacks on their own? In addition, there are a number of my direct family who are living with neurological conditions (neurodiversity). As they are not accommodated well in the workplace, many people living with neurodiversity struggle at work or even to find work.

On one of their regular visits to a Church and Community Transformation (CCT) church group, a colleague was incensed by the church's lack of concern for people with disability. (note 2) While this particular incident was in one local church, it induced a sense of awareness of those with

---

1. Conradie, "Unconditional Love," 46.
2. "Church and community transformation" refers to broken relationships in churches and communities restored so that poverty in communities can be overcome, needs met with local resources and people reaching their God-given potential. See Blackham, Kariuki and Lindop, **Introduction**, for a fuller explanation.

disabilities in the church and their plight. In this case, people with disabilities were very much present in the local church but they remained practically invisible, excluded, marginalized and often stigmatized. That is even more the case when they are not healed after they have been prayed for. (note 3) Some churches have even portrayed people with disability as evil or of little faith if they are not healed by prayer.

This book, therefore, not only addresses one of the most overshadowed theological issues of our time, but it also presents in-depth theological thoughts, ideas and insights that can change the way the church serves those living with disability. The entire work engages critically with diversity in light of the African church's seemingly deafening indifference towards people with disability and proposes possible positive courses of action; this is a Kairos moment for the church. In the opening chapter, the authors have argued that changes in attitudes are critical in closing the gap between behaviour, theology and practice. Behaviour drivers such as attitudes are shaped by critical social dynamics such as culture, norms and belief at all levels of society. Changes in attitudes and perceptions are therefore only possible as far as there is change in these dynamics that

---

3. Conradie, "Neurodiversity in the Workplace."

essentially form the building blocks of individual and collective attitude. This makes the theology and teachings of the church critical in effecting changes in attitudes and consequently societal practices, and also enabling people living with disabilities to accept and even celebrate their conditions. (note 4) Disability inclusion in theological education and pastoral practice is not an option, but rather a biblical and canonical imperative. In this concluding chapter, we would like to point out specific perspectives on disability that we believe are important for the church in Africa to include in its theology and life.

Hermeneutics, Disability and the Church

The way we read, understand and apply the Bible – that is, our hermeneutical approach to the biblical text – guides our view of and response to disability (see chapter 2). Selina Palm suggests that based on our understanding and application of biblical texts, the church could become "a Spirit-filled ecclesial community of embrace" that embraces people living with disability (see chapter 3). This focus on community as reflected in an African understanding of and approach to disability is also a theme in Edwin Zulu's chapter. In the African understanding of **ubuntu**, everyone is part of a

---

4. Mugeere et al., "'Oh God!'"

larger community that cares for and supports each other, and this includes those living with disabilities. This has implications for the way the church reads the Bible and enables appreciation of "the wonderful art of God in every person" as made in the image of God (see chapter 5). Reading the Bible through such a lens enables us to understand that throughout the Bible we see a caring, protective and inclusive God who includes those living with disability in his community, the church.

Unfortunately, the church has often misinterpreted the biblical passages that talk about disability, sometimes intentionally and conveniently to justify practices in the church that are counter to the tenets of the Christian faith or to portray a villain God who should not be believed. (note 5) In her helpful presentation at the 3rd Symposium on Misleading Theologies in Africa in 2021, Veronica Ngum Ndi explained how certain readings of biblical texts can impact people living with disabilities negatively. She said, "The experiences of persons with disabilities in divine healing and wellness in Cameroon [are] a difficulty they face on a daily basis" because "men of God (pastors, prophets, evangelists, teachers,

---

5. Hitchens, "Christopher Hitchens vs John Lennox."

etc. . . . .) have different ways of interpreting the Scriptures." (note 6) Many churches, for example, use a specific reading of Leviticus 21:16–23 to exclude persons with disabilities from theological processes and limit them from having leadership roles in churches. Instead of people living with disability being embraced in the community of believers as expressed in the church, they are excluded and experience injustice because of a certain hermeneutical approach.

There is a common thread of injustice against people with disability in the Bible that brings to the fore the issue of disempowerment. Isaac's blindness is taken advantage of (Gen 27:32–33, 45); Mephibosheth is a victim of intra-community violence (2 Sam 4:4). (note 7) The story of Mephibosheth is a spectacular embroidery of injustice and disempowerment, justice and restoration weaved together. It highlights how people, especially those who care for people with disabilities, may at times perpetuate injustice relentlessly, driven by envy and abuse of power.

---

6. Ndi, "Experiences."
7. Mephibosheth, the son of Jonathan (son of Saul), was injured at a very young age when a servant who cared for him was fleeing with him from his grandfather's house. Both of his legs were broken, leading to permanent disability.

But the story also shows David as an example to the church in the way he cared for Mephibosheth (2 Sam 9:9–13). In Acts 3:1–10, Peter and John healed a man with a disability from birth. Yet they not only heal him but, like David, they bring him into the King's perpetual presence. Both of these passages present different aspects of healing, from inner healing and restoration to the physical healing of the body. Micheline Kamba calls this perspective on healing the "realization of God's purpose to bring salvation in all of its fullness to all people" (see chapter 4).

Addressing the Theological Roots of Disability Exclusion in the Church

Doctrinal diversity and religious traditions in contemporary Christian beliefs have normalized the selective application of Scripture to a diverse set of church practices in relation to human conditions. In Africa, emerging and, to some extent, established independent churches have tended to spiritualize if not demonize human conditions of disability, including those that are caused by known events and/or incidents. Disability is often seen as the result of sin by the person living with disability or his or her family or community. (note 8)

---

8. Longchar, "Sin, Suffering, and Disability."

As Palm notes in chapter 3, the inherent doctrinal and theological misunderstanding that surrounds disability in the church in Africa can be well understood if examined from its theological roots. The exclusion and stigmatization of people with disabilities are frequently based on harmful theological scripts around disability. The church should be a "just home where all are welcomed" (see chapter 3). As she explains, churches should recognize and confess the way they have been excluding people living with disabilities, which has led to their stigmatization. People living with disabilities also have spiritual gifts that should be utilized in building the body of Christ. Churches should be liberated from their exclusion of people living with disabilities from contributing to the theology and life of the church. Churches should become spaces where all are valued, participate, belong and share their spiritual gifts with each other and their wider communities. Enabling churches to become more inclusive requires more than addressing church practices. It requires a rigorous engagement with theological scripts that reinforce exclusion of those who need the church most.

How can one disentangle the web of practices and theological scripts that confine people with disability in the discriminatory and exclusionary abyss of a toxic church? The most logical place to begin is the theological minefield that is the theologies that inform the church in its local expression and therefore its practices. It can be difficult for a church entrenched in harmful local theologies to accept its complicity in the exclusion and discrimination of people with disabilities. Negative church practices find justification in these local theologies that perceive disability to be the result of sin or manifestation of demonic possession – for example, the practice of cleansing people with disabilities from their sin or delivering them from demonic possession by prophets with specific powers, quite often for financial gain. This is in contrast to the biblical view of the church as a community of God's people that has the divine duty to care for all those in need without distinction. (note 9)

The theology of divine accommodation called for by Jill Harshaw is very important for the African church to understand how God reveals himself to people with profound intellectual disabilities (see chapter 7). Anybody can have a relationship with God and witness and minister to others. It does not matter how profoundly disabled or how limited

---

9. Matt 25:34–40.

a person's intellectual understanding of God might be. (note 10) Maliszewska calls them the invisible church. (note 11)

I (Sas) experienced this when I was a house parent at a school for deaf children with learning difficulties and other forms of disability. While their chronological ages ranged from ten to seventeen, their intellectual ages were between two and six. How could they have a relationship with God if they could not understand concepts such as sin and grace? Amazingly, one of the boys, who was seventeen years old, returned after a holiday and asked to pray. Because he could not talk, he prayed using various sounds. But then he said something that had a profound impact on me and my wife. In sign language, he said that Jesus loved him and that he loved Jesus. God accommodated himself to the mental capacity of this boy and revealed himself so that the boy could have a relationship with God. My wife and I could not understand what had happened, but we could see the remarkable change in the boy's life. This boy had been included in God's kingdom through divine accommodation. With people living with profound intellectual disabilities often seen

---

10. Volck, "Silent Communion."
11. Maliszewska, "Invisible Church."

by churches in Africa as being demon possessed or cursed, an acceptance of divine accommodation by the African church is urgently needed. (note 12)

An Inclusive Church as a Community That Embraces People Living with Disabilities

Despite the challenges faced by people with disabilities, those who provide care, support, faith and spirituality remain a source of comfort and resilience. In her empirical work "Spirituality and Parents of Children with Disability: Views of Practitioners," Samta Pandya presents evidence that highlights the importance of the church as a place where parents of children with disabilities find solace, hope and support. The church should be the space where those living with disability receive care and support, and where they experience empathy and dignity as people created in the image of God. Churches should become inclusive and accessible for those living with disabilities and integrate them into the life of the church and society. (note 13) This is what Kamba calls a "transformative church for all people" in her chapter (see chapter 4).

---

12. Raffety et al., "Lonely Joy."
13. Woodall, "Pentecostal Church."

Unfortunately, various chapters in this publication indicate that the African church is often not an inclusive community. Attitudes and responses to people living with disabilities have to change in many African churches. Louise Kretzschmar explains how this change could be facilitated in her book **The Church and Disability in Southern Africa: Inclusion and Participation**. Having a disability ministry or focus in a church can ensure that people with disabilities are included and able to fully participate in the life of the church. In this way, they can use their gifts to serve in and through the church. At the same time, plans can be made to ensure that the needs of those living with disabilities are met. This will enable them to fully belong in the church.

Kretzschmar suggests a number of practical steps for a disability friendly church:

1. Provide a warm and welcoming environment for people living with disabilities. Build intentional friendships with them.

2. Improve accessibility by making necessary changes to the church facilities and worship services.

3. Provide basic disability awareness training.

4. Provide opportunities for people with disabilities to offer and be involved in the activities of the church.

5. Ensure that communication and interactions with people with disabilities respect them.

6. Provide assistance where needed to help people with disabilities.

7. Enable the holistic growth of people with disabilities.

8. Facilitate conversations about disability in the church. (note 14)

The Role of Inclusive Theological Education

As Tongriang Daspan and Noah Daspan mention in their chapter, theological education in Africa could play an important role in equipping Christian leaders to lead churches as inclusive communities where people living with disabilities can be supported to reach their full God-given potential (see chapter 9). Theologians and clergy in Africa should be educated theologically and practically to meet the spiritual and other needs of people

---

14. Kretzschmar, **Church and Disability**, 107–22.

living with disabilities. (note 15) They should be trained to have an understanding of the causes, types, degree and challenges of disabilities so as to make a clear distinction between disability and spirituality. This will reduce the barriers to including people living with disabilities in churches. (note 16)

An African theological framework based on harmonious and inclusive living should be the foundation of theological education in Africa in order to bring holistic transformation to communities in Africa. (note 17) A focus of such a framework for theological education in Africa should be the restoration of a person's and community's broken relationships with God, him-/herself, others and creation. (note 18) Reflection on the restoration of these relationships from the perspective of people living with disabilities would be essential to include in the curricula of theological institutions in Africa. Specific courses on disability could be provided as part of the core curricula of the institutions. In addition,

---

15. Ndi, "Experiences."
16. McMahon-Panther and Bornman, "Perceptions."
17. Conradie, "Church and Community Transformation."
18. This perspective is explained in Ling and Swithinbank, **Understanding Poverty.**

biblical studies and other theological subjects should be taught from the lens of people living with disabilities so that their perspectives of their lived experience can be reflected from within the biblical texts.

A Commitment to Including People with Disabilities in the African Church

Kretzschmar mentions that some churches in Southern Africa have committed themselves to an unofficial inclusion charter as an example of their intention to include people with disabilities in the life of the church. (note 19) As this charter is of relevance to the content of this book, we include it here as well:

> **Inclusion Charter:**
> **Our Commitment to Including People with Disabilities**
>
> We want to be an inclusive community whereby everybody, including people with disabilities, is enabled and free to:
>
> - Participate in any activity – therefore our buildings and worship services should consider the needs and contributions of people with impairments.

---
19. Kretzschmar, **Church and Disability**, 128.

- Serve with their gifts – therefore people with disabilities are an integral part of our programmes, taking leadership roles and making contributions to the enrichment of all members.

- Cultivate reciprocal relationships, friendships and koinonia (fellowship) – therefore people with disabilities are not merely the recipients of charity and ministry, but accepted as fellow believers who take full responsibility for their part in enriching relationships.

We see our (faith) community as a creative space, where the diversity that people with disabilities bring is welcomed and enhanced. Therefore we live, serve and worship in this space for the purpose of new and growing interaction amongst us all. We respect one another because of the image of God in each other which is not diminished by a different level of physical or intellectual functioning. (note 20)

---

20. Kretzschmar, 128.

We would encourage all readers of this book to commit themselves and their churches to this charter. To some extent it also summarizes the core message of this publication.

Conclusion

In our roles working for Tearfund in Africa, a faith-based international relief, development and advocacy organization, we have observed how the principles outlined in the book are reflected in many of the churches that Tearfund is working with. People living with disabilities are empowered to unlock their God-given potential through church and community transformation (CCT) approaches and processes. One of the best illustrations of how this is possible is the story of Jantille, a single mother from the Ruhanga Parish in the Kigali Diocese of the Anglican Church in Rwanda. She was born physically disabled and grew up without hope for the future. It was very hard for her to move around due to her disability and she was stigmatized by her family and community members. When her church started the CCT journey, they identified and gathered information about vulnerable people in their community. Jantille was included in a small group of ladies for spiritual, emotional, social and economic support. Although she was rejected by family members, the church supported her and integrated her in their small group.

As part of the CCT journey the group conducted a Bible study on 2 Kings 4:1–7 about Elisha and the widow's oil. They asked the question in verse 2, "Tell me, what do you have in the house?" Jantille surprised everyone when she told them that during her childhood, her mother taught her how to weave and she was an expert in weaving mats. She said that if she could get raw materials and someone to take her product to the market, she could start a business. The group brought her raw materials and started taking her mats to the market. She developed her business to such an extent that she was able to employ other women as well. Every week the women's group gathered at Jantille's home for Bible study and support. The church became her new family and the pastor advocated for her and her son to be supported for school fees and scholastic materials. The church gave Jantille a wheelchair to enable her to attend church, as previously she had had to crawl for five hours to reach the church. Through this "Spirit-filled ecclesial community of embrace," Jantille is reaching her God-given potential.

There would be more Jantilles in Africa if the African church would embrace the principles suggested in this book and become inclusive communities that embrace and support those living with disabilities.

Bibliography

Blackham, Jodi, Grace Kariuki and Esther Lindop. **An Introduction to Church and Community Transformation (CCT): Overcoming Poverty through a Whole-Life Response to the Gospel.** Teddington: Tearfund, 2021. https://res.cloudinary.com/tearfund/image/fetch/https://learn.tearfund.org/-/media/learn/resources/tools-and-guides/2021/2021-tearfund-an-introduction-to-cct-landscape-en.pdf.

Conradie, Sas. "Church and Community Transformation and the Implications for Theological Education in Africa: An NGO Perspective." In **A Critical Engagement with Theological Education in Africa: A South African Perspective**, edited by Johannes J. Knoetze and Alfred R. Brunsdon, 205–20. Cape Town: AOSIS, 2021.

———. "Neurodiversity in the Workplace and the Implications for Tearfund." Unpublished blog, 9 February 2021.

——— "Unconditional Love and the Jubilee." In **Jubilee: 50 Bible Studies on Poverty and Justice**, 46–47. Teddington: Tearfund, 2018.

Hitchens, Christopher. "Christopher Hitchens vs John Lennox | Is God Great? Debate." 20 June 2017. 1:53:24. YouTube. https://www.youtube.com/watch?v=5OXPlUCGScY&t=2411s.

Kretzschmar, Louise. **The Church and Disability in Southern Africa: Inclusion and Participation.** Pietermaritzburg: Cluster, 2019.

Ling, Anna, and Hannah Swithinbank, with Seren Boyd. **Understanding Poverty: Restoring Broken Relationships**. Teddington: Tearfund, 2019. https://res.cloudinary.com/tearfund/image/fetch/https://learn.tearfund.org/-/media/learn/resources/tools-and-guides/2019-tearfund-understanding-poverty-en.pdf.

Longchar, Wati. "Sin, Suffering, and Disability in God's World." In **Disability, Society, and Theology: Voices from Africa**, edited by Samuel Kabue, Esther Mombo, Joseph Galgalo and C. B. Peter, 47–58. Limuru: Zapf Chancery Publishers Africa, 2011.

Maliszewska, Anna. "The Invisible Church: People with Profound Intellectual Disabilities and the Eucharist – A Catholic Perspective." **Journal of Disability & Religion** 23, no. 2 (2019): 197–210.

McMahon-Panther, Gail, and Juan Bornman. "The Perceptions of Persons with Disabilities, Primary Caregivers and Church Leaders Regarding Barriers and Facilitators to Participation in a Methodist Congregation." **Journal of Disability and Religion** 27, no. 1 (2023). https://doi.org/10.1080/23312521.2020.1859040.

Mugeere, Anthony Buyinza, Julius Omona, Andrew Ellias State and Tom Shakespeare. "'Oh God! Why Did You Let Me Have This Disability?' Religion, Spirituality and Disability in Three African Countries." **Journal of Disability & Religion** 24, no. 1 (2020): 64–81.

Ndi, Veronica Ngum. "Experiences of Persons with Disabilities on Divine Healing and Wellness." Unpublished presentation given at the 3rd Symposium on Misleading Theologies, 23 November 2021.

Pandya, Samta P. "Spirituality and Parents of Children with Disability: Views of Practitioners." **Journal of Disability & Religion** 21, no. 1 (2017): 64–83.

Raffety, Erin, Kevin Vollrath, Emily Harris and Laura Foote. "Lonely Joy: How Families with Nonverbal Children with Disabilities Communicate, Collaborate, and Resist in a World That Values Words." **Journal of Pastoral Theology** 29, no. 2 (2019): 101–15.

Volck, Brian. "Silent Communion: The Prophetic Witness of the Profoundly Disabled." **Journal of Disability & Religion** 22, no. 2 (2018): 211–18.

Woodall, Judith. "The Pentecostal Church: Hospitality and Disability Inclusion; Becoming an Inclusive Christian Community by Welcoming Mutual Vulnerability." **Journal of the European Pentecostal Theological Association** 36, no. 2 (2016): 131–44.

Appendix 1

The Use of Terms Describing People and Places

In this volume we have given much thought to the language and key terms we use in relation to disability. (note 1) These discussions have come out of the editorial process, with authors using a range of terms in their submitted chapters posing an editorial challenge for consistency and reflexivity. We use this Appendix 1 to make this process on the use of terminologies clear and transparent to the reader.

---

1. As a reference point, CBM (2020), a leading Christian disability rights NGO, emphasizes four key principles to foster disability inclusion through language and communications: 1) avoid negative language and stereotypes; 2) avoid messages of "curing" or "treating" people with disabilities; 3) always keep the person first; 4) promote the capabilities and contributions of people with disabilities through the choice of language.

Terms describing people living with disabilities have evolved over time and we can expect them to evolve further in the future. Like all language expressions, they reflect the socio-political landscape at the time in which they are being used. Terms such as "the handicapped," "the impaired," or even "the crippled," which are considered highly offensive now, were thought to be appropriate when in common use. Tsitsi Chataika captured the challenge of terminology in her Introduction to the **Routledge Handbook of Disability in Southern Africa** as follows: "definitions are powerful and words we choose to use when making reference to disability issues play an essential part in the way we view people. . . . Hence, the language used to describe impairments and the people who experience them is constantly evolving. It is almost impossible to always 'get it right'." (note 2) Kabue has pointed out that engaging with the controversies over terms could have the benefit of "encouraging ongoing discourse that leads to deeper understanding of the essence of the several terms." (note 3)

---

2. Chataika, **Routledge Handbook of Disability**, 1.
3. Kabue, "Persons with disabilities in church and society," 6.

Important to highlight at the outset is the distinction between "person first" and "identity first" language. Those who advocate "person first" language tend to use the term "people/persons living with disabilities," which is interchangeable with the shorter form "people with disabilities." Underlying this approach is the desire to describe, "affirm and define a person first, before the impairment or disability." (note 4) The term has its roots in North America in the 1970s and is currently the preferred term in the development sector. (note 5) However, some critics argue that attempting to separate personhood from disability in this way betrays a negative view of disability, and that "[m]ore effort should be put into incorporating disability into the concept of personhood [. . .] rather than on attempting to put distance between them." (note 6) Conversely, those who advocate "identity first" language will use disability as a descriptor for people/persons on the basis that disability is fundamental to and inseparable from a person's identity. The "identity first" term "disabled person" is widely used in the current literature, and also across public life, institutions and common

---

4. Al Ju'beh, **Disability Inclusive Development Toolkit**, 25.
5. Wehmeyer, Bersani and Gagne, "Riding the third wave."
6. Collier, "Person-first language," E935.

life. It is currently the preferred term in disability studies, although a diversity of approaches is still observable. (note 7) It is also acceptable to use "identity first" and "person first" terminology interchangeably. (note 8)

In this volume, we allow authors to take a "person first" or "identity first" approach, according to their preference and positionality. Thus, some have used terms such as "disabled person" or "autistic person," whereas others have used "people with disabilities," We like to avoid the acronym "PwD,"

---

7. A search of terms across the **Routledge Handbook of Disability Studies** (Watson and Vehmas, 2020) showed that the most commonly used term was "disabled people" (1086 times) and "disabled person" (121 times), indicating preference for an "identity first" approach across disability studies. "People with disabilities" and "persons with disabilities" were less frequently used (235 times and 145 times respectively). "People living with disabilities" was only used once, while the terms "person(s) living with disability/disabilities" were not used at all. "Living with" however was used 75 times in descriptions of "living with a [particular] disability," "living with a condition" or "living with an impairment."

8. See, for example, Brueggemann, "Disability Studies / Disability Culture."

which is sometimes used for greater ease of writing in the literature as it is shorter. There is, however, a danger that this can turn into a label, and we tend to only use "PwD" when in a quotation. We do not use the earlier term "handicapped," although we have accommodated for the use of the word "handicap" in Micheline Kamba's chapter in this volume which is a reprint of an original article. (note 9)

The same care in how we speak about people applies to how we speak about places. The intention is that how we label places entails deeper meaning than just being a choice of terminology. Terms such as "third world" or "developing country" can entail an implicit (even if unintended) meaning of lesser value or even "backwardness" for which reason we do not use them. More acceptable terms include low- and middle-income countries (LMICs) and Global South. Most authors in this volume use the term Global South (and Global North), when referring to economically poorer (and richer) countries. Some authors use the term "the West" when referring to the "western nations" in the Global North. This is not meant to divide the world into greater

---

9. The word for "disability" in French is "handicap," and since the author is a French speaker, this might account for the use of the word.

and lesser countries by geography, but simply makes use of common terminology at the time of writing. Although the term "Global South" has been critiqued, it is still in wide use in scholarly literature, whilst there also seems to be a current trend to move to the term "Majority World" instead. All of these terms are likely to evolve over time and may already be outdated at the time of print.

When referring to **Africa** in this volume, we speak about the African continent as a whole, not specific to any country or region within it. The volume does not include contributions from Northern Africa. This is not by intentional choice, but simply because we had no submissions to the call for this volume from Northern African countries. We selected the highest quality of submitted draft chapters for this volume, irrespective of their geographic locale within Africa. Only one chapter in this volume has a regional focus (on Southern Africa), while other contributions are located in particular African country contexts. In addition, we have included two chapters from the UK that we believe are important contributions to the volume as a whole (on biblical hermeneutics and profound intellectual disabilities).

Lastly, when referring to **the church** in Africa, we refer to the Body of Christ, all followers of Jesus who are organized in networks of congregations, nonspecific to any particular denominations or particular groups of Christians.

Bibliography

Al Ju'beh, Kathy. **Disability Inclusive Development Toolkit**. Bensheim: CBM, 2017.

Brueggemann, Brenda. "Disability Studies / Disability Culture." In **The Oxford Handbook of Positive Psychology and Disability**, edited by Michael L. Wehmeyer, 273–300. Oxford: Oxford University Press, 2013.

CBM. **Disability Inclusion: communications and language guide.** Cambridge: CBM, 2020.

Chataika, Tsitsi. "Introduction: critical connections and gaps in disability and development." In **The Routledge Handbook of Disability in Southern Africa**, edited by Tsitsi Chataika, 3–13. London: Routledge, 2019.

Collier, Roger. "Person-first language: What it means to be a 'person'." **Canadian Medical Association Journal** 184 (18), 11 December 2012: E935–E936.

Kabue, Samuel. "Persons with disabilities in church and society: a historical and sociological perspective." In **Disability, Society, and Theology: Voices from Africa**, edited by Samuel Kabue,

Esther Mombo, Joseph Galgalo and C. B. Peter, 3–25. Limuru: Zapf Chancery Publishers Africa, 2011.

Watson, Nick, and Simo Vehmas (eds). **Routledge Handbook of Disability Studies**. London: Routledge, 2020.

Wehmeyer, Michael, Hank Bersani Jr. and Ray Gagne. "Riding the third wave: self-determination and self-advocacy in the 21st century." In **Focus on Autism Other Developmental Disabilities** 15(2) (2000): 106–15.

www.ingramcontent.com/pod-product-compliance
Lightning Source LLC
Chambersburg PA
CBHW081143290426
44108CB00018B/2425